KT-233-957

CAMBRIDGE STUDIES IN CRIMINOLOGY

Borstal Reassessed, R. Hood

Murder followed by Suicide, D. J. West

Crime in England and Wales, F. H. McClintock and N. H. Avison

Delinquency in Girls, J. Cowie, V. Cowie and E. Slater

The Police: a Study in Manpower, J. Martin and Gail Wilson

Present Conduct and Future Delinquency, D. J. West

Crime, Law and the Scholars, G. O. Mueller

Principles of Sentencing, D. A. Thomas

Social Consequences of Conviction, J. Martin and D. Webster

Suspended Sentence, M. Ancel

Local Prisons: The Crisis in the English Penal System, R. F. Sparks

Sentencing the Motoring Offender, R. Hood

Criminals Coming of Age, A. E. Bottoms and F. H. McClintock

Drivers After Sentence, T. C. Willett

Who Becomes Delinquent? D. J. West and D. P. Farrington

CAMBRIDGE STUDIES IN CRIMINOLOGY XXXIV
General Editor: Sir Leon Radzinowicz

Who Becomes Delinquent?

THE HEINEMANN LIBRARY OF CRIMINOLOGY
AND PENAL REFORM

WHO BECOMES DELINQUENT?

Second Report of the Cambridge Study in Delinquent Development

by

D. J. West

in collaboration with

D. P. Farrington

HEINEMANN

LONDON

Heinemann Educational Books Ltd
LONDON EDINBURGH MELBOURNE AUCKLAND
TORONTO SINGAPORE HONG KONG
KUALA LUMPUR IBADAN NAIROBI
JOHANNESBURG LUSAKA NEW DELHI

ISBN 0 435 82937 8

First published 1973
Reprinted 1975

Publisher's note: This series is continuous with the Cambridge Studies in Criminology, Volumes I to XIX, published by Macmillan & Co., London

Published by
Heinemann Educational Books Ltd
48 Charles Street, London W1X 8AH
Printed in Great Britain by Butler & Tanner Ltd
Frome and London

Foreword

BY SIR LEON RADZINOWICZ

A bold and sustained venture in criminological research comes to fruition with the publication of this second volume on the Cambridge Study in Delinquent Development. Ten years ago, Dr West and his collaborators investigated, from many angles, a sample of eight-year-old schoolboys. They have been keeping watch ever since to see how they would turn out and which of them would prove to be delinquents.

Since this was a genuinely prospective study it has thrown a penetrating light upon the extent to which delinquency can be predicted from knowledge of personality, family and social background. Some factors have been found to make a very significant contribution, whereas others, in spite of expectations to the contrary, have proved to be relatively unimportant, except as reflections of other more fundamental conditions.

One of the most interesting findings is that the boys eventually brought before the juvenile courts, and especially the recidivists among them, had, from the outset, tended to differ from their schoolmates in many other respects. Dr West raises the question of whether this undermines the fashionable contention of some modern criminologists that it is the system of criminal justice that makes delinquents by the very process of labelling them.

The Cambridge study has been concerned with a typical working-class urban neighbourhood. The ideas which have emerged will need testing on other samples. How far, for instance, do the results apply to middle-class delinquents, or to girls, or to another generation? Good research raises questions and stimulates further investigation. But I predict that the findings recorded here will hold their own as a point of reference for discussion of juvenile delinquency and criminal behaviour for many years to come.

Dr West and his collaborators are to be congratulated on carrying through this undertaking so long and so successfully. It has been a combined effort, to which many workers over the years have contributed their different skills. The fact that few parents declined to co-operate, and that the investigators were in touch with ninety-five per cent of the boys after ten years of follow-up, is a considerable tribute to the interviewers. The fact that a report as detailed as this can be issued only one year after the delinquency records became available is in large part due to the skill of Dr D. P. Farrington in making maximum use of modern computer facilities.

The Home Office has consistently and ungrudgingly supported this elaborate and costly piece of research. To T. S. Lodge, to the Consultative Committee, and especially to its Chairman, Dr J. W. B. Douglas, we are deeply indebted.

But it is the fact that Dr West himself has stayed with the project from the start, and maintained an enthusiastic interest, that has been of paramount importance in guiding and co-ordinating the work and in bringing out the essentials. We welcome his book as a major contribution to the Cambridge Series.

Cambridge, July 1973

Table of Contents

List of Tables

List of Figures

Past and Present Members of the Consultative Committee

J. W. B. Douglas
Miss S. Cunliffe
J. B. Howard
*Lady Hilda Lewis
A. N. Little
T. S. Lodge, C.B.E.
*D. H. Morrell
Professor J. N. Morris
*R. L. Morrison
Miss J. J. Nunn, C.B.E.
Professor Sir Leon Radzinowicz
Peter D. Scott
Professor J. Tizard
Professor Nigel Walker.

**deceased.*

List of past and present Research Officers working full-time on the Cambridge Study in Delinquent Development

Joan Beales
John Blackmore
Joan Court
Peter Didcot
Susan Ellis
David Farrington
Janet Finney
H. B. Gibson
Gwen Gundry
Ruth Hanson
Andrew Irving
Hilary King
Barry Knight
Thomas Knox
Sylvia Morrison
Martin Murphy
Eve Road
David Scott
Ruth Williams.

Introduction

1. *Origin and Purpose of the Study*

This report is a sequel to *Present Conduct and Future Delinquency* by D. J. West (published in 1969 by Heinemann Educational Books), which described the original aims of the Cambridge Study in Delinquent Development and gave an account of the setting up of the enquiry and of the methods used. To obtain full particulars, reference must be made to that earlier report, but the present volume has been compiled so as to be comprehensible on its own.

The purpose of the Study was to investigate the development of juvenile delinquency in a normal population of boys. The boys, 411 in all, were drawn from six state primary schools in the vicinity of the research office. They were 'recruited' at age 8, and as much information about them and their families as possible was collected by the time they were 10, before the onset of court appearances for delinquency. In this way, it was hoped to avoid the bias that may affect retrospective assessments of the backgrounds of known delinquents.

All the boys were interviewed and tested in their schools, and information about their families was obtained by home visits and enquiries to social agencies. The boys were followed over a span of 10 years, and 97 per cent were interviewed on one or more occasions after leaving school. One-fifth of them became juvenile delinquents. This report compares the minority who became delinquents with their non-delinquent classmates.

The results of this Study indicate that boys destined to become involved with the law differ from their peers in many important ways. In general, their backgrounds and personal characteristics are less fortunate. Although no one can say for sure that a particular individual will become delinquent, certain groups, identifiable at an early age, are peculiarly vulnerable. The extent of this vulnerability, and the reasons for it, are the key topics of this report.

2. *The Particular Features of the Present Study*

The Cambridge Study in Delinquent Development is a survey with a unique combination of features. It is based upon an unselected group of boys from a normal population. It is a longitudinal survey in which personal contact with the subjects has been maintained for more than a decade. The size of the sample is large enough to furnish statistical conclusions, yet small enough to permit individual interviews and a detailed examination of each case. Finally, the main focus of interest is on delinquency, and information about this aspect has been collected both from official records and from the boys themselves.

While no other study is precisely similar, we have been able to draw ideas from other long-term surveys which have included delinquency or related topics in their investigations. In Britain, the most important and, in some respects, most directly comparable project is the National Survey of Health and Development under the direction of Dr J. W. B. Douglas (Douglas, 1964; Douglas *et al.*, 1968), which has now been in progress for more than 25 years. Up to the present, its focus of interest has been on educational progress, but a number of publications concerned with delinquency have been produced (Mulligan *et al.*, 1963; Douglas *et al.*, 1966; Douglas, 1966). The National Survey sample consisted of some 5,000 children selected from all legitimate single births occurring in England, Scotland and Wales during the first week of March 1946. This large sample size has precluded detailed case studies. Although the children and their parents have been continuously investigated since birth, none of them has been seen personally by members of the research team, with the exception of a small group of university entrants.

The National Child Development Study (Pringle *et al.*, 1966; Davie *et al.* 1972) was modelled on Douglas' survey. Its sample consists of every one of the 16,000 children born in England, Scotland and Wales in the first week of March 1958. The children and their parents have not been seen personally by the researchers, and no information about delinquency has been published as yet. These investigators are also following up another representative sample of children born in 1970.

S. and E. Glueck have been responsible for the most famous long-term surveys concerned with crime and delinquency. In one of their most important projects, 500 men leaving the Massachusetts reformatory between 1911 and 1922 were followed up for 15 years (Glueck and Glueck, 1930, 1937, 1943). The men, or their close relatives, were interviewed by members of the research team at five-year intervals. Another investigation consisted of a 15-year follow-up of 500 Boston delinquents and a matched group of 500 non-delinquents (Glueck and Glueck, 1950, 1968). Both groups were re-interviewed by the researchers at ages 25 and 31. However, the Gluecks have never followed up an unselected sample of normal children; their work has been based on contrasts between well-established delinquents and specially selected non-delinquent controls.

Another long-term survey arose out of an attempt to test the Gluecks' delinquency prediction criteria (see p. 134). The New York City Youth Board (Craig and Glick, 1963; Craig and Budd, 1967) followed up an unselected group of 300 boys aged 5–6 in 1952 for a period of 10 years. The boys were initially living in high delinquency areas, but only about one in six became delinquent. The researchers did not maintain personal contact with the boys and with their parents, but obtained their follow-up information in interviews with teachers, guidance counsellors and other persons.

There are other longitudinal surveys which might have been cited (see Appendix H), but the ones mentioned are those whose methods and findings are most easily compared to our own. They will be referred to again at appropriate points throughout the present report.

Longitudinal surveys have obvious advantages for research into the origins and development of delinquency. Unfortunately, they are costly and difficult to carry through, and this probably explains why so few have been done. We are pleased to have brought one such enterprise to fruition, thanks to long continued support and the efforts of several generations of research officers who have worked on the project. The task has not been easy, but an introduction is hardly the place to dwell upon methodological problems. The interested reader is referred to Appendix J.

I

The Extent and Nature of Delinquency

1. *Preliminary Facts about the Population*

The Study population of 411 included all the boys in the age group 8–9 (that is, in their fourth year of compulsory education) who were attending six typical local primary schools. Twelve boys from a school for the educationally subnormal were also included, in order to make the sample more like a total population (see Note 1). The enquiry was limited to males because a much larger sample would have been needed to produce sufficient numbers of delinquent girls (cf. p. 46).

The neighbourhood was a crowded, working-class area of London where there were no private schools and where the bulk of the housing belonged to the local authority. The Study boys were thought to be substantially representative of their generation in the locality.

Ninety per cent of the boys were both white in racial appearance and reared by parents who were themselves brought up in the United Kingdom or Eire. Most boys of immigrant parents were of European or White Commonwealth origin, although there were a few Cypriots and a few West Indian negroes. Migration of families was not a serious problem. When the boys were aged 16, 90 per cent were still living in the London area, the majority being in or reasonably near the same neighbourhood, and only five had departed overseas. The fact that the boys came from a stable and traditionally English working-class urban area needs emphasis, because it follows that the findings of this Study are likely to be true for many other similar places.

Further details of how information was collected about the boys are given in Note 1.

2. *Identifying the Delinquents*

Most of the comparisons in this report consist of contrasts between the minority who acquired some entry in the Criminal Record Office (the official delinquents) and the remainder of the boys (the non-delinquents). This way of defining delinquents has been severely criticized by some sociologists, on the grounds that official convictions measure society's reaction to selected incidents rather than actual behaviour. It has also been suggested that the important question is not why certain people and not others break the law, but why certain acts but not others are prohibited. Sutherland and Cressey (1970, pp. 46–7), in a prestigious textbook on criminology, stated that 'Once, sociologists simply analysed the available statistical "facts" about crime . . . now, they are beginning to show that the datum for study is the process by which the statistical information is manufactured, assembled and published.'

Admittedly, the numbers and types of persons who appear in official statistics are greatly affected by changes in policy of the police or courts. More than a quarter of a century ago Murphy *et al.* (1946, p. 696) noted that 'even a moderate increase in the amount of attention paid to [the misdeeds of youth] by law enforcement agencies could create the semblance of a "delinquency wave" without there being the slightest change in adolescent behaviour'. It seems likely, as suggested by Bloch (1958), that official convictions do not reflect the real level of delinquent behaviour in a community, but merely measure the volume of traffic through the courts.

Although fluctuations in the absolute number of convictions are difficult to interpret, official conviction statistics are still useful for research. Whatever prosecution standards are in vogue, the individuals selected for official action are probably, by and large, more seriously or more frequently delinquent in behaviour than the average citizen. This is confirmed by a number of investigations in which people were asked to report delinquent acts which they had committed (e.g. Erickson and Empey, 1963; Christie *et al.*, 1965; Kulik *et al.*, 1968). In these researches, as in the present Study (p. 165), it was found that official delinquents had committed more delinquent acts, according to their own admissions, than non-delinquents. It may not be justifiable to use official statistics to discover whether or not crime is increasing, but it seems reasonable to use them, as we have done, to isolate a relatively delinquent group.

Defining delinquents by official convictions has the added advantage of enabling the findings of this Study to be directly compared with the findings of many other researchers using the same method.

3. *The Prevalence of Juvenile Delinquency in the Study Sample*

The first step was to identify the officially 'convicted' delinquent minority. In legal terminology, juveniles have 'findings of guilt' rather than criminal convictions, but the term 'conviction' will be used throughout this report as an easily understood, if somewhat inaccurate, shortened form.

It was decided at an early stage to define as a delinquency conviction any proved offence sufficiently serious to belong to the categories routinely reported by the police to the Criminal Record Office, and any offence (e.g. insult, threat or assault) involving an element of personal aggression. A total of 84 boys (20·4 per cent of the sample) were juvenile delinquents on this definition. In the event, all these 84 boys had delinquency convictions for offences routinely registered in the CRO, except for one whose only conviction was for insulting behaviour. This boy subsequently became a recidivist as a young adult.

Although we have counted only 84 as delinquents, 102 boys (24·8 per cent) actually made a court appearance at age 10 or later and had some sort of juvenile misbehaviour proved (see Note 2). The extra boys consisted of 15 who were found guilty only of traffic offences (e.g. driving without a licence or without insurance or under age) and three found guilty only of non-attendance at school. These offences were located from Children's Department records, as they were only occasionally registered in the Criminal Record Office. Such offences are not regarded as criminal, and are usually ignored in criminological surveys, so it seemed best to classify the 18 boys in question as non-delinquents.

4. *The Prevalence of Juvenile Delinquency in Other Studies*

During their juvenile years, from 10 to 17, nearly one in four of our boys appeared before a court and were found guilty of misconduct of some kind. Another estimate of the prevalence of all court appearances in a working-class area of London (Tower Hamlets) was made by Power (1965), who arrived at an almost identical result—one boy in four. Margaret Shaw (1971) of the Home Office Research Unit estimated that the comparable figure for all London was rather less (20·4 per cent), but she was surveying a slightly earlier generation, boys born in March 1946.

These estimates refer to court appearances of all kinds, but it is commoner to base delinquency rates upon findings of guilt for indictable offences. Douglas *et al.* (1966), using their national sample of children born in one week of March 1946, calculated that 10·4 per cent of males would be convicted of an indictable offence as juveniles. According to the latest National Survey figures available (Wadsworth, 1972), 13·7 per cent of London boys born in March 1946 should be found guilty as juveniles of indictable and akin-to-indictable offences. It is difficult to obtain a comparable figure in the present Study, as the offences classed as indictable changed several times between the first of our boys being convicted in 1963 and the last in 1971. However, as a rough comparison, 67 boys (16·3 per cent) were convicted as juveniles of offences which were indictable in 1962. Rather more (77, or 18·7 per cent) were convicted of offences classed as indictable in 1971, the difference being mainly due to the addition of 'taking and driving away' to the indictable category.

The smaller percentage of boys with an indictable juvenile conviction in Douglas' research is only to be expected. His sample came from all areas, whereas the present Study was based on a working-class urban neighbourhood where the incidence of convictions might be presumed to be higher. In an ecological analysis of London, Wallis and Maliphant (1967) found that delinquency rates were high in areas with high unemployment rates, large numbers of manual workers, low school leaving ages, high incidences of local authority housing, and large numbers of overcrowded houses lacking in basic amenities. The last four of the features, at least, were characteristic of the Study neighbourhood.

The resemblance between our figures and Power's shows that our boys were no different, as regards prevalence of delinquency, from boys in a comparable urban area. Certainly, the figures give no support to the suggestion that awareness of being under investigation decreased delinquency among boys in this Study. Indeed, one would not have expected it, when deliberate and massive social work interventions have been found to leave the incidence of delinquency unchanged (e.g. McCord and McCord, 1959). In the National

Survey conducted by Douglas, a research with some similarity to our own, the fact of being under investigation appeared to have little effect on the children involved. Some of the children were continuously surveyed over a long period, while others were not followed up, but the two groups proved to be very similar in educational attainment, judging by their 'O level' results in examinations for the General Certificate of Education (Douglas *et al.*, 1968; Douglas, 1970).

Studies of official statistics (see Note 3) show that the label delinquent has become so commonplace that it can hardly signify a serious deviation from the norm in most cases. Nevertheless, and perhaps somewhat surprisingly, the results to be described will show that, as a group, the delinquents in this Study did differ in important respects from their non-delinquent peers, both in family backgrounds and in individual characteristics. Recidivist delinquents deviated even more, many of them having quite serious social and personal handicaps.

5. *Age at Conviction*

Our 84 juvenile delinquents were convicted on a total of 191 occasions, which means that nearly half of the convictions were of first offenders. Table I (1) shows the ages of the boys at the times of their convictions, and also shows separately the ages when they were convicted for the first time. Offences committed at age 16, which led to convictions at age 17, are included in our statistics as juvenile

TABLE I (1)

Conviction at Each Age

	Juvenile delinquents									*Adult offenders*	
	Age in years								*Total convictions of juvenile delinquents*	*Age in years*	
	10	11	12	13	14	15	16	17*		17†	18+
Number of convictions	7	10	12	23	47	43	43	6	191	49	59
Number of first convictions	6	6	7	12	22	17	12	2	84	16	10

* Committed at age 16. † Committed at age 17.

convictions (see Note 2), but are shown separately in the table. The figures for convictions sustained at age 18 or later are as yet incomplete, being based on the latest CRO search in November 1972, when the younger boys in the sample had not reached 19. Nearly half of the boys so far convicted as adults (26 out of 62) had no previous juvenile convictions.

Table I (1) shows that the incidence of both first convictions and convictions in general increased between ages 10 and 14. However, whereas the incidence of first convictions was at its peak at age 14, the incidence of convictions in general showed no falling off, and was in fact slightly greater at age 17 than at age 14 (55 as opposed to 47). The incidence of convictions at age 18 also seems likely to be greater than at age 14, since the present incomplete figures show that 46 convictions have already occurred at that age.

In England, the peak incidence of convictions for indictable offences used to be 14 (Rose, 1968). However, with the increasing use of cautioning for younger offenders, the peak age shifted to 17 in 1968, and has remained at this point since. The majority of the Study sample were born in 1953, and so reached 14 in 1967, the last year in which the peak age was 14. However, the incidence of convictions among 14-year-olds in 1967 (3,493 per 100,000) was far less than that of 17-year-olds in 1970 (5,878 per 100,000) and that of 18-year-olds in 1971 (5,705 per 100,000). The finding that our boys have more convictions at 17 or 18 than at 14 was therefore only to be expected from national trends.

Several researches (e.g. McKissack, 1967) have linked the peak incidence of convictions to the last year of compulsory schooling. Certainly, the peak age was 13 before the Second World War, when the school-leaving age was 14, and it became 14 in the post-war years, when the school-leaving age was 15. However, the recent change in the peak age is unrelated to school leaving. Moreover, the crime peak does not necessarily coincide with the last year at school in other countries, where the age of criminal responsibility and the age of maximum criminality are both apt to occur later (Lunden, 1967). Mannheim (1965) suggested that the peak age merely reflected variations in the willingness of police and public to bring young persons before the courts. In England, recent legislation encouraging alternatives to prosecution has resulted in convictions of children under 14 years of age forming a much smaller proportion of the total of juvenile convictions.

6. *Types of Offences*

Table I (2) displays the types of juvenile offences recorded against boys in this Study. The 84 juvenile delinquents had a total of 255 delinquency charges sustained on their 191 separate occasions of conviction. The great majority of these offences (89 per cent) could be described as crimes of dishonesty, principally burglaries, thefts, and taking away vehicles. As far as can be seen from the published national statistics, such a preponderance of crimes of dishonesty is typical of English juvenile delinquents (see Note 4). It is true of most countries that the majority of young offenders are convicted for burglary, theft and similar crimes.

The business of the courts is not restricted to dealing with the offences we have classified as delinquent. Table I (2) shows that, even after setting aside offences 'taken into consideration', only about three-fifths of the charges proved against our boys fell into categories included in our juvenile delinquency count.

The exclusion of certain minor offences from the delinquency count, although logically justifiable and in accordance with criminological practice, may have been somewhat unrealistic, since the excluded offences were often indicative of a definite delinquent tendency. Thus, the fifth of the sample who were delinquents included two-thirds (8 out of 12) of the boys who had findings for 'being beyond control' or 'non-attendance at school'. The delinquent group also included 42·3 per cent (11 out of 26) of the boys found guilty of minor traffic offences as juveniles. Almost all of these minor traffic infractions were committed at 16 years of age.

The distribution of offences changed as the boys grew older. The 107 adult convictions so far recorded, involving 153 findings of guilt for delinquency offences, include larger proportions of aggressive crimes and takings of motor vehicles. Burglaries increased from 9·5 per cent of all charges at ages 10–13 to 26·0 per cent at ages 14–16, but decreased again to 13·7 per cent at ages 17–19. These changing distributions of offences with age follow the trends expected from the Criminal Statistics. For example, the 1967 figures show that burglary comprised 34 per cent of convictions at age 14–16 but only 26 per cent at age 17–20, while crimes of violence, which were 4·5 per cent at age 14–16, were as high as 10·1 per cent at age 17–20.

There was little sign of any exclusively violent offenders among our

TABLE I (2)

Delinquency Charges Sustained against 84 Juvenile Offenders

(1)	*Crimes of Dishonesty*	227	(89·0%)
	Theft* from shops or market stalls	24	
	Theft* from and of motor vehicles	30	
	Unauthorized taking* of motor vehicles	32	
	Theft* of cycles or parts of cycles	9	
	Theft* from automatic machines	10	
	Other theft*	29	
	Burglary*	56	
	Fraud, forgery, fare evasion, etc.	6	
	Handling stolen property, receiving, unlawful possession, etc.	10	
	Equipped to steal, being a suspected person, etc.	21	
(2)	*Aggressive Crimes*	16	(6·3%)
	Robbery	3	
	Assault	4	
	Insulting or threatening behaviour	5	
	Carrying an offensive weapon	4	
(3)	*Damage to Property*	8	(3·1%)
	Wilful or malicious damage	7	
	Arson	1	
(4)	*Sex Offences*	4	(1·6%)
	Indecent assault on female	1	
	Unlawful sexual intercourse	1	
	Indecent exposure	1	
	Indecent telephone message	1	
	TOTAL	255	(100·0%)

Offences Excluded from the Figures given above but Recorded against 84 Delinquents and 18 other Boys in the Study

Offences 'taken into consideration'	87
Breaches of probation and conditional discharge	17
Non-attendance at school, or being beyond control	12
Minor offences dealt with at the same time as delinquency offences†	52
Other minor offences of delinquents†	57
Minor offences of non-delinquents†	48
Total Excluded Offences	273

* Including attempts.

† The excluded minor offences were all traffic offences, with two exceptions: one instance of purchasing and one of possessing an air pistol under age 17, both concerning the same boy, and both dealt with at the same time as delinquency offences.

84 juvenile delinquents. The 13 boys who were found guilty of violent offences (such as robbery, assault, insulting or threatening behaviour and carrying an offensive weapon) were generally property offenders as well. Excluding robbery, which is clearly also a crime of dishonesty, all but two of these 13 boys had additional convictions for dishonesty. A similar association between violent and other offences was reported by Walker *et al.* (1967), who found that, the more non-violent offences a person had committed, the more likely it was that his next conviction would be for a violent offence. They concluded that 'most [violent] convictions are an occupational risk of a career of non-violent crime'. McClintock (1963), in a study of violent offenders in London, also reported that nearly half of those being convicted for violence for the first time had previous convictions for non-violent offences. In our Study, there was more sign of specialization among the small number of sex offenders. Three out of the four had no other convictions apart from their single sexual offence. It is noteworthy that there were no juvenile drug offenders in the sample. The 84 delinquents were almost all convicted of at least one crime of dishonesty. In view of this, it was not feasible, when analysing our results, to subdivide the delinquents on the basis of type of offence.

7. *Companions in Crime*

According to police records, most of the offences of our 84 delinquents were committed together with one or more other persons. The companions were usually other boys of similar age. About five-sixths of the burglaries (46 out of 56), and three-quarters of the thefts from shops (18 out of 24) were recorded by the police as having been committed with (typically, two) others. Nine-tenths (27 out of 30) of the thefts from vehicles were committed with (typically, one) other, but nearly half (14 out of 32) of the offences of taking vehicles were apparently committed alone. However, it must be remembered that most of the vehicles taken by these juveniles were mopeds and scooters, not cars. A quarter of the delinquents (21 out of 84) were actually convicted for an offence committed with one or more other boys in the Study. Only 13 boys had no offence recorded as committed with others. These 13 solitary offenders included two of the four convicted of sexual offences. The fact that young delinquents in London tend to commit their offences in small groups is corroborated by the 1967 Report of the Commissioner of Police of the Metropolis. This stated that 63 per cent of persons under 21 arrested in London for indictable offences in that year were operating with other persons. The majority of groups were of two or three, and most could not by any stretch of the imagination be termed 'gangs'. Scott (1956) analysed group offences in London, and concluded that only about 12 per cent of the juveniles concerned were in structured gangs.

Similar findings have been obtained in other countries. Eynon and Reckless (1961) investigated white delinquents admitted to an institution in Ohio, and found that 75 per cent of boys were with companions when they committed the act that first brought them official attention. Craig and Budd (1967) reported that 63 per cent of a sample of (predominantly negro) delinquents in New York convicted of burglary and theft were with companions at the time of the offence. Sveri (1965) studied Norwegian police statistics, and showed that only 17 per cent of offenders aged 13–14 were alone, 46 per cent were with one or two others, and 37 per cent were with three or more others, when they committed offences. Several researchers have shown that the proportion of offences committed alone increases with age.

The finding that juvenile delinquency is a group activity accords with some sociological theories. In particular, the theory of differential association (Sutherland and Cressey, 1970) suggests that delinquent behaviour is learned as a result of interaction processes in small groups. This topic will be discussed further in connection with the questioning of boys about the delinquent activities of their friends (pp. 155–7).

8. *Court Disposals*

The majority of convictions were followed by non-custodial sentences. Counting only the most serious of the court's decisions on any given occasion, the 191 convictions led to 77 conditional or absolute discharges, 39 fines, 38 probation orders, 14 attendance centre orders, 4 detention centre orders, 18 approved school or fit person orders and one committal to Borstal training. In all, only 16 boys were sent to residential institutions following convictions for juvenile delinquency. The comparatively light sentences awarded in most cases reflect the generally trivial nature of the offences brought before the London juvenile courts. Although direct comparison is not possible, there seem to have been slightly more discharges and rather fewer probation orders in the Study sample than might have been expected on the basis of the 1967 Criminal Statistics for the Metropolitan Police District. This may be because these statistics are restricted to indictable offences.

9. *Criminal Careers*

Longitudinal surveys, if carried through for long enough, provide information about individuals whose delinquency careers start later in life, as well as about those who begin to have convictions at an early age. There is evidence from the data already available that young delinquents differ in character according to age at first conviction (see e.g. p. 29). Equally interesting, a longitudinal survey can provide information about the termination of delinquent careers, and perhaps show differences between recidivists whose convictions cease after a short period and those whose convictions spread over many years. Previous investigations of criminal careers have nearly always been retrospective, and have been hampered by the difficulty of obtaining a complete coverage of juvenile records. Some of these, such as the survey of professional criminals by Mack (1972) and the surveys by Taylor (1960) and West (1963) of preventive detainees, suggest that a significant proportion of persistent adult criminals have had no juvenile or early adult convictions. Time will tell how many true latecomers to crime will emerge from the present sample, and whether they will have distinctive characteristics.

Investigations of recidivist offenders in a number of countries suggest that, the earlier in life an offender is convicted, the greater the likelihood that he will go on committing crimes over a long period (Sellin, 1958). Some evidence that this may become true of the Study boys has already emerged. The 19 boys first found guilty between the ages of 10 and 12 amassed between them a further 67 juvenile convictions, and so far have had another 21 convictions as adults. Even allowing for their longer period 'at risk' of reconviction, this represents a much higher reconviction rate than that of the boys convicted for the first time at later ages.

Among the 84 delinquents, over half (47) were convicted as juveniles on one occasion only. Of the 37 recidivists, the most persistently delinquent boy had a total of 14 juvenile convictions, and was subsequently convicted twice more within the three months following his seventeenth birthday. One boy had 9 juvenile convictions, one had 8 and five others had 6. It is illuminating to summarize the career of the boy with the most juvenile convictions, as revealed by official records. Although he was unusual in having so many offences recorded, the kinds of offences he committed were typical of the delinquent boys in this Study.

Case 341
Age 2 *years*—3*m*. Brought before the court as being in need of care and protection. Three years' supervision order made. A police officer stated she was called to the boy's home and found it in a deplorable condition. The children were badly clothed and smelt badly. The bedding was poor and insufficient.

8 *years*—7*m*. In company with another boy, he was caught by the police stealing a box of chocolates from a milk float. He admitted the theft. He was not taken to court.

10 *years*—7*m*. Convicted of breaking into a warehouse and stealing a football and other property to the value of £3.50, together with three other boys and one girl. Arrested at the scene of the crime. Pleaded not guilty. Put on probation for three years.

11 *years*—0*m*. Seen by a police constable to take a box of mushrooms from a market stall and run away. He was with another boy. The owners of the property declined to prosecute.

11 *years*—2*m*. Taken to court for entering a block of flats and stealing lead. Case dismissed.

13 *years*—0*m*. Taken to court for stealing from a railway station 71 postcards, one map and three guide books; total value £2. Appeared before the court with his sister and another boy. Case dismissed.

13 *years*—2*m*. Convicted with another boy of stealing a camera valued at £15. Given one year conditional discharge. No separate penalty imposed in respect of the breach of probation incurred by this offence.

13 *years*—7*m*. Convicted with three other boys of stealing coins from a slot machine by forcing a wire up the slot. Ordered to go to an attendance centre for 12 hours and to pay £1 costs.

13 *years*—10*m*. Convicted of stealing an anorak from a shop, value £2.25, and also of being beyond control. A woman police constable stated in her evidence that she saw the boy and his sister at the police station with their parents after they had run away from home. The father complained that the children were always truanting from school and had been running away from home at intervals over a year. He also stated that they were both beyond the control of his wife and himself. The file included a note that the parents were *very anti-police* and

should be treated with caution. At the court hearing, a Fit Person Order was made to the local authority.

14 *years—0m.* Charged, together with his brother, with attempted taking and driving away and with tampering with the mechanism of a motor vehicle. He pleaded guilty to the second charge and was fined £0.20. The first charge was not proceeded with.

14 *years—3m.* Convicted, together with others, of breaking into a house and stealing cash to value of £7.50. Given a conditional discharge for a year.

14 *years—7m.* Convicted, with his brother and three other boys, of taking and driving away a moped. Pleaded guilty. Sent to an approved school.

14 *years—7m.* Convicted of burglary, and given a one year conditional discharge. He had opened the window of a ground-floor flat and entered as a trespasser with intent to steal. Caught by the occupant. Pleaded guilty. At the time, he was an absconder from a remand home and had been sleeping rough.

14 *years—7m.* Convicted and sent to an approved school for three offences. (1) Broke the glass in a rear ground floor window and entered. Forced inner doors with bodily pressure. Stole money to the value of £4.50. (2) Entered a café as a trespasser and stole money and cigarettes valued at £51. (3) Theft from a shop of trousers, shirt and shoes valued at £5. Pleaded guilty. Legally represented at the court hearing. Certified unruly and ordered to be detained in a remand centre pending classification.

14 *years—9m.* Convicted of taking and driving away a moped, driving with no insurance and driving under age. Committed to an approved school for the first and second offences, and given a one year conditional discharge for the third. Pleaded guilty. The police notes recorded that he admitted burglary and theft from a motor vehicle in the area, and that he was suspected of other offences.

15 *years—2m.* Convicted of being found, with one other boy, on enclosed premises for an unlawful purpose. Pleaded guilty. Committed to an approved school.

16 *years—2m.* Convicted with one other boy of stealing grapes valued at £0.50 from a market stall. Pleaded not guilty. Given a one year conditional discharge.

16 *years—6m.* Convicted of two offences of burglary. (1) With three other youths, entered some unlocked and unattended offices and stole purses containing £34.50 in cash. (2) Kept watch outside while another youth broke into a school house and stole one electric razor. He was given three months in a detention centre on each charge, the sentences to run concurrently.

16 *years*—11*m*. Convicted of four offences. (1) Stealing by finding a rail season ticket. (2) Obtaining pecuniary advantage by using the season ticket to avoid payment for a train journey. (3) Burglary: removed a window pane, entered and stole property. (4) Burglary: forced a door using bodily pressure, entered and stole property. One other offence of burglary was also taken into consideration. He was fined £10 for each of the first two offences and conditionally discharged for two years on the third and fourth.

17 *years*—2*m*. Convicted of theft from a person and sent to Borstal. With two other youths, he jostled a woman who was waiting at a bus stop and took a purse from her basket. All three youths were stopped by police a short time later, and the property found in their possession was traced back to the loser. The offence was denied at first, but all three youths subsequently pleaded guilty. It was thought that our boy's accomplice was responsible for the physical act of theft, although all were considered equally responsible for the commission of the offence. Given one day's detention (to run concurrently) in respect of the breach of a conditional discharge incurred by his offence.

17 *years*—2*m*. Convicted, with one other youth, of being a suspected person loitering with intent to commit an arrestable offence. He was seen to try car door handles on three separate occasions. Fined £5 or 1 day imprisonment. Served 1 day.

10. *Boys' Descriptions of their Offences and Convictions*

Judging by the decisions of the courts, most of the juvenile offences were not very serious crimes. This impression is confirmed by police descriptions and by the boys' own versions of what happened. When they were re-interviewed at 18 years, the boys were questioned about their past delinquencies, and their comments were recorded on tape. Some examples, quoted verbatim, are given below. Even after making allowance for the self-exculpatory bias in some of these accounts, one was left with the impression, especially in the case of boys with one conviction only, that their misbehaviour was often less grave than the ponderous legal terminology might suggest. Recidivists, however, frequently expressed an opportunistic and nonchalant attitude to law-breaking which revealed a more serious commitment to delinquent habits. There was a widespread tendency among the boys to blame the police for making too much out of their misdemeanours. The significance of the legal decisions made by the court were very often lost upon these boys, who failed to appreciate the difference between costs and fines, or between a conditional discharge and a case dismissed. Any decision other than a custodial sentence was often regarded as being 'let off'.

Case 640
The criminal records stated that this boy 'forced the quarter light of an unattended motor vehicle and stole property from it, value not stated'. He was found guilty of 'larceny from a vehicle'. He was aged 13 years and one month at the time, and this was his only conviction. He was remanded in custody for one month and a Fit Person Order to the local authority was made. The boy's own version was as follows:

'I was going around in a gang, and me and some other kids broke into this ice-cream van—it sold cigarettes. We were going for the cigarettes and the money. At the time I thought I saw some bloke who went and told the owner we were in there. He came in and caught us. He took us in his house and rang for the police. There were two of us caught, but there were more. He held us until the police arrived. The police took the particulars at the Station. I was kept in. They took me to my house and my mother said: "Do what you want with him." I was sent to [a remand home], put on remand 6 weeks and appeared in court three times. They put me under care, that was all they did.'

The Children's Department record made this offence appear even more trivial, describing it as 'larceny of three bars of chocolate'.

Case 811
This was another example of a one-time delinquent. At age 15 years and one month he was convicted of attempted store-breaking, and fined £1, plus £1 costs. The official record stated: 'With two other youths, also in custody, smashed window of cycle shop with brick and removed cycle tyre. . . . Pleaded guilty, legally represented.' At age 18 the boy gave an amusing version of what took place:

'We was going to have just a laugh and smash a shop window. I threw the brick, didn't I, and the brick bounced off. So I ran up and got on my bike and rode off. But my mate, he said, "I ain't mucking about I'll smash it." So he chucked a brick and got caught. So when the police came to the shop one of them nicked an inner tube out of the shop to make it look like a smash and grab. When he got back to the Station, he was taking his overcoat off, and the Superintendent saw it fall out of his pocket, and they tried to have us on that, but the Superintendent spoke up for us and we got let off. I think I got a £2 fine. They discharged us, but we had to pay costs. They never had no evidence. I got squealed on. I was with three mates. One was sent to Borstal because he was on Probation. The other one did not get nothing because he was not caught. One of my mates squealed on me, but he did not squeal on the other one. I didn't squeal on the other, I said it was just the two of us.'

Cases 240, 482 *and* 911
These examples illustrate a kind of offence typical of the older juvenile. Three boys from the Study, all one-time delinquents, were involved

together. All three were nearly 17 years of age at the time. The official records of the boys ran as follows:

Case 911
'(i) Theft of a motor scooter. Fined £7. (ii) No insurance. Fined £2 and licence endorsed. £0.05 costs. On 3 Jan. [—] at [—] stole a motor scooter left unattended, by removing parts. Convicted with two others, neither of whom had previous convictions.'

Case 240
'Theft of a motor scooter. Fined £8, 28 days to pay. Convicted with two others.'

Case 482
'Taking a motor scooter and dismantling it. Pleaded guilty. Fined £8, 28 days to pay. Convicted with 2 others.'

The boys' versions were all in substantial agreement, indicating surprisingly truthful reporting to the interviewers. They ran as follows:

Case 911
'The next time I was in trouble over driving was when I nicked the bike. It must have been about 15 months ago. I got an endorsement for it. There was no insurance on it when I was driving the bike. We got the bike up to my house—right—put it in the shed. We nicked it down [—]. There was three of us altogether. We knew whose it was—we knew the kid who had it. I don't know him—I just know who he is—he just used to go to my mate's school. I drove this scooter back to the house because I never had my bike, it was all smashed up, that's why I wanted it. I put it in the back shed—stripped it down. We done it through the night, someone must have heard us. We just had it in bits and we took the frame and left it round the corner on a bomb site. Next morning the police arrived. There was two scooters parked outside and all—my mate's scooter. They both stayed with me over that night. They got the same except they never got done for no insurance because I was the one driving.'

Case 482
'Me and a couple of my mates—they nicked a scooter. . . . They said I stole the bike. I was there when they stole it. I drove with them, as I had my scooter with me, up to my friend's house and helped him to take it apart and throw the rest of it away—like dump it. My mate wanted the bits, the wheels for his scooter and other bits and pieces. I dumped it down the road about 50 yards from up there. It was obvious really, it was stupid. We all had our scooters parked outside my mate's house, and one of them was exactly the same colour as the one we had dumped. So the policeman just put two and two together, you know. He went into the back garden before we even knew about it, and he found some parts. Then he knocked at the door. He was talking to us and said "You don't mind if I look in the back shed do you?". He went out and found the stuff and that was that. . . . We all got the

same fine, but one of my mates got [another] £10 fine because he drove it without insurance.'

Case 240
'It was January I went to court—before I was 17. I got an £8 fine and my licence endorsed. The reason I done it was, there was this geezer down [—]—used to hang about—had this scooter. Well, he did not hang about with us—he was always out on his own like, and he had a scooter exactly the same colour as mine. It was metallic gold. That was the only thing interested me because I could have side panels and all sorts of things off it. It would not make any difference to my own bike because it was exactly the same colour. We knew where the bloke lived so we went down there—I broke the steering and my mate drove it away—we drove it around to this geezer's house in [—]. His Mum and Dad had gone to bed by that time. We went out the back and stripped it down, hid most of the parts in the old shed at the back—I dumped the engine which was numbered, we didn't want that—and my two mates dumped the frames. I said, "Dump it well—don't leave it out in the streets or something." Anyway, they left it out in the streets and the law found it. They were just patrolling around, and they saw my bike exactly the same colour—so they came and made enquiries. They said. "We know you nicked that bike", sort of thing. So eventually I gave in and said, "Yes, I done it" and we owned up. We found out afterwards they didn't even know it had been nicked—they conned us like. It hadn't been reported that it had been nicked—the geezer hadn't reported it. It was Sunday morning.'

The victim of this offence, who also happened to be one of the boys in the Study, gave the following version of the incident:

Case 573
'I had me scooter nicked and stripped down by me mates. I used to go to school with this bloke—I don't know why he nicked it. They got caught anyway. They'd stripped it down—all that was left was the frame. They found it over in [—]. Just the frame. I used to go to school with one of the blokes. They all had scooters and I suppose they wanted the parts—but they put the parts on straight away, so they got caught. This bloke was riding along on a black scooter with an orange side panel or something stupid like that. A policeman knew the bloke and wondered where he'd got the coloured side panel from.'

Case 411
In contrast to the previous cases, this is an example of a boy more deeply committed to delinquency, who was convicted on three separate occasions as a juvenile, and reconvicted in an adult court at age 18. The official record of his first conviction at age 13 years 10 months stated 'Unlawful possession of 40 lbs. of scrap lead. Probation order two years. With two other youths was stopped in possession of lead and failed to give a satisfactory explanation as to how he had obtained same. [All three] convicted'. At 14 years 2 months he was convicted,

together with another boy, for housebreaking, and was committed to an approved school. No action was taken in respect of the breach of probation involved. It was stated that he 'opened a window, entered and stole property. Pleaded guilty.' Six offences were taken into consideration, namely: (1) Breaking into a house and stealing £2 from a meter. (2) Entering a house and stealing £3 from a gas meter. (3) Stealing £0.35 from a prepayment meter. (4) Entering an open door and stealing a gas lighter, and two oranges, value £20 cash from a house. (5) Breaking and entering a house and stealing £1.50. (6) Breaking and entering a store and stealing cash from a meter, also a clock and watch. The first five offences taken into consideration were committed at three different houses in the street where he was living.

At age 14 years 8 months, he was convicted at a court in another town of: (1) Taking and driving away a motor cycle. (2) Store-breaking and larceny. (3) Driving without insurance. (4) Aiding and abetting another boy to drive under age. For (1), (2) and (3), he was again committed to approved school, and for (4) he was given an absolute discharge. He was convicted with two associates. Twenty-two offences were taken into consideration, mostly taking and driving away or breaking and stealing from houses and stores, always together with the same two associates.

When seen at 18 years of age, the boy's version of the offences was as follows: 'The first time I got done was when I was 13. I got done for unlawful possession of lead. I nicked some lead from an old house—I'd done it before a couple of times. We was walking along the road with a big box and they said "Where did you get this?" so we said "We found it." You know we couldn't say anything else because we had it with us. So they took us down to the police station and charged us. . . . [The following year] I done a lot of housebreaking down [—] Green. I got caught for most of the housebreakings. I got charged for two of the housebreakings and got remanded in custody at [—], and then I went back to court and I got approved school. I stayed 7 months and then absconded. I did all the housebreakings with one mate. I think my mate grassed on me. I didn't get caught, I was in the house and there was someone in there. We ran out and he caught my mate. The police came and my mate got away but they caught him again. They came around to my house [later] and said "We are taking you down to the police station for questioning." The police had pulled us up in the morning [before the housebreaking] and searched us and asked us why we wasn't at school. They remembered us. [After] they caught my mate they came and got me because I'd been with him. I denied it you know but they said "You did it. Your mate has already told us you did it." I did admit it in the end because they had all the fingerprints. . . . [When] I was on the run from approved school I nicked about 7 cars and did a couple of housebreakings . . . [Why did you abscond?] For something to do you know, you get fed up. I was just sitting in the yard and a geezer said to me "Do you want to do a bunk?" So I said "Yeah!" and he said we'd be going next Saturday, bonfire night. They had a big bonfire. We went back to the dormitory and when everybody was out we got dressed and got out through the fire exit. We walked to [the nearest town] along the railway lines, nicked a car and got to [—]. We nicked another and drove to [—] and then another one and went somewhere else . . . Till we landed up in [—]. [How did you feed yourself?] We just broke into a garage and nicked a load of cigarettes and sweets and stuff, and there was a load of food in there and we started cooking the food. We wore approved school clothes all the time. The jackets were all different colours. We got another jacket we found in one of the cases with a jumper and that. We didn't see many coppers on the way down. [How did you get caught?] Well, we had done a load of jobs and that. We had nicked another car and we was just going to come back in this other car when the cop car sees us and chased us. I got out of the car and run and the others run. They caught one of them and the other one got caught later. They caught me in the evening walking down the road. They took us to the police station and we stayed there the night. . . .'

Asked about undetected offences, he said: 'Yes, loads of things. I've been pulled up a couple of times and when they tried to bring something on me, housebreaking and things like that, they took me down to the Station, but nothing ever happened. . . . They even tried to do me for doing my own house. Someone broke into our house and done the gas meter. They made me go down to the Station to take my finger-prints. Silly sods!'

11. *A Scale of Delinquency*

Returning to the crucial question of the measurement of delinquency, it is clear that the official delinquent/non-delinquent dichotomy, for all its simplicity, has many drawbacks. The official delinquents are not all equally committed to delinquency, and the official non-delinquents are not equally free from delinquent tendencies. From the point of view of comparison with other research, however, it is helpful to maintain the cut-off point between official delinquents and others. The problem then resolves itself into how to subdivide the delinquent group, and how to subdivide the non-delinquent group, so that the boys are ordered according to their respective degrees of delinquent behaviour.

In this report, the officially delinquent group has simply been divided into two, the 37 recidivists with two or more convictions for juvenile offences, and the 47 convicted once only as juveniles. Ranking offenders according to the number of their convictions appears crude, since offences differ in kind and in seriousness, and quality might be considered more important than quantity. There are precedents for scaling delinquents by grading each offence according to seriousness. The most famous attempt to do this was carried out by Sellin and Wolfgang (1964), on the basis of ratings of perceived severity made by policemen, judges and students. In the present instance, however, a simple count of convictions seemed the best method. As pointed out earlier, convictions for offences other than crimes of dishonesty were the exception, and most boys who acquired them had also been found guilty of dishonesty. In this working class area, official convictions were very largely an index of police action against thieving. Since other forms of delinquency hardly entered the picture, number of convictions might well be the best available index of severity of delinquency.

This suggestion was supported by evidence that more seriously delinquent behaviour tends to go hand in hand with more convictions. For example, McClintock and Avison (1968), in their survey of crime in England and Wales, reported that 70 per cent of persons with five or more convictions had been found guilty of an offence at least as serious as burglary. This could also be seen in the present Study. Only 10 of the 47 one-time delinquents were convicted of burglary, robbery, arson or causing bodily harm, in comparison with 11 of the 14 boys having four or more convictions. A simple count of a boy's convictions, therefore, should provide a reasonable index of the severity of his delinquent behaviour. The limited number of Study delinquents unfortunately precluded any further subdivision beyond the one-timer and recidivist groups.

The non-delinquents were also subdivided according to degree of delinquent tendency, by taking account of police action short of prosecution. Many boys caught misbehaving by the police were released with an unofficial warning or 'telling off', and a few received official cautions (Steer, 1970). During most of the juvenile life span of the boys, it was official police policy, in the area where we were based, to prosecute nearly all apprehended juvenile offenders rather than to administer official cautions. With the partial implementation of the Children's and Young Persons' Act (1969), and the setting up of a police juvenile bureau system, that policy changed. Official cautions began to take the place of prosecutions in cases where the juvenile's offence history and the results of social enquiries by the police appeared to warrant such action. However, only four of the unconvicted boys in this Study received cautions through local police bureaux for delinquent offences, so the new policy could not have had much effect on our juvenile delinquency rate.

In order to investigate what might be called the borderland of official delinquency, we isolated from the remainder of the non-delinquents a group of 56 boys who we called police contact cases. These were boys who had experienced some official police action resulting from their misbehaviour, although they had not reached the point of acquiring an entry in the Criminal Record Office. The criteria for membership of this group were as follows:

(a) Any finding of guilt for a minor offence not normally recorded in the CRO.
(b) Police prosecutions that failed or were not proceeded with.
(c) Misconduct notified by police to a Children's Department or dealt with by a police juvenile bureau without prosecution.
(d) Official cautions or serious warnings by the police involving a summons to the police station or a visit to the parents.

These incidents were counted only if the information came from official sources, or if a report by the boy was corroborated by his parents.

It was recognized that the definition of this group was somewhat arbitrary, and their identification perhaps not absolutely complete, but nevertheless the criteria succeeded in producing a group of boys who were clearly half-way delinquents. Of the 56 police contact boys, 33 had been dealt with for acts which would have come within our definition of delinquency convictions if they have been proved in court. The remaining 23 had been dealt with for more minor offences, and 14 of them had actually been found guilty by the courts, all for traffic offences. Already, 16·1 per cent of the police contact group have been convicted as adults, compared with only 6·3 per cent of the remaining non-delinquents.

The final scale of official delinquency used in the main body of this report was as follows:

Recidivist juvenile delinquents—37 (9·0 per cent);
One-time juvenile delinquents (i.e. having only one delinquency conviction)—47 (11·4 per cent);
Non-delinquents with police contacts—56 (13·6 per cent);
Non-delinquents with no police contacts—271 (65·9 per cent).

This scale of delinquency, derived from official records, does seem to provide a realistic, if rather rough and ready, measure of severity. As will be shown later, most of the observations on these boys, in regard to conduct, personality and achievement (whether by parents, teachers, peers, or the boys themselves), tended to rank the four groups of the delinquency scale in the same order, the recidivists being worst and the non-delinquents without police contacts best.

An alternative scale of delinquency, taking into account the boys' ratings of their own delinquent behaviour, will be discussed later (see pp. 162–3).

12. *Conclusions*

The boys' delinquency records have been described in some detail in order to substantiate some points of importance for the interpretation of the results to follow. First, findings from the Study sample (such as the prevalence of convictions, the distribution of charges and of court actions taken, the ages of the offenders involved, and the tendency for them to be caught in the company of others) are fairly typical of the young male population in working class areas of London. This means that the findings of this research probably apply to many communities besides the particular neighbourhood from which these boys were recruited. Second, for all their limitations and apparent arbitrariness, official delinquency convictions and police records do appear to distinguish, surprisingly realistically and effectively, between sections of the population with very different levels of delinquency involvement and delinquency potential. A scale based upon numbers of official convictions does appear to reflect genuine gradations of delinquency. Finally, inspection of the nature and circumstances of offences leading to convictions suggests that a large proportion were seemingly trivial. However, a delinquency conviction probably reflects far more in the way of disturbed behaviour than is officially recorded at the time, and is therefore of more serious import than might appear. As this report will show, boys with even a single juvenile delinquency conviction, or merely a record of contact with the police, are significantly different from their peers in many respects.

NOTES

[1] *Sources and Dates of Data Collection*

The intention was to include at least 400 boys in the Study, but this was too many to be interviewed in the space of a single year, so two successive classroom generations were recruited. Essentially, the sample consisted of two groups, 231 boys born between 1 September 1952 and 31 August 1953, who were recruited during the academic year beginning September 1961, and 157 boys born between

1 September 1953 and 31 August 1954, who were recruited during the academic year beginning September 1962. We refer to these as the older and younger cohorts. The younger cohort was smaller because, in two of the schools, no more boys were included after the first year of intake. This was decided upon to prevent numbers becoming unmanageably large. In addition, a small pilot group of 23, including all the boys from a particular class in one of the schools, was recruited at an earlier stage, actually towards the end of the academic year beginning September 1960. These boys, born between 1 September 1951 and 31 August 1952, were a year older than the older cohort. Throughout the research, they have been the first to be contacted each time the sample has been surveyed.

The first steps in planning and making arrangements for this Study took place in 1960, and the first contacts with the oldest boys were made in 1961. It was September 1971, more than 10 years later, before the youngest boy had turned 17 years of age and passed out of the jurisdiction of the juvenile courts. Complete records of official findings of guilt during the entire juvenile life span of all the boys became available by the end of 1971, thereby permitting a final analysis of the characteristics of the juvenile delinquent group.

The boys were interviewed on five occasions, initially at age 8–9, at 10–11 during their last year of primary education, and again at 14–15 shortly before the earliest date at which they could leave school. They were seen a fourth time at 16–17, when most of them had in fact left school, and yet again at 18–19. The first three interviews, which were conducted by psychologists employed full time on the Study, consisted almost entirely of questionnaires and tests. This approach fitted naturally into the school setting, where tests of various kinds were commonplace. It also fulfilled the requirements of the Education Authority, who permitted access to the boys in school on the understanding that personal questions were to be avoided. The interviews at age 16 were less formal, and were mostly conducted at the research office in the evenings by psychologists or social scientists working part-time. In the main, they consisted of a schedule of questions about employment and leisure pursuits. The boys were paid a small fee and expenses for attendance. At this age, 398 out of the 411 (96·8 per cent) were successfully traced and interviewed. The interviews at age 18 were more extensive, being concerned with social attitudes and delinquent experiences, as well as with personal histories and work records. Over 94 per cent of the original sample, 389 were successfully re-interviewed.

Information from the parents was obtained initially by means of unstructured interviews conducted by three experienced female psychiatric social workers, who visited the homes and talked whenever possible with both mother and father. A large schedule of information was recorded, necessitating three to four interviews, each an hour or so in duration. The response was variable, but with persistence at least some information was gained from over 90 per cent of the parents, and full cooperation was secured from the great majority. Efforts were made to complete the basic home background information while the boys were under 10 years of age, and in fact the case record forms were for the most part completed during the first year of contact with the family. Thereafter, the three social workers (and their successors) re-interviewed the parents approximately once a year, in order to maintain contact, record changes and administer various questionnaires. The social workers also kept in touch with a variety of outside agencies, such as health visitors, the local Family Service Unit and the local childrens' officers, in order to supplement the data about the families, and especially about the small minority who were uncooperative or reluctant to divulge information. Visiting of parents ceased when the boys were 14–15 and began to leave school.

The family background information relating to the boys' development up to 10 years of age, together with the data collected from the schools at the same time, were coded and transferred to punched cards by November 1964. These data form the main basis of the present report. Information from subsequent social enquiries, and from repeat interviews with the boys at ages 14, 16 and 18, has been drawn upon only to a limited extent, either to confirm earlier observations or to supplement official criminal records. For instance, the boys' own admissions of delinquent acts have been used to provide an alternative means of assessing involvement in delinquency.

Only the more important factors are discussed in this report, namely those that were reasonably well defined and had been assessed in a comparatively objective manner when the boys were 10 years of age or younger. In addition, some factors were chosen for discussion because they proved to be closely related to delinquency, and others were chosen because they have been cited frequently in the criminological literature.

[2] *Information on Delinquency Convictions of Boys in the Study*

Information about the juvenile court appearances of the 411 boys was obtained by repeated name searches at the Criminal Record Office and at the relevant local authority Children's Departments, now the Children's Sections of the Social Service Departments. Apart from the need for repeated searches as boys grew older, repetition proved to be necessary to ensure accuracy. In a few cases in which information from the boy or elsewhere did not agree with that in the CRO files, the discrepancies were resolved by reference to local police or court records. Convictions for minor offences occurring in the provinces were not invariably on record in the CRO. Six boys spent over a year of their juvenile life span outside England and Wales. In their cases, approaches were made to the appropriate authorities, as a result of which one was counted as a delinquent. The official conviction records were thus effectively complete for the whole sample.

A count was made of all court appearances resulting from offences committed between the boys' tenth and seventeenth birthdays. The lower age limit was set by the age of criminal responsibility, and the upper one by the legal definition of a juvenile for the purpose of juvenile court jurisdiction. The age of criminal responsibility was raised from 8 to 10 with effect from 1 February 1964, at which time the younger boys in the Study were aged 9. Consequently, only the older boys were exposed to the risk of conviction for the full period between their eighth and tenth birthdays. Convictions sustained under age 10 (three in all) were therefore discounted. It seemed logical to use the date the offence was committed rather than the date of appearance in court to decide whether to classify a conviction as 'juvenile'. Two boys were counted as delinquents, even though their first findings of guilt (owing to delays in apprehension or in legal procedure) did not take place until they had turned 17, because the offences in question had been committed at age 16.

Juvenile delinquency convictions were defined as findings of guilt for offences normally registered in the CRO. This meant excluding minor non-indictable traffic offences and breaches of regulations, as well as appearances for non-attendance at school, for care and protection proceedings, or for non-payment of fines. Breaches of conditional discharges, probation orders or attendance centre orders were also excluded. These exceptions were necessary in order to avoid one criminal offence being counted as two convictions, thereby exaggerating the statistics of recidivism. Moreover, minor traffic offences not counted as convictions could result in breaches. In the case of juvenile offenders, any findings for assaultive or disorderly behaviour (e.g. common assault, insulting behaviour) were counted as delinquency convictions, regardless of whether or not they were in the CRO.

In addition to the 84 juvenile delinquents, and the 18 other juveniles against whom some positive court findings were recorded, one other boy was found guilty but then successfully appealed against his conviction, and four others made court appearances in which the case was dismissed. Other boys were taken to court but then their charges were 'not proceeded with' (e.g. because the police offered no evidence). After the age of 10, only one boy was found 'in need of care, protection or control', and he had delinquency convictions as well.

[3] *Further Statistics on the Prevalence of Juvenile Delinquency*

The prevalence estimates cited in the text were based on samples of people, but estimates can be obtained from the whole population of offenders revealed in the national statistics. Until 1963, the Supplementary Criminal Statistics set out the number of persons of each age convicted for the first time in a given year. By relating these figures to the population in each age group, it was possible to estimate how many persons would be convicted as juveniles. On the basis of the 1962 statistics, Little (1965) and McClintock and Avison (1968) deduced that 10·9 per cent of males would be convicted of an indictable offence as juveniles. This figure confirms that obtained by Douglas. In all probability these prevalence estimates are still substantially applicable, since the total number of juveniles convicted of indictable crimes in 1963 (61,140) and in 1971 (62,041) were much the same, although convictions under age 14 were less frequent at the later date.

It is difficult to make exact comparisons, but the prevalence of official delinquency appears to be at least as great in the United States as in England. For example, Savitz (1970) found that 59 per cent of boys living in one area of the city of Philadelphia acquired court records by age 18, while Hathaway *et al.* (1960) found that 34 per cent of boys in a large sample representative of the whole state of Minnesota had police or court records by age 17. Turning to studies based on official statistics, Christensen (1967) estimated on the Uniform Crime Reports (covering the majority of the United States) that 25 per cent of the country's male population were arrested before age 17. For urban areas, Monahan (1960) calculated that 22 per cent of Philadelphia's male population appeared in court on a delinquency charge before age 18, while Ball *et al.* (1964) obtained a figure of 21 per cent for a metropolitan area in Kentucky.

[4] *The Distribution of Convictions according to Type of Offence*

It is difficult to compare the figures in Table I (2) with those in the Criminal Statistics, because in the latter only indictable convictions are recorded, and the 'principal' offence is registered on each occasion of conviction. The 'principal' offence is the one in respect of which proceedings were carried farthest. If there are two or more findings of guilt, it is the offence for which the heaviest punishment is awarded, while, if two or more equal punishments are awarded, the principal offence is the one with the maximum permissible penalty. However, ignoring this complication, and considering the year 1967 (being the year half way between the first and last juvenile Study conviction), nearly 92 per cent of indictable juvenile convictions were for crimes of dishonesty.

II

The Home Background

1. *Family Income*

The material standards of the families among the working class population in this Study varied considerably. While some could afford to run cars and have ambitious holidays, others had a struggle to provide adequate food and clothing. Standards depended mainly upon the father's earnings and the number of dependent children. The psychiatric social workers (PSWs) who visited the homes when the boys were aged 8 to 9 asked about all sources of income, including the mother's own earnings, state assistance, and contributions from lodgers or other members of the household. They also enquired about particular items of expenditure, such as rent and hire purchase, and whether the mother kept to a weekly housekeeping budget.

Accurate information about family income proved difficult to obtain, since some parents were sensitive about this, and many a woman was vague about or genuinely ignorant of her husband's total earnings. Ultimately, the PSWs had to make an impressionistic judgment, categorizing each family's financial situation as comfortable, adequate or poor, taking into account all circumstances, including the number of children. As a rough guide, a family of two adults and four children were classified as 'comfortable' if they received more than £20 per week, and as 'poor' if they had less than £15 weekly. This was in the years 1962–3. In all, 93 boys were said to come from poor families, 193 from adequate income families, and the remaining 125 from families whose incomes were comfortable.

Where information was not forthcoming, or was obviously unreliable, the PSWs judged by appearances, taking note of visible possessions and style of living. As a check on consistency of standards, all records were read and reclassified by other members of the research team, and discrepant cases were referred back to the PSWs for confirmation or reconsideration. Sixteen cases left unclassified by the PSWs were allocated later, using data about the situation at age 8–9 obtained from outside agencies and subsequent enquiries. Despite the rough and ready nature of these assessments, they did appear to reflect realistic and important differences between families.

Income was merely the first of a large number of factors that were examined in relation to delinquency. The results of these comparisons are set out in Appendix A, with family income the first of 151 numbered entries. The first column of the table gives the title of the factor, in this case family income, while the second shows the age at which it was measured, in this case 8–9. The third column gives the description of the worst category, while the fourth shows the number of boys in it and the percentage of them who were delinquents. In this instance, the worst category comprises poor boys, 93 in number, of whom 33·3 per cent became delinquents. The fifth column gives the remaining boys, in this case 318, who were rated as not poor, and shows that only 16·7 per cent of them became delinquents. Finally, the statistical significance of this contrast is given as $\chi^2 = 11{\cdot}3$, $p < {\cdot}001$. This degree of significance places poor income among the background factors most closely linked with delinquency.

A glance at Appendix A will show that many of the factors investigated proved to be significantly associated with delinquency. On any particular factor, it was almost invariably the category which, on common sense grounds, one could define as the most adverse that included the highest percentage who were delinquents. To take the first few factors listed, the boys from *poor* families, from *unsatisfactory* housing, from *neglected* accommodation, and from the *lowest* socio-economic class were, in each case, more prone to delinquency than those rated more favourably. One exception to this general rule was that boys whose mothers had a full-time job included, unexpectedly, a smaller percentage of delinquents (factors 12 and 13 in Appendix A). The reason for this may have been that mothers in full-time work tended to produce a higher family income and fewer children, both of which were factors associated with absence of delinquency (West, 1969, p. 66). The finding is in conformity with the results of the National Child Development Study (Davie *et al.*, 1972), which demonstrated that at age 7 the children of full-time working mothers showed no marked ill-effects in terms of their attainment or adjustment in school. The factors of family size and social class far outweighed any effect that could be attributed to working mothers.

Another variable, exceptional in being associated with a decreased likelihood of delinquency, was the rating nervous-withdrawn (factor 125 in Appendix A), which is described later (see p. 115).

The relationship between income and delinquency is displayed in detail in Table II (1). The delinquents are divided into recidivists and one-timers, and the non-delinquents into police contact cases and the rest. It can be seen that, compared with boys from comfortable homes, the poor boys included a much higher proportion of recidivists (21·5 per cent against 5·6 per cent), as well as somewhat higher

TABLE II (1)

Delinquency and Inadequate Incomes

	Delinquency								
Family	*No police record*		*Police contact boys*		*One-time delinquents*		*Recidivists*		*Tota*
income	(%)	(*N*)	(%)	(*N*)	(%)	(*N*)	(%)	(*N*)	*boys*
Comfortable	78·4	(98)	8·0	(10)	8·0	(10)	5·6	(7)	100% (125)
Adequate	66·8	(129)	14·5	(28)	13·5	(26)	5·2	(10)	100% (193)
Poor	47·3	(44)	19·4	(18)	11·8	(11)	21·5	(20)	100% (93)
Total boys	65·9	(271)	13·6	(56)	11·4	(47)	9·0	(37)	100% (411)

Significance Test: Comparing 93 poor income boys with the remaining 318, and comparing 84 delinquents with the remaining 327, $\chi^2 = 11{\cdot}3$, $p < {\cdot}001$. (In this instance, and throughout this report, χ^2 has one degree of freedom.)

percentages of one-time delinquents (11·8 per cent against 8·0 per cent) and police contact boys (19·4 per cent against 8·0 per cent). In contrast, boys without police contacts were less common among the poor than among the comfortable group (47·3 per cent against 78·4 per cent). These figures illustrate the general rule that unfavourable features, such as low income, which are associated with delinquency and especially with recidivism, are also characteristic of police contact boys.

Having illustrated this trend in connection with income, it will not be necessary to labour the point every time some fresh factor comes under review. For most purposes, it suffices to contrast delinquents with non-delinquents. In general, the recidivists were the extreme category, while the police contact group and the one-time delinquents shared to a lesser content the same unfavourable features. Usually the police contact group was intermediate between the no contact cases and the one-time delinquents. In regard to income, however, while the recidivists included the highest proportion of poor boys, the one-time delinquents were actually slightly better off than the police contact boys. (The percentages of 'poor' boys in the four categories were as follows: recidivists, 54·1 per cent; one-time delinquents, 23·4 per cent; police contact boys, 32·3 per cent; boys with no record, 16·2 per cent.)

The association between poverty and delinquency was particularly evident for boys first convicted at an early age. Of the 19 boys first convicted at age 10 or 11, 57·9 per cent came from poor families, compared with only 30·8 per cent of those first convicted at 12 to 16. This finding was the first of many examples showing that boys convicted early tended to be extreme cases.

2. *Interpreting the Findings on Income and Delinquency*

Most of the families classified as poor were existing at a level little different from those who qualified for or were actually receiving National Assistance at that time, so the degree of material deprivation among them was quite severe. In their ratings of family income, the PSWs tried to ignore the mother's competence in managing a limited budget. Since some cases had to be judged on appearances, it is likely that this factor could not be ruled out completely. However, even if the ratings had been precise and based purely on amounts of money, low income must to some extent have reflected incompetence, or at least lack of success. In modern times, family income is not completely fixed by outside pressures, but is at least partly determined by motivation and ability. Parental income was in fact closely related to many of the measures of unsatisfactory parental behaviour, such as poor supervision (p. 55), separations (p. 69), parental conflict (p. 53) and large families (p. 31). In short, low family income usually stood for a constellation of unfavourable home background features. The boys from poor homes lacked a great deal besides pocket money. The chain of cause and effect underlying the association between poverty and delinquency is far from simple.

The association between low family income and juvenile delinquency reported here may seem surprising in view of recent research which suggests that the lower class bias of delinquent populations no longer holds true. Palmai *et al.* (1967), who made a survey of a randomly selected sample of young people appearing before London juvenile courts, found them to be derived fairly evenly from all social classes. Their criterion of social class was the one commonly used in English research, namely the Registrar General's scale based upon a categorization of the occupation of the head of the household.

Our income classification was probably a more realistic measure of social class within the sample than the Registrar General's scale, although the two measures were related. Low income was closely correlated with other assessments of family background which were also indicative of poor material standards, such as 'poor housing', 'interior of rooms neglected', 'family supported by social agencies', 'mother has no paid job', 'erratic paternal work record' and 'boy physically neglected'. In an attempt to obtain a more accurate evaluation of material standards, a number of these assessments were amalgamated into a combined scale of 'social handicap' (see p. 128, West 1969, pp. 67 ff., and Gibson and West, 1970). The classification so produced was found to be related to other background variables and to future delinquency in much the same way and to much the same extent as the categorization of family income.

Since the combined scale was not markedly more effective than income alone, it was decided to use the income categorization throughout this report as the simplest and most easily reproducible index of socio-economic class. When we used the Registrar General's scale, applied to the current occupation of the family breadwinner, there proved to be no significant association between socio-economic status and delinquency (21·2 per cent of 151 boys in the lowest social classes IV and V becoming delinquents, as opposed to 20·0 per cent of 260 boys in classes I, II and III). This negative result was almost certainly due to the inadequacies of this method of measuring social class (see Note 1).

In recent English studies, where indices other than the Registrar General's scale have been used, significant associations between social class and delinquency have been reported. Douglas *et al.* (1966), with his national sample of children born in one week of March 1946, reported a variation in the prevalence of male juvenile delinquency from 2·7 per cent to 18·7 per cent between the top and bottom ranks of a four-point scale of social class. Their scale, although based primarily upon father's occupation, modified the Registrar General's groupings, and also took into account the educational status and social class background of both parents. Lynn McDonald (1969) investigated a sample of children from schools in central and suburban London and in a provincial city. She found a highly significant association between low social class, rated on father's occupation, and the incidence of juvenile court appearances. However, this finding emerged only after she had discovered that the Registrar General's scale was unsatisfactory and modified it accordingly (McDonald 1969, pp. 69–71).

McDonald also pointed out that some authorities have suggested that the social class membership of individuals is less important than the characteristics of the neighbourhood in which they happen to live. In the present Study, it was clear that differences between families, reflected in income, housing and number of children, were of considerable importance even though all were living in the same neighbourhood. Since the range of variation in income was limited by the character of the neighbourhood, it is probable that the contrast between delinquents and non-delinquents in this respect would have been even more striking if it had been possible to investigate a national sample.

3. *Family Size*

Many criminological surveys have reported that delinquents tend to come from large families. This has been found in England (e.g. Lees and Newson, 1954), Scotland (e.g. Ferguson, 1952), Australia (e.g. Biles, 1971) and the United States (e.g. Tuckman and Regan, 1967). Other studies with similar findings have been reviewed by Wootton (1959).

We obtained a similar result. The percentage of delinquents among boys from large families, that is boys with four or more siblings (see Note 2), was significantly higher than among the remainder of the sample (32·3 per cent of 99, as opposed to 16·7 per cent of 312; $\chi^2 = 10{\cdot}39$, $p < {\cdot}005$). Recidivists, one-time delinquents and police contact boys were all over-represented among the 99 boys from large families. Like low family income, large family size was particularly evident among boys first convicted at an early age. Of the 19 boys first convicted at 10–12, 57·9 per cent were from large families, compared with only 32·4 per cent of the 34 boys first convicted at 13–14 and 32·3 per cent of the 31 first convicted at 15–16.

Many of the factors associated with delinquency were themselves interlinked (see Appendix C), so that it was not immediately evident which ones were the most important. Low family income and large family size were particularly closely associated. A majority of the boys from the quarter of the sample defined as poor also belonged to the quarter coming from large families (56 of the 93 poor boys being among the 99 from large families: $\chi^2 = 83{\cdot}3$, $p < {\cdot}001$). Large family size also correlated closely with all the other indices of low social level, such as 'poor housing', 'interior of house neglected', 'boy physically neglected' and 'erratic paternal work record'. It seemed that in the present population some social deprivation became almost inevitable as the size of the family increased. The converse trend, an over-representation among the comfortable income group of only children or boys with only one sibling, did not occur to any significant degree.

Despite the close inter-relationship between the two, family income was not just a reflection of family size. Both factors were independently important as precursors of delinquency. To demonstrate this, each delinquent was matched with a non-delinquent from the same income level. The members of each pair still differed significantly in family size. Conversely, when each delinquent was matched with a non-delinquent from the same sized family, the members of each pair still differed significantly in income. This matching technique has been used many times in the present Study to show the extent to which factors were important independently of each other. The rationale behind these analyses, and the results obtained, are set out more fully in Appendix B (pp. 215–18).

One hypothesis to explain the link between large families and delinquency suggests that the presence of brothers leads to delinquency by infectious example. In fact, the number of sisters of each boy was only slightly less closely correlated with delinquency ($r_{bis} = {\cdot}22$, see Note 5) than the number of brothers ($r_{bis} = {\cdot}23$), and the number of younger brothers was just as closely correlated as the number of older brothers ($r_{bis} = {\cdot}18$ in both cases). This suggests that it was the actual size of the sibship rather than its composition by age or sex which was associated with future delinquency.

Another explanation suggests that large family size, by virtue of its concomitant overcrowding, produces its effects indirectly. Ferguson (1952) found that boys from large families were more delinquent-prone if they were also in the most overcrowded homes, but that there was no relationship between family size and delinquency in the least overcrowded homes. This point was investigated here, with rather similar results. In overcrowded homes most of the boys were by definition from large families, and boys from large families were particularly delinquent-prone. In homes with an ample number of rooms, however, a boy's chances of becoming delinquent were not increased by having several siblings (see Note 3). Since the influence of family size was also much reduced after matching for income (see Appendix B), one may perhaps conclude that, with ample accommodation and a comfortable income, the baleful implications of a large sized family are substantially mitigated.

It has been reported by various investigators, such as Lees and Newson (1954) in England and Glueck and Glueck (1950) in America, that the oldest and youngest children in families are less likely to become delinquents than those born into an intermediate position. Such results have led to some discussion about the influence of birth order on delinquency (e.g. Biles, 1971). Our own findings confirm that oldest and youngest born children are less likely to become delinquents. Of 170 middle-born children, 24·7 per cent became delinquents. This compares with 19·0 per cent of 100 youngest born, and 16·3 per cent of 141 oldest born or only children.

Closer examination of our data suggested that the relationship between birth order and delinquency was merely a secondary consequence of family size, because middle-born children tended to come from larger families with higher delinquency potential. Comparisons based on very large or very small families are misleading, because there are no middle-born children in small families of one or two children, whereas the great majority of children in families of five or more are necessarily middle-born. Considering only the 165 boys from families of three or four children, there was no evidence that the ones in intermediate positions were more delinquent—rather the reverse, in fact (16·0 per cent delinquents of 75 middle-born boys, 21·4 per cent of 42 oldest boys, 25·0 per cent of 48 youngest boys).

4. *Criminality in Families*

A number of older English studies, by Burt, Bagot, Mannheim and Carr-Saunders (reviewed by Wootton, 1959), showed that a boy was particularly likely to become a delinquent if other members of his family had criminal records. In his Glasgow survey, Ferguson (1952) showed that boys with criminal fathers were twice as likely to become delinquents as other boys (24·1 per cent as opposed to 11·6 per cent), and boys with delinquent older brothers were more than three times as likely (33·3 per cent as opposed to 9·8 per cent). Ferguson was able to demonstrate that criminality in the family was a significant precursor of delinquency independently of other social factors, such as overcrowding or a boy's scholastic attainment. A study by Jonsson (1967) confirmed that, in Sweden also, delinquent boys were especially likely to have criminal parents. In the well-known American study of Glueck and Glueck (1950, p. 102), it was found that two-thirds of the fathers of delinquents had a history of criminality, compared with only one-third of the fathers of the non-delinquent control group. McCord *et al* (1959, p. 93), in the Cambridge–Somerville study, followed up the criminal records of 253 boys over a long period. They also reported a significant tendency for boys with criminal fathers to become delinquents.

The present investigation confirmed that criminality in the family is as important a factor in juvenile delinquency today as it has appeared to be in previous generations. Among our boys there were 97 who, by the age of 10, had at least one convicted parent (see Note 4). These boys became delinquents more than twice as often as other boys (36·1 per cent of 97, compared with 15·6 per cent of 314: $\chi^2 = 17{\cdot}9$, $p < {\cdot}001$). Having a convicted father or a convicted mother were about equally deleterious, both being associated with a significantly increased risk of delinquency (38·6 per cent of 83 boys with convicted fathers, 37·8 per cent of the 37 boys with criminal mothers). This was a consequence of the strong tendency of criminal mothers to be married to criminal fathers; most boys with a criminal mother (23 out of 37) also had a criminal father. The 14 boys with mother but not father convicted produced only three delinquents. Apparently fathers were the trend-setters. It might be thought that fathers with a record of repeated convictions would have a particularly bad influence upon their sons, but the figures gave no support to this idea, except in the few instances of fathers who were very persistent recidivists (see Note 4).

Figure II(1) shows the proportions falling into the official delinquency categories in two groups of boys, those with and those without criminal parents. Nearly three-quarters (72·3 per cent) of boys with non-criminal parents were themselves free from any police record or criminal conviction, but among boys with a criminal parent less than half (45·4 per cent) fitted this description. The figure brings

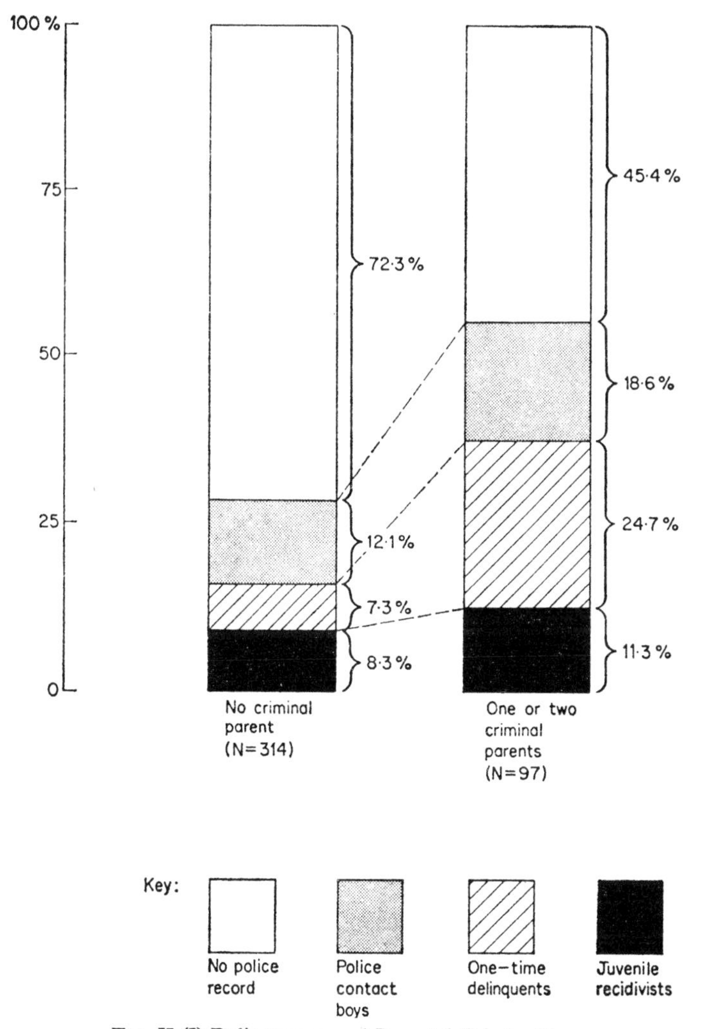

FIG. II (I) Delinquency and Parental Criminality

out one curious point. Unlike most other factors investigated, parental criminality was less closely associated with recidivism than with one-time delinquency. One-timers were more than three times as common among those with criminal parents (24·7 per cent as opposed to 7·3 per cent), but recidivists were only slightly more prevalent (11·3 per cent as opposed to 8·3 per cent). This puzzling result was due to the fact that parental criminality was particularly frequent among boys first convicted later in their juvenile life span. In fact, five of the 19 one-time juvenile delinquents first convicted after their fifteenth birthdays became recidivists as young adults, and all five had criminal parents.

In a further attempt to investigate recidivism and parental criminality, the juvenile delinquents were re-categorized into one-timers and recidivists. For this analysis, a recidivist was defined as a boy who was first convicted as a juvenile and then reconvicted either as a juvenile or as an adult. The results are displayed in Table II (2), with the delinquents subdivided by age on first conviction. It can be seen that, once later recidivism was taken into account, more of the

TABLE II (2)

The Percentage of Delinquent Boys with Criminal Parents (Subdivided by Age on First Conviction, and Recidivism as Adult or Juvenile)

Age on first conviction	*All delinquents* (%)	(*figures*)	*One-time delinquents* (%)	(*figures*)	*Recidivists (adult and juvenile)* (%)	(*figures*)
10–13	32·3	(10/31)	28·6	(2/7)	33·3	(8/24)
14–16	47·2	(25/53)	38·5	(10/26)	55·6	(15/27)
All juvenile delinquents	41·7	(35/84)	36·4	(12/33)	45·1	(23/51)
17 and over*	50·0	(13/26)				

* In this case, the follow-up period was not long enough for the boys to be classified realistically into one-time delinquents and recidivists.

recidivists than the one-time delinquents had criminal parents. There was a strong tendency for the incidence of criminal parents to increase with age on first conviction (from 32·3 per cent at age 10–13 to 50·0 per cent at age 17 and over). The finding reported previously (West, 1969, p. 106), that official delinquency at an early age was not very closely related to parental criminality, still holds true.

It is difficult to say why parental criminality should become important only in relation to delinquency of later onset. Presumably many boys become delinquents because they have failed to learn to conform to the rules of society. This learning failure may sometimes be due, as Eysenck suggests, to innate individual peculiarities, such as an unusual difficulty in establishing conditioned responses. In other cases, where there has been serious neglect or faulty upbringing by parents or guardians at critical stages of infant development, the failure may be due to lack of opportunity for learning. Again, some boys who are successful in social learning may nevertheless become delinquents because they have learned to conform to the wrong rules. This is liable to occur when boys are reared by parents belonging to an anti-social subculture which encourages crime (Eysenck, 1970, p. 160). It could be that delinquents of early onset belong to the first type, while those who begin to follow a criminal father's footsteps when they reach maturity belong to the second. This explanation is highly speculative, but it does account for the observation that most of the other adverse factors related to delinquency—such as low income (pp. 26 ff.), poor parental behaviour (pp. 59 ff.) and low intelligence (pp. 84 ff.)—are of the kind likely to hamper social learning, and are particularly connected with delinquency of early onset.

In our Study parental criminality, family size and low income were among the factors most closely interlinked (see Appendix C). Boys from poor families had a particularly high incidence of criminal parents (37·6 per cent in the poor group, as opposed to 19·5 per cent among the remainder: $\chi^2 = 12{\cdot}1$, $p < {\cdot}001$), and so had boys from large sized families (39·4 per cent of 99, as opposed to 18·6 per cent of 312: $\chi^2 = 16{\cdot}9$, $p < {\cdot}001$). However, when each delinquent was matched with a non-delinquent from the same income level, the delinquents still had significantly more criminal parents. The same held true after matching for family size. (As in all these matching analyses, Appendix B should be consulted for fuller details.) It seems, therefore, that criminality of parents made a specific contribution to delinquency independently of the social level of the family. There was, however, evidence of some interaction between income and criminality. Criminality of parents was less closely associated with delinquency in the comfortable income group. This suggests that relative affluence may afford some protection from the effects of parental criminality.

Delinquency among our boys was also found to have a close association with delinquency among their siblings. Of 83 boys with a known delinquent sibling (see Note 4), 44·6 per cent were delinquents, compared with only 14·5 per cent delinquent among the remaining 276 ($\chi^2 = 32{\cdot}5$, $p > {\cdot}001$).

Some of the convictions of siblings were contemporaneous with those of our own boys. In order to determine how far delinquency was foreshadowed by convictions of older brothers, only convictions occurring before our boys reached the age of 10 were counted (see again Note 4). On this basis, 37 of our boys had one or more older brothers previously convicted. They proved much more likely to become delinquents than the 136 boys who had one or more older brothers but none with a conviction. The difference was statistically significant, in spite of the small numbers involved (40·5 per cent becoming delinquents out of 37, as opposed to 22·1 per cent of 136: $\chi^2 = 4{\cdot}25$, $p > {\cdot}05$). The boys with delinquent older brothers were also much more likely to have criminal parents (37·8% of 37, as opposed to 21·3% of 136: $\chi^2 = 4{\cdot}39$, $p < {\cdot}05$). These two factors, both precursors of delinquency, were thus interlinked.

Where a boy already had a criminal parent, the presence of a delinquent older brother made little difference to his chances of becoming a delinquent. The presence of a delinquent brother was important particularly if the parents were non-criminal (in which case 30·4 per cent of those with a delinquent brother became delinquent, as opposed to only 15·0 per cent of those with non-delinquent brothers).

Finally, we looked to see how important as a precursor of a boy's own delinquency record it was to have any older member of his family convicted (i.e. father, mother, older brother or older sister). In all, 122 boys, by the time they reached 10 years of age, had one or other of these family members convicted. Among these boys, the likelihood of becoming delinquent was increased more than two and a half times (36·1 per cent of 122, in comparison with 13·8 per cent of 289: $\chi^2 = 24{\cdot}7$, $p < {\cdot}001$).

A most striking feature of the criminal records was the uneven distribution in the community of individuals with convictions. Of the 353 family members convicted (out of 2,054 names searched), half were concentrated among 47 (11·8 per cent) of the 397 families. In these 47 families, the number of persons searched was 339, or 16·5 per cent of the total number of persons searched. Half of them (176) had criminal records. Even more strikingly, 18 families accounted for half of the 1,076 criminal convictions.

The histories of boys from highly criminal families were quite revealing. Of the 397 families in the Study, there were 10 that had at least five members with a criminal conviction. Eleven of the Study boys, two of whom were brothers, belonged to these families. Five of these 11 boys were juvenile recidivists, and the rest all became recidivists as young adults. Evidently these families had a very strong tendency to produce persistently delinquent sons. They merit closer examination.

All 11 boys were in the bottom half of the sample of Matrices IQ (p. 84), and six were in the lowest quarter. Nine were from poor families. Seven were rated as having experienced unsatisfactory parental behaviour, although, in the population as a whole, this adversity was not particularly associated with parental criminality (see p. 42 and Appendix C).

The extreme degree of social pathology typical of highly criminal families has been amusingly illustrated by McCullough (1967) in a composite case history drawn from a number of such cases. In this Study also, inspection of individual case records showed that the families with many convicted members were usually unfortunate in many respects besides their conviction records. One case is quoted later (Case 851, p. 61) to illustrate particularly bad parental behaviour. Here are some other examples from the 10 most criminal families.

Case 310

On first contact with this family when the boy was 9 years of age, the PSW summed up the situation as follows: 'All the family in bed at 10.30 a.m. Indescribable squalor! . . . Father is a well-known problem-person with a long record of work-shyness, dishonesty, criminal convictions and anti-authoritarian attitude. He is brutal and violent to his wife, and extremely brutal and violent to his children, particularly when he is drunk. Mother is in poor health, of low mentality, unable to write, frightened and tyrannized by the father.'

When the boy was 14, a probation officer reported on his absence from school as follows: 'The reasons appear to be partly practical ones, such as lack of clothes and shoes on occasion, but mainly because [father] forces [mother] to stay up to the early hours of the morning, so that she is very tired and does not get up in time to see that the elder children get to work or the younger ones to school. There are many rows and violent scenes, making it difficult for the children to get enough sleep. . . .'

Case 560

This was a family in which the parents had no criminal records, but most of their children were delinquents. Mother cooperated with the PSW only reluctantly, after numerous attempts to see her had failed. Both parents were thought to be not very bright. They were in poor circumstances, and father was off work a lot with ill health. The PSW's initial impressions noted a good maternal attitude, 'kindly, affectionate, certainly not tough. Does not have any disciplinary problems'. Parental behaviour was rated satisfactory.

Different information emerged later from outside sources. When the boy was aged 15 his probation officer noted 'an unhappy domestic situation'. The parents were occupying separate rooms and were at least partially estranged. The probation officer felt that the mother despised the father and that her attitude was partially shared by the children. He considered the father a weak, passive, inadequate man who made little effort to control the children. In earlier years, the NSPCC had been involved with the family on account of physical neglect of the children, and later there were constant problems of non-attendance at school. A psychiatric report on one of the boy's sisters noted: 'She misses school with her parents' connivance, with excuses of ill health which are not impressive.' The girl (then aged 11) was admitted to a remand home 'in an appalling physical state. Arrangements had to be made immediately to have her admitted in hospital for treatment of scabies and head lice'. The parents finally separated when the boy was 16.

Mother had told the PSW that the boy 'liked school very much and would never truant' but his school teacher at the time reported a poor attendance record, and this remained the case throughout his school career. His school reports indicated that he was backward, poor in concentration, and (at age 10) 'a boy who hasn't the strength of character to understand right from wrong. He doesn't understand he is a member of a community and not just an individual.'

When this boy was seen at age 18, the interviewer commented: 'He is the stereotype of the juvenile delinquent. He tried very hard in the interview to cooperate. Unfortunately, he is not used to thinking about or justifying any of his actions, and his schedule is full of inconsistencies which it was not possible to iron out. . . .' His face was scarred with glass from a pub fight. 'I don't really know what happened—I was blind drunk,' he explained. He had had frequent periods of unemployment, and been dismissed on the spot on one occasion for fighting with a workmate. Although a juvenile recidivist, and with several further convictions against him since his seventeenth birthday, he admitted 'I've got away with hundreds of things . . . I've been thieving all the time since I was the age of 13. The only times I've been caught in five years is 8 times—now that's not bad!'

Case 440

A large poor family. Mother was, according to the PSW, 'very friendly, but of dull intelligence, and there is no doubt she sometimes deliberately misleads me'. Her children were of various parentage, and her current 'husband' (who, it subsequently transpired, had gone through a marriage ceremony with another woman) was frequently unemployed and thought to be work-shy. The PSW noted: 'Severe marital discord, parents sleeping in separate rooms. Constant rows—they throw things at each other. Mother used to be afraid of father, but now she gives as good as she gets.'

Discipline in the home appeared to be erratic and ineffectual. Mother told the PSW she had never wanted children, particularly not boys, because they got out of hand and she could not manage them. The PSW noted: 'While I was there, mother was constantly threatening or bribing the children with little apparent effect either way.' Mother complained that her husband was too soft in discipline. The PSW thought there was 'totally erratic handling from both parents'.

At first, the boy was reported to be submissive and bullied by other boys. Father said: 'He don't hit back—he's scared. . . . When you punish him he cries like breaking the heart because he's got no guts.' A teacher's report categorized the boy at age 8 as a hard worker and commented: 'A careful boy. Poor home, but very well mannered.'

He became more assertive as he grew older, but remained officially non-delinquent. He was, however, convicted as a young adult, and when interviewed at age 18 it was clear that he had been involved in many delinquent acts without being caught. He said he used to help a man steal lead from roofs because he was sorry for him. Shoplifting, he said, 'I've done loads of times. . . . I think its wrong now, but when I was smaller I didn't use to care. I did it and felt proud of myself.' He also described stealing a radio from a car and selling it because he wanted money. 'I don't see anything wrong in buying [stolen] stuff. If a copper pulls you up, you say you don't know it's stolen and they can't really have you.' He mentioned his recent conviction, but insisted he wasn't guilty of that offence. However, he intended to join the army to get away and avoid more trouble. At the time, he was still living with his mother and a new stepfather.

Case 504

After considerable persuasion, the mother agreed to be seen for the first time when the boy was aged 9. At that stage, the PSW noted: 'Father has been divorced from mother. It was an appalling marriage. He was a violent drinker, irritable, inconsistent, erratic and harsh to his children, giving them many beatings. He was interested in other women and led the family a terrible dance. He was apparently against authority, and resisted getting school uniforms for the children. He is now remarried. . . . If he sees his children in the street he ignores them.' Father left the home when the boy was aged 8. Mother had to cope with a large family. She was thought to be somewhat anxious and over-protective. 'She certainly appears to have her children very closely identified with her, and all of them spend their time running round helping her. . . . [In her opinion] they are perfection. She reiterates it with monotonous regularity and great pride.'

At age 8, the teacher's report on this boy indicated poor attendance, untidy appearance and lack of concentration, and commented that he was 'easily influenced by other children'. Later reports suggested that he had become a more satisfactory pupil of average conduct. At age 9, and again at age 13, his mother described him as a quiet, obedient, friendly boy who gave no trouble and was less tough than some of his siblings who had delinquency convictions. However, she tended to paint a very rosy picture of all her children.

The boy had only one conviction for a juvenile offence, committed at age 16, but he had further convictions as a young adult. When seen at age 18, the interviewer commented: 'Quite cooperative, but quite a liar and rather indifferent to what story he told me. . . . A charming, extraverted and apparently non-violent delinquent. His mother and sister waited on him hand and foot.' He had recently absconded from a detention centre and claimed that, following his recapture, he had been severely punched by the police.

Our findings concerning family criminality are open to a variety of interpretations. They are compatible with an explanation in terms of an hereditary predisposition to crime, but they are equally compatible with the transmission of criminal tendency through example and shared attitudes. The means of transmission could be quite subtle. Direct instruction in criminal techniques is unlikely to play much part for two reasons. First, most paternal convictions occurred in youth, often before our boys were born, and few fathers were still active criminals when the Study began. Second, the PSWs reported that even parents who had been delinquents themselves were censorious towards delinquent behaviour in their own sons.

If criminal parents tend to mishandle their children, that might explain the findings. In a subsequent section (see Chapter III), parental behaviour is considered in some detail. The general unsatisfactoriness in child-rearing which we have labelled poor parental behaviour was probably a serious hindrance to social learning. It was associated with poor intellectual performance among the boys concerned, and also with delinquency of early onset. Criminal parents, however, were not significantly worse than the rest in regard to parental behaviour (see Appendix C), so an explanation for the delinquency of their sons must be sought elsewhere.

One specific aspect of the conduct of criminal parents did seem relevant, namely their tendency to exercise poor supervision over their boys (see Appendix C). This defect in supervision was gauged by the PSWs from laxness in enforcing parental rules and in watching over the child's activities (see p. 55). After matching for parental supervision, there was only a slight association between parental criminality and subsequent delinquency (see Appendix B). It seems possible, therefore, that the link between a parent's criminality and a boy's delinquency was due to some lack of social responsibility among the criminal parents which revealed itself in a lax attitude to the social training of their sons.

Parental criminality was linked with delinquency of late onset.

It was suggested earlier (see p. 37) that this might be due to a natural take-over at adolescence of the standards of a criminogenic environment. Poor supervision, which tended to go with parental criminality, was possibly just a reflection of these standards, rather than an indication of serious disturbance to social learning due to bad parent–child relationships.

The PSWs' opinions about parental supervision could have been biased by their awareness of the criminal records of certain fathers. This possibility was discussed in the previous publication (West, 1969, pp. 126–9), but it does not amount to a very serious objection. If the PSWs were seriously influenced by the negative halo of criminality, this should have emerged in relation to most aspects of poor parental behaviour, and not just the poor supervision assessment.

NOTES

[1] *Difficulties in the Use of the Registrar General's Scale as a Measure of Social Class*

In the present Study (as can be seen in Table I and II in Gibson and West, 1970), six out of seven indices of 'social handicap' were all significantly intercorrelated, and were all significantly correlated with delinquency. Apart from family income, these indices were large family, poor housing, boy physically neglected, interior of rooms neglected and family supported by social agencies, all of which appear to be facets of low social class. The only social class measure which was not significantly correlated with most of the others, or with delinquency, was the occupational status of the family breadwinner on the Registrar General's Scale.

The reasons why the Registrar General's Scale proved unsatisfactory are easy to see. The classification is not up to date, and does not always reflect the current status or level of earnings of a particular job. When it is applied to a neighbourhood sample, in which the range of occupations is rather limited, the proportions of cases allocated to the different classes become too unbalanced for effective statistical comparisons. In this Study, only 6 per cent of families were in the upper classes I and II (see West, 1969, pp. 17 ff.), and only 18·0 per cent were classified as non-manual. Of 74 in the non-manual group, 17·6 per cent became delinquents, compared with 21·1 per cent of the 337 in the manual group. It is probable that the manual/non-manual classification was less distinctive in the Study sample than in a total population. Several jobs proved difficult to categorize in these terms.

Lynn MacDonald (1969), who found a positive association between delinquency and low social class when she used a modified version of the Registrar General's Scale, failed to demonstrate any association when, in one small section of her study, she applied the Scale in the normal way. She did this in order to compare the social class distribution of a group of delinquents dealt with by a police juvenile liaison scheme in East London with that of the neighbourhood population as revealed by published statistics. Although the delinquents were predominantly working class, she was unable to show that they were any more so than the population of the district. This negative result was in all probability just another example of the inappropriateness of the Registrar General's Scale for a working class neighbourhood survey. As McDonald points out (1969, p. 159), 'There is probably less to distinguish middle from working class people in an area such as East London than in most places'.

Our reassertion of the association between delinquency and low social class, as reflected in family income, may seem old-fashioned. Some recent American researchers have challenged the theory that low social class, and hence poverty and social deprivation, are important causes of delinquency. For example, Empey and Lubeck (1971), in a study of juvenile delinquents and non-delinquents in Los Angeles and Utah, were unable to demonstrate any association between the possession of a delinquency record and low social class membership. As a measure of social class, they used an 8-point ranking of the prestige of the occupation of each boy's father, and were confident about the validity of that index (Empey and Lubeck, 1971, p. 17). They shared the sociological preference for occupational rankings rather than more objective measures, such as wages or housing. Even if they had used what we would consider a more effective measure of social class, and had found it unrelated to delinquency, this would not necessarily invalidate the results of English research. Social conditions in the two countries are so different that one cannot assume that delinquency has the same connotations in both places.

[2] *The Definition of Family Size*

For the analyses in this report, family size was defined as the number of children, surviving three months or more, who were born to a boy's mother before his tenth birthday. It transpired that, on this definition, 46 boys were only children, 101 had only one sibling, 165 had two or three siblings, and 99 had four or more. These 99 were considered to belong to 'large' families. Information about the number of siblings in each family was obtained from parental interviews, from the boys themselves, from school records and from outside agencies, including birth registrations at Somerset House. In all probability, the figures are substantially accurate, although they became so only after repeated inquiries from these different sources. Except where it is specifically stated to the contrary, this count and others in this report are based on the total of 411 individual boys, ignoring the fact that these included 14 pairs of brothers, of whom five pairs were twins, and hence that the sample was drawn from only 397 different families.

The sibling count was taken at a stage when the families were not all fully completed. Subsequent births occurred in the families of 79 boys, and three who had been only children up to age 10 ceased to be so. The definition was biological rather than social. Usually, but not invariably, the count corresponded to the number of children living in the household, but it included siblings who had died or left home, so far as these could be ascertained, and it excluded paternal half-siblings. The reasons for using a biological definition were twofold. First, in the investigation of medical histories of births, it was the number of children born to the mother, rather than the number living with her, that mattered. Second, the number of children actually at home was subject to fluctuation, and parentage was not always clear, so the biological criterion was preferred as being more precise.

The analysis of the effect of being an oldest or youngest child, reported on p. 33 was an exception in that it did take into account all the most recent maternal births known to the investigators.

[3] *An Index of Overcrowding Related to Family Size and Delinquency*

At age 10–11, when the social workers made some observations on the point, 75 boys were counted as being in overcrowded conditions, because there were more children in their families than rooms in their houses. At the opposite extreme, 173 boys were living in the least crowded conditions, with two or more rooms than there were children. The remaining 138 boys were in 'average' conditions, while 25 were 'not known'. Bathrooms were not counted as rooms, but kitchens were, unless they had no living space—as with a scullery. The count was subject to a slight inaccuracy, as the number of children in the family was taken from the 'biological' family size which, as pointed out in Note 2 above, did not invariably correspond to the number actually living in the house. A further inaccuracy was introduced because the number of adults, other than parents, living in the house was neglected. This must have affected the degree of overcrowding.

Among the least crowded boys, family size was unrelated to delinquency. Sixty of these boys, of whom 11·7 per cent became delinquents, were from families with three or more children; 113 boys, of whom 10·6 per cent became delinquents, were from families with only one or two children. In contrast, among the overcrowded group, those from large families were more often delinquents. Fifty of these boys, of whom 38·0 per cent became delinquents, were from families of six or more; 25 boys, of whom 28·0 per cent became delinquents, were from families of five or fewer children.

[4] *Definition of a Criminal Parent or Sibling*

In estimating the criminal convictions of parents, only offences routinely recorded in the Criminal Record Office at the time were counted. Breaches of probation were discounted, as were minor motoring offences and minor non-indictable offences not normally recorded unless the offender already had a CRO file. Convictions by both juvenile and adult courts were included, although it was realised that the juvenile records of the parents' generation were incomplete. For the purposes of these searches, the term 'father' or 'mother' was defined as the man or woman who mostly filled that role in the boy's upbringing during his first 10 years. Even on this criterion, 10 boys had no father and three had no mother, but, since every boy had at least one parent whose record was searched, no case was counted 'not known' on parental criminality. However, a few parents had spent a substantial part of their lives abroad, and the incomplete identifying particulars of three mothers did not permit a search. It is possible, therefore, that a few parental convictions as adults may have escaped notice. Several searches were made over a five-year period to ensure accuracy. In two instances, a mother's conviction for a relatively minor crime had been 'weeded' from the records between the first and last searches, but these were counted all the same.

On these criteria, 83 boys had criminal fathers, 37 had criminal mothers, and 97 had at least one convicted parent. Had the small number of parents who were first convicted after their sons' tenth birthdays been included, there would have been 91 boys with a criminal father, 42 with a criminal mother, and 109 with at least one convicted parent. The actual prevalence of fathers with convictions was 87 out of 387 names searched (22·5 per cent), and of mothers with convictions it was 39 out of 395 searched (9·9 per cent). The slight increase in prevalence over the figures reported earlier (West, 1969, p. 100) was the result of repeating the CRO searches after discovering more maiden surnames of mothers.

The criminal records of fathers were categorized as slight (juvenile convictions only, and/or no more than one conviction as an adult) or serious (two or more convictions as an adult). Of the 46 boys whose fathers had a slight record, 41·3 per cent became delinquents, while of the 37 boys with seriously criminal fathers only 25·1 per cent became delinquents. However, the majority of cases (7 out of 13) in which the father had a really persistent record (four or more adult convictions) became delinquents.

Information was also obtained from the Criminal Record Office about convictions of the boys' brothers and sisters. Only full siblings and maternal half-siblings (i.e. other children born to our boys' mothers) were searched. Convictions were defined as findings of guilt, both juvenile and adult, located in the Criminal Record Office, provided the offences were of the kind that were routinely recorded. This definition was adopted because minor offences may be recorded in the Criminal Record Office if committed by a person with a prior criminal record. Including these would have had the effect of exaggerating the convictions of known criminals.

At the time of our most recent search in 1970, 83 boys in the Study were found to have delinquent siblings. Of the remaining boys, 276 had the criminal records of one or more siblings searched for with no positive result, 44 were only children, and 8 had siblings not searched for, because they had died, or were too young, or had insufficient identifying particulars.

In order to investigate the extent to which delinquency of our boys was preceded by the delinquency of their older brothers, a recount was made of the convictions of each boy's older brothers, including only those convictions that had occurred before our boys reached 10 years of age. This investigation was restricted to brothers because they were so much more often convicted than sisters, and also because the surnames of older married sisters were not known and could not be searched. Sixty-three (25·0 per cent) of 252 older brothers searched, and 15 (6·0 per cent) of 250 older sisters searched, had had juvenile convictions. This count was based on 397 different families, boys who were older brothers or 'presumptively' older twins of other boys in the Study being discounted. The fact that these older brothers had a slightly higher incidence of juvenile convictions than the boys in the Study may be because, by definition, they came from families with a minimum of two children.

[5] *Correlations*

The biserial correlation (r_{bis}) has been used whenever the delinquent/non-delinquent dichotomy was compared with some reasonably continuous variable, such as number of siblings. In this report, virtually every biserial correlation has a standard error of 0·07, so that any value of 0·14 or greater is statistically significant at $p = \cdot05$. The product–moment correlation (r) has been used to estimate the relationship between two factors whenever both were measured on a reasonably continuous scale (e.g. IQ scores at two different ages; see p. 94). With 400 boys, any product–moment correlation of 0·10 or greater is statistically significant at $p = \cdot05$. The word 'correlated' is used in this report for any positive relationship and should not necessarily be taken to refer to either of these two statistics.

III

Parental Behaviour

1. *Present Findings and Previous Studies*

Many aspects of the behaviour of parents were rated by the PSWs in this Study. The emotional attitudes of the parents towards their boys, the disciplinary methods used by parents, and their marital relationships, all proved to be associated with future delinquency. These features were closely interlinked and will be discussed together in the present chapter.

The relevance of these factors of family interaction to the development of juvenile delinquency has been indicated by many previous investigations, and admirable reviews of the evidence have been published (Peterson and Becker, 1965; Rodman and Grams, 1967). Family factors have been assessed by personal interviews or structured questionnaires directed to parents, children or both. Most of our measures were derived from the PSWs' interviews with parents although questionnaires addressed to parents were also used to some extent (see pp. 73–6). Neither method produced wholly satisfactory results, as will become apparent. Interview assessments were subjective, and the PSWs found difficulty in disentangling one aspect of parental behaviour from another. On the other hand, parents were not strongly motivated to fill in questionnaires, so information from that source was often lacking (see also West, 1969, pp. 124–34).

The present Study appears to be unique in Britain in relating data about family interaction to future delinquency in a normal population. The technical difficulties of eliciting reliable information from families who have no particular reason to cooperate, and the time and trouble needed to follow up the children afterwards, no doubt explain why this has not been done before. In the United States, however, something on these lines was accomplished in the sequel by McCord *et al.* (1959) to the Cambridge–Somerville Youth Study (see Appendix H). In that project, the family factors were assessed from extensive case records, compiled over a five-year period while the boys were about 11–16 years of age. Since many court appearances must have occurred during these years, the McCords' assessments could not always have been based upon material recorded in advance of actual convictions. Aside from that complication, however, their findings are substantially comparable to ours, particularly since our parental behaviour assessments were largely inspired by the categorizations used by the McCords.

Our ratings also resemble quite closely the family factors derived by the Gluecks (1950) from their retrospective comparison of the backgrounds of 500 delinquents and 500 non-delinquents (p. xv), which they later used as the basis of their Social Prediction Table (p. 134). The Glueck factors have been tested prospectively, by measuring them in samples of young children and then following to see who became delinquent. These longitudinal surveys carried out in the United States, and investigations of the Glueck factors in other countries (Veverka, 1971), are not very relevant in the context of this chapter. They have been concerned with the validity of the combination of measures contained in the prediction table, rather than with estimating the importance of any particular one, such as paternal discipline. The follow-up surveys do, however, confirm the importance of family factors generally as predictors of delinquency.

The resemblance between the Glueck predictors and those assessed in the present Study is sufficiently close for comparisons of broad conclusions to be of interest. It is not claimed, however, that the Glueck assessments have been repeated exactly. The specifications for carrying out the Glueck evaluations, as given in the most recent publication (Craig and Glick, 1964) and amplified in personal communications, were not available to the PSWs when they carried out the interviews.

Among the better known criminological surveys, there appear to be no other prospective investigations into the effect of family circumstances on delinquency. Andry (1960) investigated family interaction mainly through retrospective reports from sons. Bandura and Walters (1959) interviewed boys and their parents separately with interesting results, but they were investigating a special group of aggressive boys and not juvenile delinquents in general. Nye (1958), who used self-report measures of delinquency, evaluated family interaction solely from questionnaires filled in by children.

The findings in this chapter will therefore be compared primarily with those of the McCords and the Gluecks.

2. *Parental Attitude*

Psychoanalysts have laid great emphasis upon the emotional attitudes of parents, and especially of mothers, in the formation of the characters of their offspring. When our boys were aged 8–9, the PSWs categorized their mothers' attitudes towards them as 'loving normal', 'loving anxious', 'over-protective' or 'cruel, passive or neglecting'. The definitions of these labels, and of others quoted in this section, have been given by West, 1969, pp. 78–85. (See also Note 1.) The descriptions cruel, passive and neglecting were meant to include mothers who were indifferent, lacking affection or positively and cruelly rejecting. The small group of boys whose mothers were given these labels frequently became delinquents (33·3 per cent of 42 boys, compared with 17·4 per cent of 339: $\chi^2 = 5{\cdot}14$, $p < {\cdot}025$).

These findings may be compared with those of the McCords, who showed that 59 per cent of the sons of cruel, passive or neglecting mothers were convicted as juveniles, compared with only 34 per cent of the remainder. The boys studied by the McCords were specially selected for high delinquency potential, so the total percentage of delinquents was much higher than ours. Nevertheless, the two surveys agree about the greatly increased risk of becoming delinquent if, at an early age, maternal attitude appeared unfavourable. Glueck and Glueck (1950) also found that mothers of delinquents were much more likely to be rated indifferent, hostile or rejective in attitude, and correspondingly less likely to be rated warm, than mothers of non-delinquents. However, the summary table in Appendix C of Glueck and Glueck (1962) shows that maternal attitude discriminated between delinquents and non-delinquents less effectively than any of the other four factors in their Social Prediction Table, namely paternal attitude, paternal discipline, maternal supervision, and family cohesiveness.

Since our immediate concern is with the links between later delinquency and family background at an early age, observations made when the boys were older are not strictly relevant. Nevertheless, it is of some interest to record the findings of different social workers who reassessed mothers' attitudes when the boys were aged 10–11, and again when they were 14–15. The association between cruel, passive or neglecting mothers and delinquent sons was actually closer at these later ages than at 8–9 (37·0 per cent of 27 at age 10–11, and 37·5 per cent of 32 at 14–15). Pooling the assessments at the three ages, 42 boys were consistently rated unfavourably in maternal attitude (i.e. rated cruel, passive or neglecting on at least two occasions out of three), and 38·1 per cent of them were delinquents. This shows that a combination of the assessments by different social workers at different ages was capable of identifying a larger number of vulnerable boys, and was more closely correlated with delinquency, than any single measure. Of course, it must be remembered that the later ratings could have been contaminated by the knowledge of which boys were already delinquents.

At the same time as they assessed maternal attitudes, the PSWs also rated the operative fathers' attitudes towards their boys, classifying the fathers as warm, passive, neglectful or cruel. It was found that the minority of boys with fathers categorized as anything other than warm were particularly likely to become delinquents (30·9 per cent of 68, as opposed to 16·1 per cent of 286 : $\chi^2 = 6{\cdot}91$, $p < {\cdot}01$). It seems that cruel, passive or neglectful fathers were just as damaging as cruel, passive or neglectful mothers. This contrasts with the findings of the McCords' survey, in which bad fathers were not quite as deleterious as bad mothers. The Gluecks, however, found that unsatisfactory paternal attitude—indifferent, rejecting or hostile—was slightly more characteristic of delinquents than unsatisfactory maternal attitude.

As with maternal attitude, other social workers repeated the assessments of paternal attitude at later ages. It was again found that an overall rating taken from all three ages was more closely correlated with delinquency than any single one.

3. *Parental Discipline*

Parental discipline is of special interest to social psychologists because of the central role of punishment in social learning theory. According to this theory as applied to criminality (Trasler, 1962; Eysenck, 1970), young children naturally behave in a hedonistic and delinquent manner which is liable to attract punishment. The pain and fear engendered by punishment become linked with the commission of the delinquent act, so that each time the child contemplates such an act he experiences fear, which inhibits him from carrying the intention through. According to the theory, fear will not become associated with delinquent behaviour unless punishment is administered consistently whenever misconduct occurs. It therefore follows that lax or erratic discipline should be ineffectual in suppressing delinquent behaviour.

Most of the evidence for social learning theory comes from laboratory experiments purporting to measure the effect of punishment on delinquent behaviour in children (see Becker, 1964; Parke, 1970). However, since the 'punishment' has usually consisted of verbal reprimands or loud noises, and the delinquent behaviour involved has usually been cheating, the relevance of the results to real life child-rearing and delinquent behaviour is problematical. In a real life family, misbehaviour and punishment occur in a complex emotional context of social expectations and on-going personal relationships. Field surveys in the community to investigate the association between parental discipline and official delinquency are badly needed if the theory is to have practical application. Understandably, however, few learning theorists are prepared to forsake the protected laboratory setting for real life situations where there are so many uncontrollable factors to interfere with their predictions (Baldwin, 1967).

In the present Study, the PSWs attempted to follow the system described by McCord *et al.* (1959), and to categorize the operative mothers' styles of discipline as normal, lax, strict, very strict or erratic. These assessments were primarily concerned with the nature and severity of methods of control and punishment. The standard of the boy's behaviour which the parents attempted to enforce, and the consistency with which they applied their rules, were considered under the heading of parental supervision (see p. 55). The boys thought to have had very strict or erratic discipline were significantly more delinquent-prone than those who had experienced other disciplinary methods (26·7 per cent of 135, as opposed to 15·8 per cent of 241 : $\chi^2 = 5{\cdot}83$, $p < {\cdot}025$; 25 boys not rated).

The PSWs also rated the emotional quality of the operative mother's discipline, classifying this as normal, spoiling, harsh or disinterested. The boys whose mothers' methods of discipline were thought to have a 'harsh' quality were especially likely to become delinquents (37·2 per cent of 43, as opposed to 17·4 per cent of 334 : $\chi^2 = 8{\cdot}29$, $p < {\cdot}005$).

The father's discipline was similarly rated, with similar results.

Discipline that was erratic or very strict in style, and discipline that was harsh in emotional quality, were both associated with an increased likelihood of subsequent delinquency (see Appendix A, factors 25 and 26).

These results agree in most respects with those of previous surveys. The Gluecks found that their delinquents were much more likely than their non-delinquents to have had lax, overstrict or erratic discipline from both parents. The McCords also found that erratic or lax discipline was associated with delinquency, although they did not find punitive discipline (physical punishment or aggressive threats) to be deleterious. The only substantial point on which our results differ from these is in the finding that lax discipline was not associated with delinquency (17·1 per cent of 41 boys with lax fathers, and 25·0 per cent of 16 boys with lax mothers, becoming delinquents). The reason for this difference may lie in the way our ratings were made. The PSWs' categories were mutually exclusive, and the erratic category had priority. So long as discipline was thought to be to some extent erratic, it was classified as such, even though it might at the same time be predominantly lax.

The topic of parental discipline was investigated again more systematically at a later stage, but without producing any clearer results (see p. 183).

4. *Parental Attitude and Discipline Combined*

There was a great overlap between the various ratings of parental attitude and discipline. For example, 36 of the 42 boys said to have been exposed to maternal discipline of a harsh quality, and 27 of the 42 said to have experienced cruel, passive or neglecting maternal attitudes, also figured among the minority of 134 who received erratic or very strict discipline. It could be argued that even such extensive overlapping faithfully reflects the family situations if, for some reason, certain parental attitudes and disciplinary methods are genuinely interlinked. However, as previously reported (West, 1969, pp. 129–31), it was apparent that the intercorrelations among PSWs' ratings were much higher in regard to factors requiring subjective judgments than in the case of the more direct and objective observations. This suggested that the overlap between the attitude and discipline scales was largely due to a tendency to view each parent either positively or negatively, and to rate accordingly on all three scales.

It therefore seemed more meaningful to score each boy on just two combined scales, one reflecting maternal attitude and discipline, and the other reflecting paternal attitude and discipline (see Note 1). Both assessments were significantly associated with delinquency, the relationship being slightly closer in the case of maternal attitude and discipline (see Appendix A, factors 23 and 27).

Many other investigators have reported that parental attitude and discipline were closely interlinked. For example, the McCords found that loving parents tended not to be lax or erratic in discipline. Researchers such as Sears *et al.* (1957) have distinguished two contrasting general methods of child-rearing, called 'love-oriented' and 'object-oriented'. The love-oriented parents tend to feel warmly towards their children, praise them, employ reasoning and use withdrawal of love as the main punitive device. The object-oriented parents tend to feel rejecting and hostile toward their children, to use material rewards and to apply physical punishments. It is claimed that love-oriented methods are favoured by middle-class parents (Bronfenbrenner, 1958), and that these methods are more effective in producing well socialized and less delinquent children (Trasler, 1962). In so far as unfavourable ratings on attitude and discipline correspond to the concept of object-oriented parents, our findings are in agreement with this suggestion.

5. *Parental Conflict*

The PSWs found that 89 boys came from homes in which there was a noticeable degree of marital disharmony. These boys included a significantly high percentage who became delinquents (31·5 per cent of 89, as opposed to 14·8 per cent of 284: $\chi^2 = 11{\cdot}3$, $p < {\cdot}001$).

Marital disharmony was further assessed at later ages by different social workers. However, in this instance, although the ratings on all three occasions were significantly intercorrelated, a combined score was not more closely associated with delinquency than the original assessment at age 8–9. This result can be contrasted with the improved relationships with delinquency obtained by combining the ratings from different ages on other parental factors such as maternal attitude. It could be that parental disharmony has a more damaging effect on children when it occurs relatively early in life.

The Gluecks also found that the conjugal relations of the parents of their delinquents tended to be unsatisfactory. Both they and the

McCords reported that delinquents came from less cohesive homes, in which there was less warmth between the two parents and between the parents and their children.

Disharmony between parents was often associated with inconsistency between them in the handling of their children, or with an undue dominance by one parent in family matters. The PSWs tried to assess both these aspects. They identified 100 boys whose parents differed in their handling of the child so much that he could play off one against the other or avoid conforming with either. Such parental inconsistency was found to predict delinquency, although not to the same extent as other factors described in this section (26·0 per cent of 100, as opposed to 16·9 per cent of 261 : $\chi^2 = 3{\cdot}30$, $p < {\cdot}10$). This result follows the trend reported by Bandura and Walters (1959), who found that parents of aggressive boys were particularly likely to disagree about aspects of the child-rearing process. Andry (1960) also concluded that delinquents tended to have inconsistent parents (strict fathers and lax mothers).

The PSWs also rated the relative dominance of each parent. A parent was said to be dominant if he or she took the lead in the organization of family life, excluding the other partner from decisions or leaving the partner very little say. The rating of neither dominant indicated that the parents discussed plans together and arrived at joint decisions. It was found that paternal and maternal dominance were almost equally deleterious (21·7 per cent of the 83 boys said to have dominant fathers becoming delinquents, as opposed to 24·6 per cent of the 118 with dominant mothers). The boys with neither parent dominant were much less likely to become delinquents (12·1 per cent of 149, as opposed to 23·4 per cent of 201 : $\chi^2 = 6{\cdot}50$, $p < {\cdot}025$). This result appears to differ from the Gluecks' conclusion that neither maternal nor paternal dominance was associated with delinquency. The Gluecks, however, categorized nearly all their cases as either mother dominant or father dominant, thereby obscuring the possibility that more or less equally balanced parents produced less delinquents.

Since the PSWs' assessments of marital disharmony, parental inconsistency and dominance were all closely inter-related, the three were merged into a combined scale of parental conflict (using the rules described in Note 1). It was found that the boys suffering serious parental conflict were particularly prone to delinquency (35·0 per cent of 60, as opposed to 16·2 per cent of 332 : $\chi^2 = 10{\cdot}44$, $p < {\cdot}005$).

6. *Parental Supervision*

One aspect of parental behaviour which did not seem to be closely associated with most of those previously discussed was parental supervision. The PSWs rated each boy's parents according to their vigilance and their rules when the boys were aged 8–9. Vigilance referred to parental watchfulness, concern and closeness of supervision, while rules referred to whether parents were rigid or lax in their application of rules of behaviour and penalties for non-conformity (see West, 1969, pp. 73–4). The boys with 'under-vigilant' parents and those whose parents were lax in rules were particularly likely to become delinquents (44·2 per cent of 43 boys and 28·8 per cent of 66 boys respectively). The ratings of vigilance and rules overlapped considerably. Eliminating boys not known on both, 25 out of the 41 with under-vigilant parents were among the 66 whose parents were lax in rules. The two assessments were therefore combined into a single measure of parental supervision. The method of combination was similar to that previously described in connection with maternal attitude and discipline (see Note 1).

Poorly supervised boys were much more likely to become delinquents than boys whose parental supervision was assessed as average or good (31·1 per cent of 74, as opposed to 16·5 per cent of 309 : $\chi^2 = 7{\cdot}23$, $p < {\cdot}01$). Boys with poor parental supervision were also more likely to become police contact cases (23·0 per cent to 11·0 per cent). Nevertheless, in spite of this association with delinquency, matching analyses showed that delinquents and non-delinquents did not differ significantly in parental supervision once family income or parental criminality was taken into account. Apparently, this aspect of parental mismanagement was very closely bound up with low income (see Appendix C), and was not in itself an important precursor of delinquency independently of other background factors. As pointed out earlier (see p. 42), poor supervision was particularly prevalent among boys with criminal parents, and this may have been the true cause of the increased risk of delinquency among these boys. Poor supervision differed from most of the other adverse factors, but resembled parental criminality, in being no more closely associated with delinquency of early onset than with later delinquency.

The results of the matching analyses, suggesting that parental supervision was of little significance after allowing for other factors, came as a surprise. The Gluecks (1950, p. 112) found that maternal supervision was a basic factor distinguishing delinquents from non-delinquents. They wrote, 'A disproportionately lower percentage of the mothers of delinquents (7 per cent: 65·2 per cent) gave or arranged for suitable care of their children by keeping close watch over them and providing for their leisure hours. . . . Far more of the mothers of delinquents (63·9 per cent: 13 per cent) left the children to shift for themselves or in the care of an irresponsible child or adult.' Unsuitable supervision by the mother was used by the Gluecks (1950, p. 261) as one of the five important factors in their original social prediction table for identifying future delinquents. It may be that in our Study the parental supervision ratings were based on insufficiently precise criteria, and hence subject to class bias. The findings illustrate yet again the extreme difficulty of distinguishing between aspects of family life that are in practice closely interlinked.

7. *Parental Arrangements for Boy's Leisure*

Criminological research into leisure pursuits has concentrated on the supposed unwillingness or inability of juvenile delinquents to become members of organized clubs. However, Wootton (1959), reviewing this assumption as one of her 12 criminological hypotheses, found the evidence rather inconclusive. This may be because of the difficulty of obtaining adequate information to test the hypothesis (Grygier, 1955). A rather neglected aspect of leisure is the amount of time spent by delinquents with their parents. Gold (1963) found that delinquents and their parents did very few activities together.

When our boys were aged about 12–13, the social workers visited their homes and asked their mothers a prepared schedule of questions relating to their sons' leisure activities. The questions covered such topics as whether the boy spent his leisure time mainly with members of his family or with other people, whether or not his father joined in such activities, and whether he spent his leisure time mainly at home or on the street. In order to counteract the bias introduced by the fact that interviews took place at different periods of the year, when habits might differ, certain questions specified the season of the year to which they referred.

In general, the boys who spent their leisure time with other members of their family or at home tended not to be delinquents. For example, only 6·5 per cent of the 93 boys who stayed mainly at home all the year round were delinquents, in comparison with 21·4 per cent of the 182 who stayed mainly at home only during the winter, and 29·8 per cent of the 57 who never spent their leisure time mainly at home. The excess of delinquents among boys who never spent the main part of their leisure at home was noticeable at all three family income levels. Those boys with fathers who never joined in their leisure activities were particularly likely to be delinquents (35·5 per cent of 31, as opposed to 16·8 per cent of 268 : $\chi^2 = 5{\cdot}21$, $p < {\cdot}025$).

Each mother was also asked whether her boy had had a holiday away from home of at least one week's duration during the previous two years. It was found that the minority of boys who had not had holidays were particularly delinquent-prone (30·4 per cent of 46, as opposed to 16·9 per cent of 279 : $\chi^2 = 3{\cdot}93$, $p < {\cdot}05$). Having no holidays was a particularly frequent feature among boys from poor families, but the relationship with delinquency held true at all levels of family income. Of the boys who had had holidays, those who had never been away without their parents were unlikely to be delinquents (12·0 per cent of 108, as opposed to 19·9 per cent of 171), although not to a statistically significant degree.

The results of the leisure time enquiry were much as expected from Gold's previous study. Our delinquents received relatively little encouragement to spend time with their parents or to organize their leisure constructively. They tended to spend their time on the street, to be given no holidays away from home, and to have fathers who did not participate in their leisure pursuits. The minority of boys who, all the year round, spent most of their time with their family were rarely delinquents. Since most of the delinquents were first convicted after this information was collected, the leisure habits characteristic of delinquents probably preceded their official convictions.

8. *Mothers' Job Aspirations for Boys*

According to Gold (1963), American mothers have comparatively low aspirations for their delinquent sons, and these boys share their mothers' low aspirations. This is partly a consequence of the poor school records of the delinquents. Typically, the delinquent's mother thinks her son unlikely to achieve even the lowly job she wants for him. Aspirations and expectations are easily confused. Fredericks and Molnar (1969) found that, whereas both delinquents and non-delinquents aspired to higher status occupations than those of their fathers, only the non-delinquents anticipated obtaining such jobs. Elliott (1962) found that delinquents associated managerial or professional jobs with success in life, but did not anticipate obtaining them. These observations are relevant to the theories of Cohen (1955) and Cloward and Ohlin (1960), which stress the discordance between delinquents' aspirations and the opportunities available to them.

We measured mothers' job aspirations for their sons by means of a questionnaire given to the mothers by the social workers when the boys were aged about 13. The responses were scored according to the status of the job which the mother said she would like her son to have in the future (see Note 2). When the boys were divided into four equal groups according to their mothers' job aspirations, it became clear that low aspiration was very significantly related to delinquency (see Table III (1)).

Low aspiration was also very significantly related to low family income. Of the 73 boys from poor families whose mothers' job aspirations were known, more than half (38) fell in the worst quarter on job aspiration. However, the association between low job aspiration and delinquency was not merely a reflection of social class. At

TABLE III (1)

Delinquency and Mothers' Job Aspirations

Mothers' Job aspirations	*Delinquency*									
	No police record		*Police contact boys*		*One-time delinquents*		*Recidivists*		*Total boys*	
	(%)	(*N*)	(%)	(*N*)	(%)	(*N*)	(%)	(*N*)		
High (8 or below)	84·4	(65)	10·4	(8)	3·9	(3)	1·3	(1)	100%	(77)
High average (9–10)	74·7	(59)	10·1	(8)	11·4	(9)	3·8	(3)	100%	(79)
Low average (11–12)	66·7	(52)	14·1	(11)	10·3	(8)	9·0	(7)	100%	(78)
Low (13 or above)	50·0	(39)	16·7	(13)	21·8	(17)	11·5	(9)	100%	(78)
Total boys known	68·9	(215)	12·8	(40)	11·9	(37)	6·4	(20)	100%	(312)
Not known	56·6	(56)	16·2	(16)	10·1	(10)	17·2	(17)	100%	(99)

Significance Test: Comparing the 78 boys with the least aspiring mothers with the remainder, and comparing the 57 delinquents with the non-delinquents, $\chi^2 = 14{\cdot}5$, p= < ·001.

each level of family income, the boys whose mothers had low aspirations were very much more likely to be delinquents than those whose mothers had average or higher aspirations.

The job aspiration of a boy's mother was also very closely related to his own educational achievements, suggesting that the mothers were in the main being realistic. For example, nearly half (44·7 per cent) of the boys in the lowest quarter on secondary school allocation (pp. 82–9) were also in the lowest quarter on mothers' job aspiration, a highly significant association ($\chi^2 = 22{\cdot}8$, $p < {\cdot}001$). There was an interesting interaction between educational achievement and maternal aspiration. Where the boy was below-average in achievement, the aspiration of his mother appeared to have little effect on his likelihood of becoming a delinquent (26·9 per cent of 119 boys with below-average mothers' aspirations becoming delinquents, in comparison with 22·9 per cent of 48 boys with above-average mothers' aspirations). In contrast, low maternal aspirations were closely related to delinquency in the case of boys with above-average achievements (24·3 per cent of 37 boys with below-average mothers' aspirations becoming delinquents, in comparison with only 4·6 per cent of 108 boys with above-average mothers' aspirations). It would appear that high-achieving boys whose mothers nevertheless maintain low job aspirations for them are rendered especially vulnerable to delinquency. It may be that unrealistically low aspiration on the part of mothers reflects some undervaluation or rejection that is particularly damaging.

9. *Parental Behaviour: A Global Rating*

Three combined ratings of parental behaviour have been described, namely maternal attitude and discipline, paternal attitude and discipline, and parental conflict. The overlap between the three was very considerable. After eliminating those not rated on one or other assessment, there were 56 boys with serious parental conflict. Of these 56, no less than 33 were among the 77 rated unfavourably on paternal attitude and discipline, and 23 among the 59 rated unfavourably on maternal attitude and discipline. The overlap was just as extensive between the favourable as between the unfavourable categories. Parents tended to be seen as bad in many respects, or good in many respects, but rarely bad in some and good in others. Once again, the results suggested that the PSWs had found difficulty in measuring one aspect of parental behaviour independently of another.

In view of these findings, it was decided to combine all three (already combined) ratings into one global rating, termed parental behaviour (see Note 1). This final measure indicated essentially how far the PSWs approved of the way the boy was treated by his parents. As might perhaps have been expected, the boys experiencing the worst parental behaviour were more than twice as delinquent-prone as the remainder (32·3 per cent of 96, as opposed to 15·3 per cent of 300 : $\chi^2 = 12{\cdot}3$, $p < {\cdot}001$; see Table III (2). This result was similar to

TABLE III (2)

Delinquency and Poor Parental Behaviour

Parental behaviour	*Delinquency* No police record (%)	(N)	Police contact boys (%)	(N)	One-time delinquents (%)	(N)	Recidivists (%)	(N)	Total boys	
Not known	33·3	(5)	20·0	(3)	13·3	(2)	33·3	(5)	100%	(15)
Good	74·6	(94)	12·7	(16)	8·7	(11)	4·0	(5)	100%	(126)
Average	67·2	(117)	15·5	(27)	12·6	(22)	4·6	(8)	100%	(174)
Poor	57·3	(55)	10·4	(10)	12·5	(12)	19·8	(19)	100%	(96)
Total boys	65·9	(271)	13·6	(56)	11·4	(47)	9·0	(37)	100%	(411)

Significance Test: Comparing 96 boys suffering poor parental behaviour with the remainder, and comparing 77 delinquents with the remainder, $\chi^2 = 12{\cdot}3$, $p < {\cdot}001$.

that previously obtained by the McCords, when they too used a combined rating based on a number of aspects of unsatisfactory parental behaviour. They discovered a substantial minority of boys, handicapped by parental deviance, among whom the likelihood of future delinquency was more than twice that in the remainder of the sample.

In our Study, poor parental behaviour was particularly characteristic of the recidivists. Of the 96 boys with the worst parental behaviour ratings, 19·8 per cent became juvenile recidivists, in comparison with only 4·3 per cent of the remainder rated. Poor parental behaviour was not a feature of either one-time delinquents or police contact boys. As with other important factors, such as low income and low intelligence, poor parental behaviour was especially evident among boys first convicted at an early age. Among those rated on parental behaviour, 28 boys were first convicted at 10–13. Of these, 57·1 per cent experienced poor parental behaviour, compared with only 30·6 per cent of the 49 boys first convicted at 14–16.

Poor parental behaviour was particularly prevalent among the poor boys (38·2 per cent as opposed to 20·2 per cent). Nevertheless, delinquents and non-delinquents still differed significantly in parental behaviour when matched for family income, family size or parental criminality (see Appendix B). Furthermore, they differed significantly in each of these three factors when matched for parental behaviour. These results indicated that parental behaviour was an important factor associated with delinquency independently of other basic factors.

It was gratifying to be able to show that unsatisfactory parental behaviour was very significantly related to future delinquency, but disappointing that the marked halo effect present in the PSWs' ratings prevented them from distinguishing different types of unsatisfactoriness. The combined parental behaviour assessment was very much a global impression, based as it was upon an accumulation of unfavourable ratings. One suspects that much the same result would have been obtained however many or however few aspects the PSWs had tried to evaluate. Of the components of the parental behaviour scale, maternal attitude and discipline was more closely associated with delinquency than either paternal attitude and discipline or parental conflict. Of the components of maternal attitude and discipline, a harsh quality of discipline (i.e. cruel, brutal, rejecting) was most productive of delinquency. These two points, general unsatisfactoriness and harsh maternal discipline, are the nearest one can come, on the basis of the results so far described, to a delineation of criminogenic parental behaviour.

Parental behaviour is a particularly interesting factor because it is a possible cause, and not merely a precursor, of juvenile delinquency. Further insight into the meanings of the parental behaviour ratings may be obtained by studying the descriptive comments made by the PSWs after interviewing the families in question. Of the 96 boys rated unfavourably on parental behaviour, 17—the worst of the lot—had a score of 9, 28 had a score of 8 and 51 had a score of 7 (see Note 1). Here are two examples picked at random from the 17 cases with the worst parental behaviour ratings:

Case 851 (Information extracted from the PSW's notes made when the boy was aged 8–9)

This mother is a tough, aggressive, vicious woman, completely plausible, thoroughly uncooperative and untrustworthy. This is my impression, but it is confirmed by the many social agencies who know the family.

They live in a very old, dilapidated house. The whole appearance of the place is one of neglect. A window on the ground floor has been broken for 6 months. It is boarded up from the bottom so that no light can get in. At one time they lived in a local authority home for problem families.

Father is work-shy and often out of a job. At other times he works at any odd labouring job that comes to hand. He was discharged from the army with a diagnosis of psychopathic personality. Five years later he was investigated at a psychiatric hospital for 'blackouts'. No physical cause was found and he was diagnosed as an inadequate psychopath. About five years ago the parents were involved with the NSPCC because their children were running about the streets while they were inside pubs drinking.

Mother puts on a loving act in front of me with her boy, then she sloshes him one minute later for not doing what she says. A thoroughly unloving, violent mother. Up against authority, protecting her children from social workers and so on.

A children's officer reports that mother is out at work for quite lengthy hours, including every evening, so she cannot have much control over the children's activities. She is obviously the dominating person in the family. The probation officer reports that the family appear to attach little importance to their children's court appearances, and seem to accept delinquency as their normal pattern.

Marital situation not ascertainable directly, but a probation officer notes that on several occasions mother has left her husband and family, although she always showed some concern about the children. It is her husband she wanted to leave, not the children.

Information obtained subsequently

When the boy was aged 10, a report from his school noted: 'Complete lack of normal standards. Difficulty in work. . . . We cannot get him to attend regularly, but his absences are invariably covered by notes from parents, often palpably untrue. When he is absent or out of school hours he is continually in trouble.' In fact, he soon became a juvenile recidivist.

When the boy was 12, a social worker saw the parents in connection with court proceedings. She found evidence that mother had been drinking heavily and was currently living away from home. There had been trouble going on between the parents for six years or more. About the same time, a probation officer found that both parents eluded attempts to see them. 'Mother seems to have little to do with the control of the boy, and the daughters in the family play the role of mother.'

When this boy was seen at age 18, the interviewer commented: 'He seemed to be a shambles, without a clue about ordering his life. . . . The real world seems to be too complicated for him and his point about wanting to go back to [the approved school] may be of some significance since it possibly gave him the predictable environment he seems to need.' He admitted to long periods of unemployment, frequent job changes, several prosecutions for being drunk and disorderly, a recent attack of venereal disease from a casual pick-up, extensive involvement in delinquent activities, and experience with pep-pills and cannabis. He said he had been convicted for assaulting a police officer who tried to stop him while he was on a shoplifting spree with a girl. He admitted further that on one occasion he had broken a bottle and threatened to cut the throat of a youth who was arguing with him. At the time of interview, he was 'on the run' from the police for non-payment of a fine.

Case 460 (Information extracted from the PSW's notes made when the boy was just turned 10 years of age)
The initial visits to this family were delayed because mother claimed to have lost the letter asking for her cooperation. She was at first rather hostile, but then somewhat ingratiating. She thinks it doubtful if I will ever be able to see father, who has always managed to hide himself from other social workers. She has been taking the boy to a child guidance clinic for two years, because he is clinging and has a school phobia. The family is known to social agencies because of mother's illegal child-minding activities, and because they have constant worries over debts and have had much help from various charities. They have had court appearances and eviction orders for rent arrears.

The parents have not slept together for the last six years at least, and I gather the marriage is one in name only. They still have their meals together but sleep in separate rooms. There is a strong denigration of father by mother, who makes him out to be quite useless. She feels she is kept down by her husband and by having to live in a bad neighbourhood. She complains that father is a liar, takes no interest in the home, bullies and shouts at the children and constantly loses his temper with them. She remarked 'It is my fault, I only married him to get a home for my [illegitimate] boy.' Father is in poor health, often out of work, and is completely excluded, or excludes himself, from the life of the family.

It seems the parents are never in agreement over the children, and both are moody and erratic in their handling. For instance, if mother puts the children to bed father gets them up again. Mother is a strange, very neurotic woman. She certainly over-manages and protects both her boys, washing and dressing them and keeping them in too much. The boy is discouraged from taking any responsibility in the way of chores. She is very restrictive about his playmates. She says she can't let the children play with her neighbours' children because it makes trouble when the children repeat things.

Mother says it is always our boy who gets punished by father, never his brother. The brother is undoubtedly mother's favourite. She feels our boy to be hard in some way, self-willed, unresponsive, and less affectionate and obliging than his brother.

Later information
This boy had a 'police contact', but only for a motoring offence. He did not acquire a delinquency conviction. When seen at 19, he had been living on his own for a year, and said he felt a lot better for it. 'When I was with my family it didn't help me at all. My parents didn't get on with each other. . . . When I think about my family it really annoys me. . . . I've always tried to help my mother, but she's never taken any interest in me. . . . My father left me alone and I left him alone—that was the best thing about it.'

The following two examples were drawn at random from the 51 cases with parental behaviour rated 7, that is just bad enough for inclusion in the unsatisfactory category, but not so extreme as the cases quoted above:

Case 150 (Information extracted from the PSW's notes made when the boy was aged 8–9)
Both parents are highly strung, neurotic people. Father is somewhat irresponsible. He tries to relax by going to pubs drinking and by living in his work. Both parents profess to be fond of each other, but they are undoubtedly erratic and unpredictable in their handling of the children.

There is marital conflict over father's drinking. They both sulk for ages. Father, seen on his own, seemed not very interested in his children and admitted freely that he was extremely fed up and depressed about his home situation, but unwilling or unable to do anything about it. He thinks he was not really born to be married, though he is very fond of his wife and could never leave her.

Mother is tense and over-anxious in her attitude to the boy. She admits she is too soft, but also that she loses her temper, shouts and scolds and threats, and then fails to carry out her threats. Father thinks she is far too lenient and that she cannot control the children, so he is the one who is forced to be tough and shout and punish.

Later information
When our boy was aged 11, his younger brother was taken to a psychiatrist with numerous nervous symptoms. After a year the psychiatrist wrote: 'I have continued to see him regularly. . . . However, it has become clear that his family background is chronically disturbed and I feel that he is only likely to progress further if placed away from home.' The mother was seen by the social worker when our boy was aged 14. At that time, he also was showing nervous symptoms and was truanting. Mother was extremely distressed and fearful that by confiding to the boy her own troubles, fears and dissatisfactions with her husband she may have done him harm.

This boy had no juvenile police contacts and did not become a delinquent. Interviewed at 18, he was then in the forces and said he preferred living away from home. He reported continued disputes between his parents, this time because his father was having an affair with a much younger woman.

Case 450 (Information extracted from the PSW's notes made when the boy was aged 8–9)
The parents live in a comfortable, luxurious local authority flat. Both work, and there is a good income. Mother is a nervous, defensive young woman, dependent on her women friends. She does not appear to get much enjoyment out of her husband or the boy, but she says she has no means of comparison, she has never known any different. She herself had a sordid childhood, with a brutal step-father and an alcoholic mother. I think she is immature and lacking in maternal warmth. Mother expressed strong ideas about parents being unfairly blamed for their children's misdeeds. 'I had such a terrible life and nobody bothered about me.' She complains that her husband is abnormally jealous, watching her all the time, and suspecting her of going out with other men. She says he is hypochondriacal, always rushing to the doctor. The marriage seems a cold, sterile relationship with little depth of understanding. She complains that father acts like a sergeant major with the boy, always shouts, expects too much, never asks the boy anything, but always gives orders.

Later information
When the boy was 11, his father died. After that, his mother had to undergo psychiatric treatment, and developed hostility towards the Study. When he was 18, and a research worker called to ask for an interview, the mother became extremely emotional and tried to drag her son away from the door, shouting 'No, he don't want anything to do with that.' Eventually, however, the boy was persuaded to come for interview, but he was guarded and untruthful on matters concerning his family. His mother had remarried, and he was still living at home with her and his step-father.

The boy did not become a delinquent, and had no juvenile police contacts.

In contrast to the preceding examples, here are two taken at random from the 64 boys rated 3 (the best possible score) on parental behaviour:

Case 903 (Information extracted from the PSW's notes made when the boy was aged 8–9)
A family of good social standard. She is an understanding and kindly mother who is desperately keen to preserve the confidence and trust the children have in her, and she enjoys her children. Marital harmony good, sexual adjustment satisfactory. Mother says they have small arguments. The children are amused by it, they say 'Mummy stop arguing.'

Mother reported that, on the whole, very little discipline was needed to make the boy conform. He is never cheeky. 'An occasional smack, that's enough.' Father tells mother to be firm and then gives in himself. Mother thinks it is no good being too strict. Father takes the boy out and both parents tell him they are proud of him when occasion arises. Both have a normal, loving attitude. Mother was hesitant about co-operating with the Study, and did not want her boy singled out for testing at school.

Later information
This boy had no juvenile police contacts and did not become a delinquent. Interviewed at age 18, he had recently left home following his marriage. He said he was quite happy at home with his parents, but he wanted to be independent. He still visited his parents regularly. He appeared well settled. He had been on day release from his job, studying to further his career.

Case 833 (Information extracted from the PSW's notes made when the boy was aged 8–9)
Father has been in steady work all his life and earns good money. Mother is a loving, less intelligent, anxious person, obviously fond of her children and her husband. She seems anxious and over-protective, but is under stress from very bad housing conditions. Father would like to buy a house, but the Building Society will not give him a mortgage.

Mother talks warmly about her boy, obviously devoted to him. Most concerned to make sure the Study was not going to upset him. Came from a warm united family herself and has a good understanding of children. Marital relationship good. Mother says: 'We are very happy —I don't want for nothing.' She describes her husband as 'A good man, very easy and settled and nice-natured.' Sexual adjustment satisfactory and neither parent dominant.

Father is normal and loving, takes a keen interest in the children, and takes the boy out a good deal. Neither parent believes in being over-severe. Father says he never hits the boy; 'He always knows when I mean it.' Father's handling is firm, kind, even-tempered. Mother says she advises the boy about bad company, but usually lets him find out for himself.

Later information
This boy had a police contact as a juvenile for a delinquent act, but no convictions. Interviewed at 18, he was in regular work in a job he liked. He was still living with his now widowed mother. He seemed to have taken the key role in the household since his father's death.

NOTES

[1] *Further Details of Parental Behaviour Ratings*
Six boys were not rated on maternal attitude because at the time they had no one filling the role of mother, and 24 others could not be rated because their parents were too uncooperative. These 24 boys were a very delinquent-prone group (41·7 per cent delinquents). Since the same boys tended to be rated 'not known' on most items concerning family background, absence of information

was generally associated with delinquency (see pp. 77–81 and West, 1969, pp. 63–5). For this reason, in comparing boys rated unfavourably on these family factors with those rated otherwise, cases not assessed have been excluded.

When producing a combined rating of maternal attitude and discipline (see p. 53), three points were given if maternal attitude was cruel, passive or neglecting, another three if maternal discipline was erratic or very strict, and another three if quality of discipline was harsh. Two points were given if maternal attitude was loving, anxious or over-protective, if maternal discipline was lax or strict, or if quality of discipline was spoiling or disinterested. Finally, one point was given for each assessment of 'normal'. The combined score, which was obtained by simple addition, varied from 3 to 9. If a boy was not rated on one of the scales, his total points on the other two were multiplied by 1½. In the exceptional case where a boy was rated on one scale only, the points were multiplied by three.

The use of two or three points for the different categories of unsatisfactory attitude or discipline involved a decision as to which categories were the most unfavourable. This was usually fairly clear; for instance, 'cruel, passive or neglecting' was presumptively worse than 'loving anxious' or 'over-protective'. Where it was less obvious, for example that erratic discipline was worse than lax discipline, the decision was made by seeing which categories were most closely related to other parental categories that were indisputably unfavourable.

Similar rules were adopted for amalgamating the ratings of marital disharmony, parental inconsistency and parental dominance to derive the combined measure of parental conflict. In producing a final, global rating of parental behaviour, three (already combined) ratings were amalgamated. These consisted of (1) Maternal attitude and discipline, (2) Paternal attitude and discipline and (3) Parental conflict. Each boy was scored good (one point), average (two points) or poor (three points) on each of these separate ratings, and the combined parental behaviour measure was produced by adding the points.

[2] *Further Details of the Mothers' Job Aspiration Questionnaire*

This questionnaire was given by the social workers during a home visit. In the previous visit the mothers had been asked questions about the boys' leisure activities (see p. 56), and in the following one they were asked questions about discipline (see p. 183). The job aspiration questionnaire was first tried out with 98 mothers who were not in the Study, but lived in the area and had sons at secondary school or in the last year at primary school.

In its final form, the questionnaire consisted of a list of 30 jobs, all of them typical of the kind of work young school leavers in the area might take up. The list was in fact drawn up after consultation with a local youth employment officer. Each Study mother was given the list and asked to mark, in order of preference, the five jobs that she would most like for her son. She was also asked to state the age at which she wanted him to leave school.

A job aspiration questionnaire was filled in for only 312 boys, because the mothers of the remaining 99 were uncooperative, or not available, or failed to return the form despite several reminders. As usual, the 99 boys who were not known were slightly more delinquent-prone than average (27·3 per cent delinquents).

In scoring the questionnaire, the order in which the mother placed the five jobs was not taken into account. Each job chosen was given one, two or three points, according to its status. Jobs judged to be of professional or white-collar status, such as trainee bank clerk, trainee librarian and trainee surveyor, were given one point. Apprenticeships for blue-collar jobs, such as electrician, carpenter and motor mechanic, were given two. Finally, unskilled jobs such as van boy and warehouse assistant, and blue-collar jobs without apprenticeships, were given three. Consequently, boys whose mothers picked out all low status jobs obtained the highest scores on this measure. The question about school leaving was scored in the same direction, giving the highest score (three points) for the earliest leavers at age 15 (since this implied low job aspiration), down to zero points for a leaving age of 18. The total scores therefore ranged from 5 to 18, with high scores indicating that the boy's mother had low aspirations for him.

IV

More about Home Backgrounds

Chapters II and III have described home background factors that were associated with delinquency to a very significant degree and, at least to some extent, independently of each other. This Chapter describes some background factors which our figures suggest have somewhat less importance. They are of interest, however, if only because most of them have been widely believed by social workers to be determinants of delinquency.

1. *Separations and Broken Homes*

The topic of separations from parents was investigated in some detail. The successive social workers engaged on the Study made repeated inquiries about separations lasting longer than one month, whether from a natural or a substitute parent. Virtually all permanent separations (broken homes) became known to the investigators sooner or later, but some temporary separations, especially those occurring early in the boys' lives, may have escaped detection through parental uncooperativeness or forgetfulness. Since inquiries from a variety of sources were made in all cases, it has not been practicable to isolate a 'not known' category.

(a) *Broken Homes.* A broken home was defined as a (presumably) permanent separation from one or both natural parents. By the time they reached their fifteenth birthdays, 76 boys (18·5 per cent) were permanently separated. In 28 cases (6·8 per cent), the reason for the break was the death of a parent, most usually the father. In 48 cases (11·7 per cent), the reason was parental separation, desertion or divorce. This prevalence of broken homes appears to be slightly greater than obtained in the National Survey (Douglas *et al.*, 1968). However, our own figures are not directly comparable with those of

Douglas, because he excluded illegitimate births and counted a different age span. The National Child Development Study of a cohort of children born in 1958 (Davie *et al.*, 1972) used the same definition of broken homes as we did. They found that the proportion of children in broken homes by the age of seven was 7·6 per cent in England. In the present Study, the corresponding percentage was only slightly higher (9·2 per cent).

The 28 boys whose homes were broken by death were not particularly prone to be delinquents (21·4 per cent of 28, compared with 17·9 per cent of 335 boys from unbroken homes). However, the

TABLE IV (1)

Delinquency and Broken Homes (Up to a Boy's Fifteenth Birthday)

	Delinquency								
Broken homes	*No police record* (%)	(*N*)	*Police contact boys* (%)	(*N*)	*One-time delinquents* (%)	(*N*)	*Recidivists* (%)	(*N*)	*Total boys*
Not broken	69·3	(232)	12·8	(43)	9·6	(32)	8·4	(28)	100% (335)
Broken by death only	53·6	(15)	25·0	(7)	21·4	(6)	0·0	(0)	100% (28)
Broken by other reasons	50·0	(24)	12·5	(6)	18·8	(9)	18·8	(9)	100% (48)
Total boys	65·9	(271)	13·6	(56)	11·4	(47)	9·0	(37)	100% (411)

Significance Test: Comparing 84 delinquents with the remainder and comparing 48 boys from homes broken by other reasons with the remainder, $\chi^2 = 8{\cdot}58$, $p < {\cdot}005$.

48 boys whose parents deserted, separated or divorced included a high proportion (37·5 per cent) who were delinquents (see Table IV (1)). A strong association between delinquency and marital separations, rather than between delinquency and parental death, has been found in a number of previous surveys (e.g. Ferguson, 1952; Douglas *et al.*, 1968, Table 28; Banks, 1965; Bruce, 1970).

In order to estimate the predictive value of broken homes, only 31 boys whose family breaks occurred before the age of 10, and were due to parental separation or desertion, were counted. These boys were significantly delinquent-prone (38·7 per cent of 31, compared with 19·0 per cent of 380: $\chi^2 = 5{\cdot}72$, $p < {\cdot}025$). There was no evidence that homes broken at an early age were more closely associated with future delinquency than those broken in later years (Gibson, 1969c). This finding was also in conformity with previous research (McCord *et al.*, 1959, p. 83).

Twenty-five boys (6·1 per cent) were known to have been born illegitimate (see Note 1). The illegitimacy rate for the area in which the boys were born was almost 7 per cent at the time of their births. Although our information was probably incomplete, it should have yielded a higher incidence of illegitimacy than official statistics. The Registrar's estimates are based on birth certificates, whereas the social workers had additional information which enabled us to detect 13 instances in which the particulars furnished by the mother when the birth was registered gave a spurious appearance of legitimacy. One possible reason for the comparatively low illegitimacy rate in the Study sample was that, owing to the way the sample was recruited, illegitimate children reared in institutions, or adopted into middle class homes, were necessarily excluded.

Eleven of the 25 illegitimate boys were not counted as coming from broken homes because they continued, at least until age 15, living with their own parents, who were in a stable union although not legally married. In contrast, of the 14 illegitimate boys from broken homes, six had no contact whatever with their true fathers, who had deserted before they were born, while a further three were deserted soon after birth. The remaining five boys lost their parents by death or desertion at a later stage.

As a group, the 25 illegitimate boys were particularly delinquent-prone. Ten of them became juvenile delinquents, of whom seven were recidivists. When convictions as young adults were included, 11 were delinquents, of whom 10 were recidivists.

(b) *Separations from Parents.* Counting both permanent and temporary separations from a parent, it was found that a history of some disruption was quite common and was significantly associated with future delinquency. Thus, there were 90 boys who had experienced some break of more than a month's duration before reaching the age of 10, and 32·2 per cent of them became delinquents. There were 84 boys who had been separated only by virtue of death (of a parent), or hospitalization (of the boy or parent), and only 20·2 per cent of them became delinquents. Finally, of the 237 boys who, to our knowledge, had never been separated during their first 10 years, 16·0 per cent became delinquents. Once again, it appeared that separations due to a parent leaving home were much more closely related to future delinquency than separations due to illness or death.

Separations at an early age were no more deleterious than later ones. Of the 90 separated boys, those whose first break occurred under the age of six were not more delinquent-prone than those who were not separated until later (30·9 per cent delinquents, as opposed to 36·4 per cent). This result has to be treated with some caution, however, since the information from mothers about earlier separations was likely to have been incomplete. Permanent separations had a slightly worse connotation than temporary ones (38·7 per cent delinquents as opposed to 31·2 per cent).

If it were the actual physical separation that was damaging, separations due to death or illness would have been as important as those due to other causes. The contrary finding which we obtained suggests that the factor which counts most is not so much the separation itself as the underlying family problems.

Separations due to reasons other than death or illness were commoner among boys from poor families, and among those from large families. Analyses showed that, when matched for income or for parental criminality or for family size, there was no clearly significant difference between delinquents and non-delinquents in the incidence of such separations (see Appendix B). This result can be taken as further evidence suggesting that separation experience is an important precursor of delinquency only in so far as it reflects the presence of other more basic family background factors. It agrees with some recent findings from Florida (Chilton and Markle, 1972) showing that, once the effect of family income was allowed for, there was no longer a tendency for delinquents guilty of more serious offences to come from incomplete parental homes.

As far as they go, these findings are in general conformity with the trends of recent research. They confirm the many studies which have reported a statistically significant relationship between family breaks and delinquency (e.g. Eidner, 1966; Naess, 1962). They agree with the views of Grygier *et al.* (1969), who emphasized the mixture or phenomena, and the disruption of family relationships, which underlie separations. More importantly, however, they point to the need for further exploration of the nature of the link between separations and delinquency. This would require a much more detailed analysis and classification of separation situations than has been possible with the small sample in this Study.

2. *Parental Authoritarianism*

Chapter III described how parental child-rearing attitudes and behaviour were assessed by psychiatric social workers on the basis of interviews with the boys' parents. Another measure of these attitudes was obtained by asking the parents to fill in an 'opinion poll' containing statements about child-rearing with which they could agree or disagree. The value of such questionnaires is in dispute. The most famous ones were devised in the United States by Shoben (1949) and Schaefer and Bell (1958). The most important dimension measured by these parental attitude questionnaires is authoritarianism-permissiveness.

It is very doubtful whether questionnaire responses accurately reflect actual child-rearing practices. Gordon (1957) observed the behaviour of mothers toward their pre-school children during a 12-day camp, and found little relationship between behaviour ratings and questionnaire results. Brody (1965) watched the behaviour of mothers towards their pre-school children during half-hour periods at a nursery school, with the same result. Gerhart and Geismar (1969) compared questionnaire responses with behaviour ratings made over a two-year period of contact, and still found no correlation. Of course, it is always possible that the behaviour of parents in the presence of observers is somewhat artificial, but the lack of any correspondence between attitudes and behaviour is surprising. Further evidence on this point was provided by Ryle (1967) in a London survey. He gave parents questionnaires relating to authoritarianism which were similar to those used in the present Study, but the responses obtained were unrelated to a PSW's assessments of the same qualities derived from interviews with the parents. Finally, Mosher and Mosher (1965) gave delinquent girls and their parents the same questionnaire on child-rearing, and discovered that the girls' perceptions of their parents did not agree with the parents' own responses.

Attitudes expressed on questionnaires may have little to do with observable parental behaviour, but even so it is suggested that authoritarianism scores derived from questionnaires to parents are significantly related to delinquency in their children. In particular, Madoff (1959) showed that parents of delinquents were more authoritarian in their attitudes toward child-rearing than parents of non-delinquents. Chorost (1962) demonstrated that authoritarian attitudes of parents were significantly related to aggressive behaviour of boys in an institution, and Winder and Rau (1962) found that parental authoritarianism was associated with peer-rated aggression among sons. However, not all results have been positive. Zuckerman *et al.* (1960) reported that parents of children attending a child guidance clinic were less authoritarian than those of a control group, and Ryle (1967) discovered that questionnaire responses of parents were not related to teachers' ratings of the aggressiveness of their children.

When our boys were aged 9-10, an attempt was made to measure the child-rearing attitudes of their parents, using questionnaires. Gibson (1968) has described the development of the questionnaires used, one for fathers and one for mothers. The parents were required to circle the answers 'agree' or 'disagree' against each statement (see West, 1969, Appendix IV (E) and pp. 87–9). On the basis of principal component analyses, a 12-item scale of authoritarianism was derived from the mothers' questionnaire, and a 20-item scale of authoritarianism from the fathers' questionnaire. Each parent was scored according to the number of authoritarian answers he or she endorsed. The scores were ranked, and the population divided into approximate quarters. Those falling into the top quarter were considered 'authoritarian'. The major disadvantage with these measures was that, in spite of repeated requests, a large number of boys remained whose mothers (120, or 29·2 per cent) or fathers (179, or 43·6 per cent) failed to complete the questionnaire. Maternal authoritarianism was closely related to future delinquency, but paternal authoritarianism was not. The boys whose mothers gave 7 or more authoritarian answers included a much higher percentage who were delinquents than the rest (28·1 per cent of 82, as opposed to 13·9 per cent of 209 : $\chi^2 = 7{\cdot}12$, $p < {\cdot}01$). In contrast, the boys whose fathers gave 13 or more authoritarian answers were no more delinquent-prone than the remainder (17·5 per cent of 57, in comparison with 16·6 per cent of 175 : $\chi^2 = 0{\cdot}00$, not significant). The null result may perhaps have occurred through a majority of delinquents (45 out of 84) being unrated, because their fathers failed to answer. This was another example of the link between non-cooperation and delinquency. Paternal authoritarianism was, however, demonstrably associated with recidivism. The percentages of recidivists increased regularly from the boys in the lowest quarter on paternal authoritarianism to those in the highest (the figures being 1·8 per cent, 4·0 per cent, 8·8 per cent and 10·5 per cent).

Maternal and paternal authoritarianism scores were significantly correlated. Eliminating cases where one or both parents failed to complete a questionnaire, 81 of the 113 boys whose mothers had above-average scores were among the 123 boys whose fathers had above-average scores ($\chi^2 = 23{\cdot}6$, $p < {\cdot}001$). This was not in agreement with Ryle (1967), who found little relationship between the attitude scores of mothers and fathers. Our overlap may have been the result of collaboration between the parents in filling in the forms. Be that as it may, it was thought that a combined measure of parental authoritarianism might be more useful, so one was derived by averaging each boy's percentile placings on the separate maternal and paternal scores. Where a boy was not scored on one of these measures, his percentile placing on the other was taken as his 'combined' placing. This combined assessment was associated with delinquency. Of the 77 boys with scores in the highest quarter, 13·7 per cent became recidivists, 13·7 per cent became one-time delinquents and 15·1 per cent became police contact cases. The corresponding figures among the remainder of the sample were 4·9 per cent, 10·2 per cent and 10·2 per cent. It may be concluded that authoritarian parents tend to have delinquent sons.

Parental authoritarianism was significantly more common among boys from poor or large families. This agrees with previous findings (e.g. Zuckerman *et al.*, 1960; Gildea *et al.*, 1961) linking authoritarianism and low social class. On the other hand, authoritarianism was quite unrelated to parental criminality (see Appendix C). Matching analyses showed that authoritarianism was not important as a precursor of delinquency independently of family income, family size or parental behaviour (see Appendix B). This suggests that authoritarian parental attitude was of predictive value only because of its association with more basic factors. In particular, it was not important independently of the global assessment of parental behaviour.

3. *Parental Neuroticism and Parental Instability*

At age 8–9, the PSWs identified 73 boys whose mothers appeared to have neurotic tendencies, defined by the presence of such classic symptoms as anxiety, depression and phobias. In addition, they enquired whether or not each mother had ever had medical treatment for psychiatric disturbance. A third, independent assessment was obtained by giving mothers a health questionnaire derived from the Cornell Medical Index (see Note 2). This yielded a score of neuroticism based on the number of symptoms from which the mother claimed to suffer (see Gibson *et al.*, 1967, and West, 1969, pp. 93 and 184–9). Appendix A (factors 53–55) shows how these measures were related to delinquency. Since the three indices of neuroticism (i.e. PSW assessment, history of treatment and questionnaire scores) were all significantly intercorrelated, a combined rating of maternal neuroticism was derived. This proved to be associated with delinquency, but not to any great extent (24·8 per cent of 125 boys, as opposed to 16·8 per cent of 262 : $\chi^2 = 2{\cdot}98$, $p < {\cdot}10$).

Boys with neurotic mothers also tended to experience poor parental behaviour. Various matching analyses were carried out to see if other factors were masking the effect of maternal neuroticism, but, as no statistically significant results appeared, it was concluded that maternal neuroticism was not important as a precursor of delinquency.

Fathers were not given a health questionnaire, but a measure of paternal neuroticism was obtained from PSWs' ratings and from a history of treatment for psychiatric troubles. Paternal neuroticism was not significantly related to delinquency although, like maternal neuroticism, it was significantly commoner in the group rated poorly on parental behaviour (see Appendix A, factors 57–59).

In contrast to neuroticism, parental instability was significantly correlated with delinquency. The label 'unstable' was used for parents who displayed erratic behaviour, psychopathic traits or hysterical personality. It was intended to isolate a behaviour-disordered group. The 49 boys with unstable mothers were particularly delinquent-prone (44·9 per cent becoming delinquents), as were the 47 boys with unstable fathers (34·0 per cent).

As usual, maternal influences appeared to be the more important, but this may have been due to the PSWs having better contact with mothers, and hence making better assessments of them than of fathers. Although they were of predictive value, parental stability ratings were not incorporated into the global measure of parental behaviour, because they were ostensibly descriptions of personality rather than child-rearing behaviour, and because instability was not clearly defined.

4. *Parental Uncooperativeness*

As already mentioned, boys classified as 'not known' often included a higher proportion who were delinquents than those in the worst categories on the home background factors. This was because the families who were least cooperative towards the PSWs had a strong tendency to produce delinquent sons. The PSWs rated each boy's parents as being totally uncooperative (22 cases), reluctant (21 cases) or cooperative (368 cases). The first two groups were particularly delinquent-prone (40·9 per cent and 38·1 per cent, compared with 18·2 per cent). Nearly one-third of the recidivists (12 out of 37) came from the 43 boys (10·5 per cent of the sample) whose parents were not cooperative.

These results confirm impressions from other social surveys. Bebbington (1970) stated that 'it is widely accepted that non-responders show important differences from responders in almost all kinds of psychological and sociological surveys'. He found that evasive subjects tended to have low intelligence, low socio-economic status, poor school records, delinquency convictions and to be anti-social and amoral. In another investigation, Robins (1963) found that refusers tended to be poorly educated, in routine jobs and to have foreign-born parents.

The descriptions of the reactions of non-cooperative parents, by social workers and others who tried to enlist their help, leaves no doubt that many of them were markedly suspicious and hostile. It might have been predicted that uncooperative or reluctant parents would be more frequent among boys from poor or large families, or among boys with criminal parents, but this was not so. Numbers were too small for the usual matching analyses, but at each income level, and regardless of whether or not there was parental criminality, noncooperation was associated with a raised incidence of delinquency. There seems little doubt that noncooperation was in itself important as a precursor of delinquency.

It is difficult to discover an explanation for this finding, for the simple reason that the home backgrounds of the uncooperative group were not open to scrutiny. However, some information came to light subsequently, from other agencies, or as a result of interviews with the boys at ages 16 and 18, or from further attempts to see the parents when the boys were aged 14–15. Of course, this later information, being retrospective and acquired somewhat haphazardly, was relatively unreliable, but it did throw some light on the matter.

The 22 boys whose parents originally refused to be interviewed included 9 who became juvenile delinquents and one who was first convicted at age 18. At least 7 of these 10 boys would have been rated adversely as regards parental behaviour if the later information had been available when the assessments were made.

Case 141
Home described as 'stinking and verminous' by housing authority. Mother dull, suspicious, uncouth, and of dirty, neglected appearance. Boy's elder sister had an illegitimate baby when she was 15. When our boy was an infant, the health visitor noted: 'Poor maternal care, low standards, unsatisfactory home.' Seen by a social worker from the Study when the boy was aged 12, the mother was superficially cordial, and painted an agreeable picture of a problem-free family. However, since she denied several facts about her children's misconduct which were already known to the interviewer, her sincerity was open to doubt.

Case 341
Mother dirty, borderline defective, always in debt and had been to court for neglect. Scared of children being removed, but vacillating between over-protection and rejection. At age 13, this boy and his sister having run away from home, the father complained to the police that they were always running away and truanting and were beyond the control of himself and his wife. Social and psychiatric reports prepared at that time suggested that there was considerable disagreement between the parents over their handling of this boy, and that the family were too uncooperative for the boy to benefit from help outside an institution (cf. pp. 12–14).

Case 561
Accommodation squalid and depressing. The NSPCC had contact with mother over harsh treatment of her illegitimate child. Father was violent and the neighbours said to be 'terrified'. Mother was described by a social worker as a muddler who cannot cope. The headmaster felt she had a 'chip-on-the-shoulder'. It was thought that the parents treated our boy better than they had treated his older siblings, but information was largely lacking. The boy was living away with his brother when interviewed at 16.

Case 773
When our boy was 7, parents were in debt for rent, and an action for possession was taken. Father chronically unemployed and in debt, though family often away at weekends. When our boy was 13, because of his non-attendance at school, father was fined £3. Headmaster thought mother 'one of the worst managers in the school'. Elder brother was convicted of indecent assault on a small girl, and admitted many similar offences.

Case 852
School attendance officer described the family as 'dodgers'. Our boy's elder sister truanted a lot with mother's approval. Headmaster felt the boy could do much better if the parents would take an interest in him and be less aggressive in their attitude to the school. At age 13, our boy told the probation officer he was unhappy, because mother and father went out drinking and left him alone in the house. He felt he was the black sheep, and that mother was on at him all the time and father not interested. Interviewed at 18, this boy was still bitter about his parents, because of the way they had treated him. He said that until she got married, when he was 10, his elder sister was the person who was left to bring him up, and after that he just had to look after himself. He said he was continuing to live with his parents, but only to get his own back on them.

Case 941
This boys' mother refused to be interviewed until eight years after the Study began, but some information was gleaned from his father and paternal grandfather. It appeared that there was considerable marital disharmony. The mother was bitter about lack of money and having to live with her in-laws. She was working at several part-time jobs, and often did not come home until after 10 p.m. Father was also away a lot. The boy's headmaster reported that there was no support from the parents. When the boy was 16, the parents finally separated.

Case 991
Mother persistently and aggressively refused all contact, but some information was available via a child guidance unit which was visited by the parents when our boy was aged 9. At that time it was thought there were serious marital difficulties, with quarrels over the mother's dislike of sexual relations and other matters, and differences of view over the handling of the children. Mother was unsmiling and distant and no constructive contact was made. When our boy was 16, mother was prevailed upon to talk with our social worker, but only on the doorstep. She was belittling and critical about her children, and, although ostensibly permissive towards the boy, she seemed to have mixed feelings about the easy life of young people today compared with her own early difficulties and deprivations. Soon after this, our boy was interviewed. He came secretly, saying his parents would be furious if they knew. The interviewer, who had previously tried to persuade the parents to let the boy come if he wanted, found them both to be 'aggressive, bombastic and authoritarian'. At age 18, the boy was seen again and agreed readily to come for interview, but his mother called him inside and subsequently telephoned to say he was not interested to come and must under no circumstance be contacted again. He was convicted for the first time at age 18.

In contrast, at least some of the boys from uncooperative

families were from ordinary, united homes with no evidence of serious parental conflicts or mismanagement:

Case 420
When our boy was 13, the parents became cooperative. At a subsequent interview, social workers found no evidence of unloving parental attitudes, marital disorder or other indications of significant parental mishandling. At age 16 the boy was still living happily at home, but at 18 he said his parents were getting old, they did not have the same attitude as his generation, and he would like to leave home if he got the chance.

Case 202
Mother persistently refused to have anything to do with people asking personal questions, but when our boy was 15 she granted the social worker a doorstep interview. She appeared to be a warm, affectionate mother with good relations with all her children. The boy was interviewed at 18, and said he preferred to live at home with his widowed father, with whom he got on all right.

Case 210
At first, the family were in poor, overcrowded accommodation and the mother had a grudge against the housing authorities. When our boy was 15, she agreed to see a social worker briefly. She was then living in a well maintained maisonette, and reported that she was healthier and happier. Although welcoming and communicative, she had no special family problems to report. She was concerned, however, about her son, because he appeared secretive and over-sensitive, suffered from ulcerative colitis, and was not doing well at school. Both parents were anxiously concerned with the boy's social problems and career prospects. At age 18 the boy was interviewed, and reported that he was happy at home with both parents. 'They've been good to me. We get on all right. . . .'

Case 343
The parents were originally quite hostile, threatening to call the police if pestered again, but father gave the social worker a long interview when our boy, an only child, was aged 15. Father seemed a warm, intelligent man. The interviewer thought it was 'obviously a child-centred home' and that both parents were proud of and pleased with their son. At 18, the boy said he was happy living at home with both parents. 'It's always been quite good. They don't put any restrictions on me. . . . Mother never moans at me or anything. . . . Get on great with father . . . I can talk to him.'

Case 583
Mother persistently declined to be seen. A neighbour reported that mother was a worrier, and over-protective to her son, discouraging him from fighting back. The headmaster reported that the boy was doing well and that his parents were extremely interested in his progress. At age 15, father was seen briefly on the doorstep. The social worker got

the impression of an easy, relaxed relationship between father and son. Interviewed at 18, the boy was still living at home and said he felt he was best off staying there, and that he got on 'terrific' with both parents.

Case 750
At age 10, the headmaster reported that he knew of no problems with this 'independent, self-respecting family'. When father was seen a year later, he was aggressively unwilling to commit himself to the Study. When the boy was 15, his mother was seen. The social worker was not allowed beyond the doorstep, but noted: 'The family standards are considerably higher than the vast majority of their neighbours.' At 18, the boy reported he was quite happy at home and got on well with his parents.

Case 961
The headmaster reported: 'A decent family, rather superior, surprising that they are not cooperative.' When our boy was 11, mother granted an interview for the first time. She was defensive and belligerent, but considered to be reliable, conscientious, excessively concerned about her boy's trouble with his eyes, and apparently over-protective. At 18 our boy was still living at home with both parents, and said he got on with both of them pretty well.

One can see from this sketchy survey that the noncooperative families fall into two roughly equal groups. One group consisted of families who produced delinquent sons, and most of these had rather obvious and serious social or psychological difficulties of the kind typical of the families of recidivist delinquents. They may well have been uncooperative because they did not wish their troubles to be exposed. The other group consisted of families of non-delinquent sons, most of whom were free from outward signs of gross disturbance. They tended to be over-protective, self-contained, independent parents who resented inquiries, although objectively there was no special reason for them to be ashamed of being studied.

5. '*Catholic*' *Families and Ethnic Minorities*

The 73 boys with one or both parents professing affiliation to the Roman Catholic Church included a significantly high proportion (28·8 per cent) of delinquents. There was also a significant tendency for criminal parents to be Catholic. Of the boys with a criminal parent, 36·9 per cent had a Catholic parent, in comparison with only 15·8 per cent of those with non-criminal parents. Surprisingly, however, there was no significant association between coming from a large sized family, or a poor family, and having a Catholic parent.

When delinquents and non-delinquents were matched for parental criminality, they did not differ significantly in the prevalence of Catholic families. It seemed reasonable to conclude that having a Catholic parent was a precursor of delinquency only because of its link with parental criminality. In turn, criminality and Catholicism were related by virtue of so many Catholic families being Irish immigrants. It should also be pointed out that the sample excluded boys whose parents sent them to Catholic schools, and that Catholic (or Protestant) affiliation was often only a nominal attachment and did not necessarily mean that the parents attended church. The link with criminality becomes more understandable when it is realised that the label 'Catholic' had more to do with ethnic origin than religious practice.

Racial minorities were too thinly represented in the Study sample to enable valid comparisons to be made. As already pointed out (p. 1), 90·3 per cent of the boys were both white in racial appearance and reared by parents who were themselves brought up in the United Kingdom or Eire. The remaining 40 boys included 12 of negroid stock, most of whom had at least one parent of West Indian origin, and 28 others of varied foreign extraction (10 Cypriot, 5 Polish, and 13 from nine different countries). The 12 negroid boys included a high proportion who became delinquents (7, of whom 4 were recidivists), whereas the 28 of varied foreign descent included rather few delinquents (5, none a recidivist).

NOTES

[1] *Definition of Illegitimacy*

A boy was counted as illegitimate if it was known from a reliable source (e.g. the mother herself, obstetric hospital record or birth certificate) that his natural parents were not married to each other at the time of his birth. The exact definition of illegitimacy, and the accuracy of the data from which figures are derived, are little discussed in sociology texts. In this Study, it was found that a few cases were difficult to categorize because of conflicting information, and an almost arbitrary decision had to be made. The following examples, which were not counted among the illegitimates, are cases in point:

Case 712

Mrs X. was admitted to hospital for a serious illness shortly after the birth of her son. The hospital notes state categorically that the boy was the child of Mr Y. On the birth certificate, the boy's father was given as Mr X. of the same address as Mrs X. However, the hospital notes, and Mrs X's own admissions to social workers, revealed that her husband Mr X. had in fact deserted the home during her pregnancy and that she had no contact with him subsequently. On recovering from her illness, Mrs X. went to live with Mr Y. For a time, Mrs X. told the PSWs that Mr Y. was her brother. Ultimately, however, she married him and the boy accepted him as 'father'. Whether Mr X. or Mr Y. was really the father was impossible to ascertain.

Case 411
This was a delinquent boy whose mother was known to have had a number of extra-marital affairs, and had at least one child by a man racially different from her husband. For this reason, and also because the boy was of a different complexion and appearance, the husband repeatedly expressed the belief that this was not his own son.

[2] *The Cornell Medical Index (CMI)*
This is a questionnaire divided into two parts. The statements in one part enquire about purely physical ailments, while those in the other enquire about psychiatric symptoms. Several British investigators have shown that this inventory is a valid index of neurosis. In London, Culpan *et al.* (1960) showed that, on both parts of the CMI, neurotic out-patients scored significantly higher (i.e. claimed to possess more ailments) than a control group of store workers. In South Wales, Rawnsley (1966) showed that a group of patients diagnosed as psychiatrically disordered scored more highly on both parts than a group diagnosed as healthy by a psychiatrist. In a working class London borough, Ryle (1967) found that high CMI scores were associated with a diagnosis of neurosis by a general practitioner. In view of the good discrimination shown by both physical and psychiatric parts of the CMI, Gibson *et al.* (1967) derived the mother's health questionnaire used in this Study exclusively from questions about physical ailments. It was felt that these were as effective as questions about psychological symptoms, and less likely to give offence.

V

Intelligence and Attainment

1. *IQ and Delinquency*

The connection between intelligence and criminality has long been a favourite topic of research (Ferracuti, 1966). Most surveys suggest that delinquents tend to perform relatively poorly on IQ tests. The principal non-verbal intelligence measure used in the Study was Raven's Progressive Matrices, a test which can be administered without written instructions. The test problems are presented on successive pages of a printed booklet, in order of increasing difficulty. An incomplete sequence of patterns appears on the top part of each page, and underneath are printed 6 to 8 different patterns, only one of which correctly fits into and completes the sequence illustrated above. The subject has to select the one he thinks is correct.

The boys were grouped into quarters according to their IQ on Raven's Matrices (see Note 1). The lowest quarter of boys had IQs of 90 or less, while the highest had IQs of 110 or more (see Table V (1)). The percentages of future delinquents in the four quarters of the sample, from the highest to the lowest IQ groups, was 13·7 per cent, 15·7 per cent, 21·4 per cent and 31·1 per cent respectively. Delinquents were significantly over-represented among the least intelligent, and under-represented among the most. The biserial correlation between these IQ scores and the delinquent/non-delinquent dichotomy was $-0{\cdot}27$ ($p < {\cdot}001$).

The average IQs of the delinquent and non-delinquent groups were 95·1 and 100·9 respectively, a difference of less than 6 points. In previous investigations, a difference of up to 8 points has sometimes been regarded as unimportant. Fortunately, we compared the delinquent and non-delinquent groups on the prevalence of low IQ in just the same way as we compared them on other factors such as poverty, large families or criminal parents. It was thereby demonstrated that low IQ was a significant precursor of delinquency to much the same extent as other major factors. This shows the importance of comparing all factors in the same way. Although the differences were not large, intelligence proved to be an important and significantly predictive factor, because of the consistency with which recidivists tended to have below average IQs.

One other non-verbal test was given to the boys, namely the Porteus Maze (see pp. 109–10). At age 8, this was administered in standard form, and the test quotients correlated very significantly with the delinquent/non-delinquent dichotomy ($r_{bis} = 0{\cdot}26$, $p < {\cdot}001$).

TABLE V (1)

Delinquency and Intelligence (Averaging the Progressive Matrices IQ at Ages 8 and 10)

Progressive matrices IQ	*Delinquency*								*Total boys*	
	No police record		*Police contact boys*		*One-time delinquents*		*Recidivists*			
	(%)	(*N*)	(%)	(*N*)	(%)	(*N*)	(%)	(*N*)		
High (110+)	76·5	(78)	9·8	(10)	11·8	(12)	2·0	(2)	100%	(102)
High average (99–109)	68·5	(74)	15·7	(17)	11·1	(12)	4·6	(5)	100%	(108)
Low average (91–98)	68·4	(67)	10·2	(10)	12·2	(12)	9·2	(9)	100%	(98)
Low (90−)	50·5	(52)	18·4	(19)	10·7	(11)	20·4	(21)	100%	(103)
Total boys	65·9	(271)	13·6	(56)	11·4	(47)	9·0	(37)	100%	(411)

Significance Test: Comparing 103 boys with lowest IQs with the remainder, and comparing 84 delinquents with the remainder, $\chi^2 = 8{\cdot}70$, $p < {\cdot}005$.

This can be taken as confirmatory evidence that, in the present sample, non-verbal intelligence was significantly predictive of delinquency.

Low IQ was more common among boys from large families, boys with criminal parents, boys exposed to poor parental behaviour, and especially among boys from poor families (see Appendix C). However, on matching for each of these factors in turn (see Appendix B), low IQ remained an important feature distinguishing delinquents from non-delinquents (but see Note 2).

The association between low IQ and delinquency surprised the investigators, since recent criminological writings tend to underplay the factor of intelligence. It was thought that the results might be due to some flaw in the test. Gibson and West (1970) suggested that the Matrices test may be particularly sensitive to poor motivation, since it presents abstract problems of increasing difficulty, and allows the subject the opportunity to save himself the bother of concentrating and to finish more quickly by answering at random. If potential delinquents tended to be poorly motivated in the test situation, this might explain their particularly poor performance on the Matrices.

The results were re-examined with this in mind, to see if delinquents gave up more readily than non-delinquents when they reached the more difficult sections of the test. On the occasions when the test was timed, the data were also studied to see if delinquents had filled in the answers more hastily than non-delinquents. In addition, the results of the tests at three different ages were compared, to see if the delinquents gave less consistent scores, as might be expected if their motivation was more erratic. None of these analyses supported the theory that the low IQs of delinquents were due to their poor motivation (see Note 3).

The contrast between delinquents and non-delinquents in regard to intelligence was almost entirely due to the recidivists, who were dramatically frequent among boys in the lowest quarter of IQs and correspondingly infrequent among those in the highest quarter (20·4 per cent compared with 2·0 per cent). The full figures are displayed in Table V (1). The average IQs of non-delinquents and one-timers were not significantly different (100·9 and 99·7 respectively), whereas that of the juvenile recidivists was 89·1. The recidivists thus had an average IQ as low as that reported from groups of institutionalized delinquents (q.v.). These findings were in keeping with the results previously reported (Farrington and West, 1971) showing that low IQ was particularly characteristic of those delinquents who were first convicted at an early age, since these were the boys who tended to become recidivists. Low IQ was not so noticeable a feature of the boys first convicted at age 14 or later.

A special analysis was done to disentangle the relationship between intelligence and age on first conviction from that between intelligence and recidivism. Table V (2) was prepared taking into account one-time juvenile delinquents who became recidivists as young adults. It can be seen that early delinquents had lower IQs, but, whatever the age on first conviction, recidivists had a lower average IQ than one-time delinquents. It can be concluded that the two features, recidivism and being convicted at an early age, seem to be independently associated with low IQ.

There have been some previous investigations linking low intelligence with convictions at an early age. Eilenberg (1961) found that among remand home inmates the younger boys were more likely to have a low IQ than the older ones. Cowie *et al.* (1968) showed that a low IQ among female delinquents was particularly common among those first convicted at an early age. However, Anderson (1958), who compared remand home boys convicted for a first offence with those

TABLE V (2)

Average Matrices IQ of One-Time Delinquents and Recidivists (Subdivided by Age on First Conviction, and Recidivism as Adult or Juvenile)

Age on first conviction	*All delinquents*		*One-time delinquents*		*Recidivists (Adult and juvenile)*	
	No.	*Average*	*No.*	*Average*	*No.*	*Average*
10–13	31	90·3	7	93·9	24	89·2
14–16	53	97·9	26	102·1	27	93·8
All juvenile delinquents	84	95·1	33	100·4	51	91·6
17 and over*	26	97·6				

* Insufficient time has elapsed to classify these boys realistically into recidivists and one-time delinquents.

convicted for a fourth or later offence, reported no significant difference between the two groups on intelligence, as measured by the Stanford–Binet test or Raven's Matrices.

2. *Verbal Facility and Educational Attainment*

The various measures of verbal performance and educational attainment which were taken at ages 8 and 10 all yielded significant relationships with delinquency (see Appendix A, factors 71–9). The measures are listed in Note 4, while their intercorrelations with each other, with IQ, and with delinquency are displayed in Table V (3). All of the measures of verbal ability, educational attainment and non-verbal IQ were significantly intercorrelated, the lowest biseral correlation being 0·20. Moreover, with the single exception of the

Porteus TQ at age 10, all were significantly correlated with delinquency. This confirms the importance of intellectual level as an index of the likelihood of future delinquency.

The verbal and attainment measures did not, in general, correlate with delinquency any more closely than did the Matrices IQ. This

TABLE V (3)

Intercorrelations among Intelligence and Attainment Measures

	Low matrices IQ at 8	Poor mechanical reading at 8	Poor sentence reading at 8	Poor word comprehension at 8	Low Porteus TQ at 8	Low matrices IQ at 10	Poor Mill Hill vocabulary at 10	Low Porteus TQ at 10	Peer rating not clever at 10	Poor in arithmetic at 10	Poor in English at 10	Poor in verbal reasoning at 10	Poor secondary allocation at 11	Delinquency
Low matrices IQ at 8		49	41	49	40	66	46	33	29	48	49	56	54	−28
Poor mechanical reading at 8			81	67	26	46	63	24	35	63	73	74	73	−27
Poor sentence reading at 8				60	25	42	58	25	32	65	68	69	66	−24
Poor word comprehension at 8					32	46	69	21	28	54	63	64	64	−30
Low Porteus TQ at 8						41	31	38	20	29	28	33	32	−26
Low matrices IQ at 10							47	35	35	53	52	57	56	−21
Poor Mill Hill vocabulary at 10								27	29	55	64	64	62	−27
Low Porteus TQ at 10									32	29	24	29	29	−10
Peer rating not clever at 10										45	44	43	42	−23
Poor in arithmetic at 10											81	85	73	−27
Poor in English at 10												89	76	−26
Poor in verbal reasoning at 10													80	−28
Poor secondary allocation at 11														−27

N.B. The figures represent product-moment correlations ×100, except in the case of the figures under delinquency, which represent biserial correlations ×100.

result was somewhat unexpected, since it is often said that educational retardation and poor verbal ability are more characteristic of delinquents than low IQ on non-verbal tests. The discrepancy between an individual's verbal and non-verbal intelligence is supposed to be particularly related to delinquency (q.v.). In fact, when discrepancy scores were calculated, no significant association with delinquency was found (see Note 5).

Since the poor educational achievement of delinquents is a much discussed topic, the figures from the present Study are given in detail in Table V (4). Those rated low on educational achievement included a high proportion who were juvenile recidivists (20·7 per cent of 121, as opposed to only 4·1 per cent of the remaining 290 boys). Poor achievement remains a characteristic of delinquents in their later years. The 162 boys who left school at an early age (under 15½), who may be presumed to be the least effective, least welcome or least committed scholars, included a significantly high percentage (32·7%) who were juvenile delinquents. In contrast, of the 94 boys who stayed on at school until 16½ or later, only 6·4 per cent were delinquents.

TABLE V (4)

Delinquency and Educational Attainment (Assessed by Secondary School Allocation at Age 11)

	Delinquency									
*Educational attainment**	*No police record*		*Police contact boys*		*One-time delinquents*		*Recidivists*		*Total boys*	
	(%)	(*N*)	(%)	(*N*)	(%)	(*N*)	(%)	(*N*)		
High	85·7	(60)	5·7	(4)	5·7	(4)	2·9	(2)	100%	(70)
High average	70·2	(73)	14·4	(15)	11·5	(12)	3·8	(4)	100%	(104)
Low average	65·5	(76)	12·1	(14)	17·2	(20)	5·2	(6)	100%	(116)
Low	51·2	(62)	19·0	(23)	9·1	(11)	20·7	(25)	100%	(121)
Total boys	65·9	(271)	13·6	(56)	11·4	(47)	9·0	(37)	100%	(411)

* The categories are explained in Note 4.
Significance Test: Comparing 121 low attainment boys with the remainder, and comparing 84 delinquents with the remainder, $\chi^2 = 8{\cdot}36$, $p < {\cdot}005$.

3. *Present Findings and Previous Studies*

As Vernon (1969) points out, bitter controversies have arisen because some people use the term intelligence to refer to an innate, inherited capacity for mental growth, whereas others mean the individual's current capacity to grasp the essentials of a situation and to arrive at a solution by reasoning. Others, again, mean by intelligence the IQ scores an individual produces on specified tests. It is only in this last sense that the word 'intelligence' has been used in this book.

The effectiveness of the first IQ tests was measured by their ability to predict school performance. More recent tests have often been validated against earlier tests, so presumably they reflect the same thing. Doing well in school, however, is not necessarily equivalent either to innate intellectual capacity or to reasoning ability.

In recent years, IQ tests have been much criticized (e.g. Richardson *et al.*, 1972; Schmideberg, 1970). It is argued that it is misleading to reduce all the varied aspects of intellectual functioning to only one or two numbers. Nevertheless, since virtually all these aspects are significantly intercorrelated, it is not unreasonable to extract a general factor. A more relevant and more serious objection is that the tests were developed by and for the middle classes, and that some of them are biased against those from underprivileged backgrounds. To combat this, test constructors have tried to minimize the dependence of tests on particular educational and social experiences. IQ tests which do not involve words are not so likely to put the less articulate lower classes at a disadvantage. It is also suggested that the tests encourage people to give stereotyped, unoriginal, over-simplified answers quickly. Consequently, attempts have been made recently to develop more open-ended tests which involve creativity.

The IQs of delinquents have been measured in a great many surveys. At least one IQ test is included, as an aid to classification, in the routine examination of delinquents admitted to British penal institutions. Unfortunately, very few of the published reports on IQ and delinquency compare the scores of delinquents with those of a control group of non-delinquents. Instead, the test scores of the delinquents are compared with the test norms. This comparison is only valid if the sample on which the norms are based is drawn from the same population as the delinquents. Too often, English delinquents are evaluated according to test norms derived from American schoolchildren, who are racially and culturally quite different. Even when English delinquents are evaluated according to English norms, the comparison is not always valid. It has been shown (e.g. Richardson *et al.*, 1972) that past norms have often been based on samples with a higher socio-economic status than the general population. Furthermore, test norms in current use may derive from schoolchildren of 20 years ago, and may not be applicable to the present generation.

For all these reasons, it is advisable to contrast the intelligence of delinquents with that of a properly comparable control group, as in the present Study. Among the few other investigations in which this has been done, the recent survey by Wolfgang *et al.* (1972) of 10,000 boys born in Philadelphia in 1945 should be mentioned. They discovered that delinquents had a lower verbal intelligence than non-delinquents of the same race and socio-economic status. However, the differences were only of the order of three to four points, even less than we found. The McCords (1959) found no connection between low IQ and delinquency. This is the most important respect in which our results differ from theirs. It may be because they were dealing with a population of more or less deprived children, in which IQ was below average for both delinquents and non-delinquents, that the intelligence factor was masked.

According to published surveys, the average IQ scores of delinquents, both in Britain and in the United States, have gradually improved during this century (Caplan, 1965; Woodward, 1963). One of the most thorough demonstrations of this was carried out in the United States by Caplan and Siebert (1964). They studied the results of IQ tests routinely applied to all juvenile court cases in Cleveland, Ohio over a 34-year period, and found that the average IQ increased from 80 in the 1930s to 92 in the 1960s. They attributed the increase to the replacement of the original 1916 Stanford–Binet test by other tests less dependent on verbal facility. In England, Eilenberg (1961) compared admissions to Stamford House (London) remand home in 1930 and 1955, and found that the proportion of boys with above-average intelligence increased from 26 per cent to 39 per cent over this 25-year period.

Stamford House inmates are particularly relevant here because they are London boys. Anderson (1958) found that Stamford House boys were below average both in the Progressive Matrices and (slightly) in the revised Stanford–Binet. Asuni (1963) and Critchley (1968) found that they were below average in the Wechsler tests, while Gath *et al.* (1970), using the same tests, discovered only half as many highly intelligent delinquents as expected on population norms.

Turning to other English institutions for delinquents, Gittins (1952) reported that 1,300 boys admitted to Aycliffe approved school in Durham in 1948–51 had a mean IQ in the revised Stanford–Binet of 90. In the same school some 15 years later, Hoghughi and Forrest (1967) also obtained a figure of 90 for 650 boys given the Wechsler Intelligence Scale for Children (WISC), and Passingham (1968) reported an average of 92 for 50 randomly selected boys in the same test. In an unspecified English classifying school, Walton (1955) found that the boys were considerably below average in both the revised Stanford–Binet and the Progressive Matrices test, but more especially in the Matrices. Finally, Frost and Frost (1962) obtained a slightly below average IQ in the WISC with 42 approved school boys diagnosed as sociopathic or psychopathic, and Gibbens (1963) found that Borstal boys were slightly below average in the Progressive Matrices and considerably below average in a verbal IQ test.

These results are reasonably consistent in showing institutionalized delinquents to be below average in intelligence, but they differ somewhat in the extent to which the IQ falls short of the average. In most cases, the average IQs of institutionalized delinquents were no lower than the average IQ of our own recidivists. Researches with adult criminals have produced less consistent results. For example, while Marcus (1955) found British prisoners to be slightly below average on the Progressive Matrices, Blackler (1968) found them to be very much below average on the same test, and Warder *et al.* (1970) found them to be slightly above average on the same test!

There has been a good deal of interest in the hypothesis that delinquents have an average non-verbal IQ, but a low verbal IQ. Many relevant studies (mostly American) have been reviewed by Prentice and Kelly (1963), and the results generally confirm the hypothesis. Against this, it must be pointed out that two more recent American investigations by Naar (1965) and Henning and Levy (1967) are not wholly in agreement with the idea.

Most English researches using the Wechsler tests, which have sub-tests providing separate verbal and non-verbal IQs, have found that delinquents have higher non-verbal than verbal IQs. For example, Hoghughi and Forrest (1967) obtained a mean verbal IQ of 87, in comparison with a non-verbal IQ of 96. Similarly, Frost and Frost (1962) obtained a verbal IQ of 93 and a non-verbal IQ of 99. These investigations also reported the characteristic Wechsler sub-test pattern of delinquents which has been noted by many American investigators (e.g. Diller, 1955; Richardson and Surko, 1956; Foster, 1959). They found that delinquents do best in picture arrangement, picture completion and object assembly, and worst in information (general knowledge), vocabulary and comprehension. However, tests other than those of Wechsler do not always show the verbal/non-verbal discrepancy. For example, as mentioned above, both Walton (1955) and Anderson (1958) discovered that delinquents were more retarded in the non-verbal Progressive Matrices than in the predominantly verbal Stanford–Binet. This is in agreement with our results, which show that the verbal IQs of delinquents were no worse than their non-verbal IQs.

It has been suggested that delinquents are retarded verbally on the Wechsler tests because they are poor readers. Graham and Kamano (1958) have shown that unsuccessful readers obtain a pattern of scores very similar to that of delinquents. In Britain, as in the United States, there is little doubt that delinquents are poor readers. For example, Critchley (1968) found that more than half of his delinquents were retarded in reading by three years or more, and Passingham (1968) found that the average reading age of 15-year-old delinquents was 12.

Why should delinquents be just as retarded on a non-verbal test like the Progressive Matrices? According to Raven's manual (1960), 'A person's total score provides an index of his intellectual capacity, whatever his nationality or education.' On the other hand, Trasler (1970) argues that '. . . although it does not employ words, the Raven test tends to sample logical reasoning and problem-solving strategies'. These abstract reasoning skills are of the kind generally learned at school through the medium of language, and are rather different from the manual dexterity skills measured by the Wechsler performance scales. In fact, Barratt (1956) showed that Matrices scores were just as closely correlated with verbal IQ on the WISC as with non-verbal IQ, and that they were particularly closely correlated with the information (general knowledge) and vocabulary sub-tests.

Why is it that delinquents have a lower verbal or Matrices IQ than non-delinquents? Years ago, it was thought that people with a low IQ were morally retarded and unable to distinguish right from wrong, but later evidence showed that delinquents knew just as well as non-delinquents what was socially acceptable (Woodward, 1963). Another possibility is that persons with a low IQ are more likely to be caught, and, once caught, are more likely to be prosecuted and found guilty. In the course of this Study, an alternative method of defining delinquents, based upon their own admissions, was developed, and is described later in Chapter IX. For the moment, it suffices to point out that low IQ was significantly associated with self-reported delinquency (see Table IX (2), p. 158). Unless self-reported delinquency has a similar bias, due perhaps to duller boys confessing more readily, it seems unlikely that the lower intelligence of official delinquents can be explained on the basis of the duller boys being more easily caught.

Rhodes and Reiss (1969) see juvenile delinquency in large part as a reaction to the social frustrations which accompany school failure. Opinions differ about the extent to which school failure is predetermined by innate ineptitude or by acquired aversion to the scholastic approach. However that may be, IQ measures are, almost by definition, highly predictive of school performance. Hence, one would expect low IQ to be an important precursor of juvenile delinquency. The present Study re-confirms this expectation.

NOTES

[1] *Administration of Raven's Matrices Test*

The test was given to the boys first at age 8, again at age 10, and for a third time at age 14. On the last occasion it was administered individually, and on the first two occasions it was generally given as a group test, although some boys completed it individually. At ages 10 and 14 the time taken to complete the test was recorded, and at age 10 those boys who worked in groups had to note their own times.

At all three ages, a low Matrices IQ score was very significantly associated with delinquency. At age 8, for instance, among the boys in the lowest quarter of scores the proportion who became delinquents was nearly double that in the remainder of the sample (31·4 per cent of 86, as opposed to 17·5 per cent of 325: $\chi^2 = 7{\cdot}20$, $< {\cdot}01$). In order to assess the predictive value of the Matrices IQ, it was decided to average the scores obtained at ages 8 and 10, to get as reliable a measure as possible. The test/re-test correlation between ages 8 and 10 was $r = 0{\cdot}66$. It might have been greater if the test had been administered in exactly the same way to all boys on both occasions. The averaged IQ scores from the tests at 8 and 10 are referred to in the text as the Matrices IQs.

[2] *Intelligence and Income*

After matching for intelligence, delinquents still differed significantly from non-delinquents on the important background factors of large families, criminal parents and poor parental behaviour. These three factors could be said to be, at least to some extent, precursors of delinquency independently of intelligence. However, after matching for intelligence, delinquents and non-delinquents did not differ significantly in family income. This anomalous result might be interpreted to mean that income was important in relation to delinquency only as a consequence of the low intelligence of boys from poor families. This explanation seems implausible, for the poorer boys are at a disadvantage in many ways besides low intelligence. It seems more likely that the result arose from an artefact of measurement, due to the fact that intelligence was assessed more accurately than income. The family income measure was a relatively crude tripartite categorization, limited by the nature of the information available, whereas intelligence was measured with a well-tried test on a standard scale of IQ units.

[3] *Matrices IQ and Motivation*

One way to test the hypothesis that the low IQ of delinquents reflects poor motivation is to use as the measure of intelligence the highest IQ that each boy attained on any of the three occasions of testing (at ages 8, 10 and 14). On the (plausible) presumption that motivation tends to vary while intelligence tends to remain constant, the highest score should reflect intelligence more accurately. If the correlations with delinquency were due to poor motivation on particular occasions of testing, it might be expected that the highest IQ measure would be less closely associated with delinquency than the IQ scores from any single test. In fact, the correlation between the highest IQ measure and delinquency was −0·26, which was little different from the correlations at the three ages (−0·28 at 8, −0·21 at 10, −0·25 at 14), and was still highly significant ($p < ·001$). Hence, these results lend no support to the motivational hypothesis.

Another possible test of the hypothesis is to investigate the pattern of scores in the Matrices. If indeed the delinquents have low scores because they 'give up' at some stage, it might be predicted that delinquents and non-delinquents should differ in their success more in the later stages than in the earlier stages. The Matrices consists of five series, each of 12 items, labelled A–E in order of increasing difficulty. The first few items of series A are used largely for practice, and to ensure that all subjects have grasped the instructions. In view of this, it was thought that the best method of investigating changes in performance was to compare series B and C with series D and E. According to the hypothesis, delinquents and non-delinquents should differ more in series D and E than in series B and C. Table V(5) shows that, in fact, the hypothesis was not supported at any of the three ages. For example, at age 8, non-delinquents answered 47·2 per cent of items correctly in series B and C, and delinquents 38·6 per cent, a difference of 8·6 per cent. In series D and E, non-delinquents answered 23·7 per cent correctly, and delinquents 17·7 per cent, a difference of only 6·0 per cent.

TABLE V (5)

Matrices Peformance of Delinquents and Non-Delinquents

Age	*Series*	*Non-delinquents correct* (%)	*Delinquents correct* (%)	*Difference* (%)
8	B + C	47·2	38·6	8·6
	D + E	23·7	17·7	6·0
10	B + C	61·3	54·0	7·3
	D + E	36·2	29·0	7·2
14	B + C	71·0	64·1	6·9
	D + E	45·9	39·0	6·9

The figures represent the percentage of answers which were correct, averaged over all questions and all boys in the category (i.e. delinquents or non-delinquents).

The motivational question might also be studied using the time taken by a boy in the test. This was recorded at ages 10 and 14, but not at age 8. At age 14, all the boys were tested individually and their times were noted down by the testers, but at age 10 the majority of the sample (80 per cent) took the test in groups and recorded the time themselves. Since the individually tested boys tended to take longer than those who were tested in groups, each boy's time was converted into a percentile rank within the individually-tested or group-tested segments of the sample.

It might perhaps be assumed that a boy's score on the Matrices depends upon two factors, his potential intelligence and the length of time he spends trying to puzzle out the answers. It might also be assumed that time spent on the task is an index of motivation, and that highly motivated boys will spend more time and achieve higher scores than poorly motivated boys of equal intelligence. A correction for this effect can be made by giving each boy the score he might have obtained if he had taken an average amount of time over the test. On the hypothesis that the association between delinquency and Matrices scores is due to the motivational factor, the two adjusted scores should no longer correlate significantly with delinquency.

In order to carry out this correction to the results at age 10, the boys' scores were converted into percentiles in the same way as their times. The resulting percentile scores were significantly associated with the percentile times ($r = \cdot 37$), and there was every indication that the mean score increased linearly with the time taken on the test. This correlation was somewhat higher than the one obtained by Schnell and Dwarshuis (1967) in an investigation with 31 adult residents of a rehabilitation centre in the USA. The equation relating score and time was as follows:

$$(S - \bar{S}) = 0{\cdot}37\,(T - \bar{T}),$$

where S = Score, $\bar{S}$ = Mean Score (about 50) and T = Time, $\bar{T}$ = Mean Time (about 50). This equation indicates that boys tended to achieve above average scores by taking above average times. For instance, a boy whose time corresponded to the 20th percentile would be expected to achieve a score corresponding approximately to the 39th percentile. (The highest scores and times are placed in the first percentile.) If such a boy had taken an average time (i.e. at the 50th percentile), his score might have been expected to be 11 percentile points farther from the 1st percentile. Hence, this boy's score could be converted to the score he would have been expected to obtain if he had taken an average time by adding 11 percentile points to it.

The scores of all the boys were modified according to the above equation. The adjusted scores proved to be still very significantly correlated with delinquency ($r_{bis} = -\cdot 22$, $p < \cdot 005$), and the same result (i.e. $r_{bis} = -\cdot 25$) was obtained from the Matrices scores at age 14 after a similar linear regression correction. Consequently, even when an attempt was made to allow for the effects of differing motivation, Matrices scores were still significantly linked to delinquency.

The Matrices test at age 8 was not amenable to exactly this analysis, since it was not timed. However, an index of motivation during the psychological tests at age 8 was tentatively derived from the Spiral Maze (pp. 110, 124). It might be thought that the boys who were poorly motivated in the test situation would have been quick and careless in tracing through this simple maze. An index of motivation was therefore obtained from the maze by subtracting each boy's percentile placing on time from his percentile placing on errors. The highest motivation scores corresponded to the lowest errors and highest times. The results with this index of motivation were similar to those derived using the time taken in the Matrices test. The adjusted Matrices scores was still very significantly related to delinquency ($r_{bis} = -\cdot 26$, $p < \cdot 001$).

These analyses are rather speculative, but as far as they go they lend no support to the hypothesis that delinquents and non-delinquents do not differ in intelligence, but only in motivation.

[4] *Details of Verbal and Attainment Measures*

The verbal measures were a Mechanical Reading test, a Word Comprehension Test and a Sentence Reading test given at age 8, and the Mill Hill Vocabulary test given at age 10 (see West, 1969, pp. 22 ff.). Educational attainment ratings in arithmetic, English and verbal reasoning were obtained from primary school headmasters when the boys were 11. These were identical with or closely followed the assessments used for purposes of secondary school allocation, but the official figures could not be divulged owing to the refusal of the Local Education Authority to release them for research purposes. Finally, educational achievement was measured from actual secondary school placement at age 11. This was a four-category rating. The 43 boys who entered grammar schools, together with 27 who were put into top streams of comprehensive schools, were given the highest rating. The next highest rating—the high average—was given to 104 boys who were in the second streams of comprehensives or the top streams of secondary modern schools. The low average rating was given to 116 boys who were in the third streams of comprehensives and the intermediate streams of secondary modern schools. Finally, the 121 boys in the lowest category consisted of those in the lowest streams of secondary moderns or comprehensives, together with 19 boys who were in special schools for the subnormal or maladjusted. In the case of boys in schools which were not streamed, the classification was based upon position in class, and in a few cases in which information was unobtainable the boys were categorized according to attainment on leaving primary school.

[5] *Discrepancy between Verbal and Non-Verbal Scores*

It has been suggested that a discrepancy between verbal and non-verbal intelligence scores is characteristic of delinquents. An attempt was made to establish whether or not this feature was important as a predictor. To this end, 8 discrepancy scores were compiled for each boy, according to the differences between his percentile placings on verbal tests and his placings on non-verbal tests. The verbal and non-verbal measures involved are given in Table V(6), together with the biserial correlations between the resulting discrepancy scores and the delinquent/non-delinquent dichotomy. Since the standard error of each biserial correlation was again about ·07, it can be seen that none of the discrepancy scores proved to be significantly related to delinquency, although the last was not far off.

TABLE V(6)

Delinquency and Verbal/Non-verbal Discrepancy Scores

Verbal measure	*Non-verbal measure*	*Biserial correlation between discrepancy score and delinquency*
Verbal comprehension at 8	Matrices at 8	·03
Mechanical reading at 8	Matrices at 8	·01
Sentence reading at 8	Matrices at 8	—·05
Verbal comprehension at 8	Porteus TQ at 8	·04
Mechanical reading at 8	Porteus TQ at 8	·02
Sentence reading at 8	Porteus TQ at 8	—·02
Mill Hill vocabulary at 10	Matrices at 10	·07
Mill Hill vocabulary at 10	Porteus TQ at 10	·12

VI

Early Behaviour as a Precursor of Later Delinquency

1. *Troublesomeness*

(a) *Teachers' Ratings*. It is known from many previous researches that teachers are able to identify fairly accurately those boys likely to become delinquents in the future. Teachers' reports on children in the National Survey rated future delinquents significantly higher than non-delinquents in 'aggressive maladjustment' (Mulligan *et al.*, 1963). The delinquents were said to be more disobedient, more aggressive and quarrelsome, more resentful of criticism, and to lie, cheat and truant more often. These characteristics applied both to delinquents who had already been convicted and to those not yet convicted at the time the assessments were recorded.

The Bristol Social Adjustment Guides, devised by Stott (1963) are the best known of British questionnaires designed to predict delinquency on the basis of teachers' ratings. Stott (1960) showed that the Bristol Guides significantly distinguished boys on probation from a control group of boys of similar age attending the same Glasgow schools. Furthermore, Stott (1964) reported that these teachers' ratings significantly predicted success or failure on probation, and Stott and Wilson (1968) found that they predicted which juvenile offenders would be reconvicted as young adults. So far, however, it does not seem to have been proved that the Bristol Guides will identify, in a non-delinquent population, those who will be convicted in the future. Marsh (1969) suggested that their efficiency in this respect may not be very high. A firm answer on this point should eventually emerge from the National Child Development Study (Davie *et al.*, 1972), since Bristol Guides were completed for that sample when the children were aged 7.

Work in the United States also indicates that teachers can predict delinquency. Reckless and Dinitz (1967) asked teachers in Ohio to nominate, from among 12-year-old white boys, one group who would never get into trouble with the law and another who would almost certainly be the subject of police or court action in the future. During the next four years, about 4 per cent of the first group and 40 per cent of the second had contact with the courts. Hathaway and Monachesi (1963) asked teachers in Minnesota to say whether or not each of some 5,000 14-year-old boys were likely to get into trouble, and followed up the boys' court records for three years. After eliminating those who were already delinquents before being assessed by their teachers, they found that the ratings very significantly predicted future delinquency. Kvaraceus (1960), in a follow-up study in Massachusetts, also showed that teachers' opinions identified future delinquents. Finally, Conger and Miller (1966), Khleif (1964) and others have retrospectively investigated cumulative school records, and have discovered that, from an early age, delinquents were rated worse in behaviour than non-delinquents. Conger and Miller reported that, at age 8, the future delinquents were said to be poorly adapted, to have less regard for the rights and feelings of peers, to have poorer attitudes towards authority, to be more easily distracted and to be more aggressive.

It might be suggested that teachers' predictions of delinquency are self-fulfilling prophecies, brought about by their own behaviour towards boys of whom they have a low opinion. Rosenthal and Jacobsen (1968) have shown that teachers with high expectations of scholastic performance actually induce high achievement in their pupils. The same might be true in relation to delinquency. If a boy sees that nothing good is expected of him, he may feel impelled to conform to the delinquent stereotype. However, this was unlikely to have been the sole reason for the success of the teachers' predictions in the present Study. Different teachers produced similar ratings at different ages, and the opinions of teachers were significantly correlated with those of peers, indicating that teachers' assessments were realistic measures of behaviour.

A rating of each Study boy was obtained from his primary school class teachers. When the boys were aged 8, their teachers filled in questionnaires about classroom behaviour. A different set of teachers filled in similar forms when the boys were aged 10 (see Note 1). The questionnaire was a slightly modified version of the one used in 1955 by J. W. B. Douglas in the National Survey (Douglas, 1964). It was scored on a points system outlined by Gibson (1964c), based on the number and type of unfavourable descriptions endorsed by the teacher. At both ages, each boy was scored according to his ranking within his class in the opinion of his teacher, and a final score was derived by combining the ratings at the two ages (see Note 2). It was thought that the average of two different teachers' assessments would have greater validity than the report of one person.

The 'most troublesome' third of the boys included a surprisingly high proportion who were delinquents (38·1 per cent of 134, against 11·9 per cent of 277: $\chi^2 = 36{\cdot}4$, $p < {\cdot}001$). Only 4·1 per cent of the least troublesome boys became delinquents. The great majority of recidivists (30 out of 37) were rated most troublesome, and only one was rated least troublesome.

These results confirm that teachers can effectively identify two sizeable groups of boys, the first presenting a substantial risk of becoming future delinquents, and the second extremely unlikely to develop in this way. The aspects of behaviour which contributed most to the teachers' ratings (e.g. truancy, indiscipline, unkempt appearance, laziness) were different from the conduct (e.g. stealing, breaking in) which led to convictions for delinquency. It would appear that the boys who later attracted the attention of the police by blatant offences against property tended to be the same boys who, at an earlier age, had excited unfavourable comment from teachers by virtue of a quite different range of troublesome behaviour.

The contribution of truancy to the teachers' unfavourable ratings was not very great, since only 24 boys were reported to be truants at either 8 or 10 years of age. However, 14 of these (58·3 per cent) became delinquents. In contrast, frequent absences from school attributed by teachers to lax parental attitude or illness were not particularly associated with delinquency.

(b) *Peer Ratings*. In contrast to teachers' assessments, ratings by peers have rarely been used in the prediction of delinquency. Skaberne *et al.* (1965) asked elementary schoolchildren in Ljubljana to rate their peers on untruthfulness, aggression, popularity and withdrawn behaviour. Seven years later they made a complete name search in criminal records. They showed that the peer rating of untruthfulness was the best predictor of future delinquency, followed by that of aggression. They also identified about one-third of the sample as problem children using the opinions of both teachers and peers, and found that this group included two-thirds of the future delinquents.

At age 10 the Study boys were given a peer rating test. The test material consisted of an eight-page booklet, each page containing a list of all the boys in the class and headed by a different description, namely 'youngest', 'I'd like as a friend', 'daring', 'I want to be like him', 'gets into trouble most', 'honest', 'clever' or 'like I am'. The boy was told to cross out his own name and then to mark in order the four of his classmates who best fitted the description. With the exception of 'youngest', which was a buffer item inserted to facilitate

TABLE VI (1)

Attributes Rated by Peers at Age 10 and Incidence of Delinquency

Boys ranked in top quarter of class (*N* = approx. 88)	*Delinquents* (%)	*Boys ranked in bottom quarter of class* (*N* = approx. 88)	*Delinquents* (%)
Most popular ('I'd like as a friend')	13·5	Least popular	24·7
Most daring	38·0	Least daring	6·8
Most ideal ('I want to be like him')	15·1	Least ideal	14·5
Most troublesome ('Gets into trouble most')	37·5	Least troublesome	6·2
Most honest	5·3	Least honest	37·5
Most clever	12·9	Least clever	25·9
Most 'Like I am'	19·5	Least 'Like I am'	17·6

N.B. Of the total 353 boys tested, 19·3 per cent became juvenile delinquents.

explanation, the boys were scored according to their positions within the class on each of these attributes, using the scoring system published by Gibson and Hanson (1969). Largely owing to the fact that by this age some boys had moved out of their original school classes, peer ratings were obtainable for only 353 boys. On each description, approximately 88 boys were ranked in the top quarters of their classes, and another 88 in the bottom quarters.

Table VI (1) shows the percentages of delinquents among the boys placed in the highest and lowest quarters on each attribute (see also Appendix A). Boys who became delinquents were particularly prevalent among the most troublesome (37·5 per cent), most daring (38·0 per cent) and least honest (37·5 per cent) groups. Conversely, they were rarely found among the least troublesome (6·2 per cent), least daring (6·8 per cent) and most honest (5·3 per cent) boys. It can also be seen that the least popular and least clever boys were particularly prone to delinquency, but that the individuals whom boys thought most like themselves, and those whom boys most wanted to be like, were only average in this respect.

(c) *Combining the Ratings of Peers and Teachers.* Several researchers (e.g. Butcher, 1965; Wiggins and Winder, 1961; Walder *et al.*, 1961) have reported high correlations between teachers' and peer ratings of aggressive behaviour. These marked associations are in sharp contrast to the slight relationships observed between teachers' and parental ratings. Rutter *et al.* (1970), in their survey of all children on the Isle of Wight aged 9–11 in 1964 (much the same generation as in the present Study), found a correlation of only ·18 between parents' and teachers' assessments of maladjustment. Glidewell *et al.* (1959), in St. Louis reported that the extent of the association varied with the social class of the parents. Teachers' ratings of behaviour disorder agreed with those of upper class parents, but were almost unrelated to the assessments of lower class parents. This is hardly surprising, in view of the fact that teachers rarely share lower class values.

We obtained similar findings. There was only a modest correlation between teachers' ratings and the PSWs' conduct disorder judgments based upon parents' reports (see West, 1969, p. 42). In contrast, there was a close association between troublesomeness rated by teachers and peers (see Note 3). The teachers' and peer ratings were therefore combined in the usual way to produce a composite measure of troublesomeness. According to the combined assessment, future delinquents were much more common in the most troublesome category than among the remainder of the sample (44·6 per cent of 92, as opposed to 13·5 per cent of 319: $\chi^2 = 40{\cdot}5$, $p < {\cdot}001$). Figure VI (1) displays in more detail the relationship between delinquency and troublesomeness. It can be seen that the percentages of recidivists, one-time delinquents and police contact boys all tend to increase as one moves between the least and most troublesome classifications. Furthermore, while the percentage of future delinquents in the most troublesome group was strikingly high, that in the least troublesome group was even more strikingly low (44·6 per cent of 92 and 3·5 per cent of 143 respectively).

Maybe troublesomeness was the best predictor of delinquency because both were to some extent indices of persistent misconduct. The findings set out in previous Chapters suggest that five background factors made independent contributions to the likelihood of future delinquency, namely low family income, large family size,

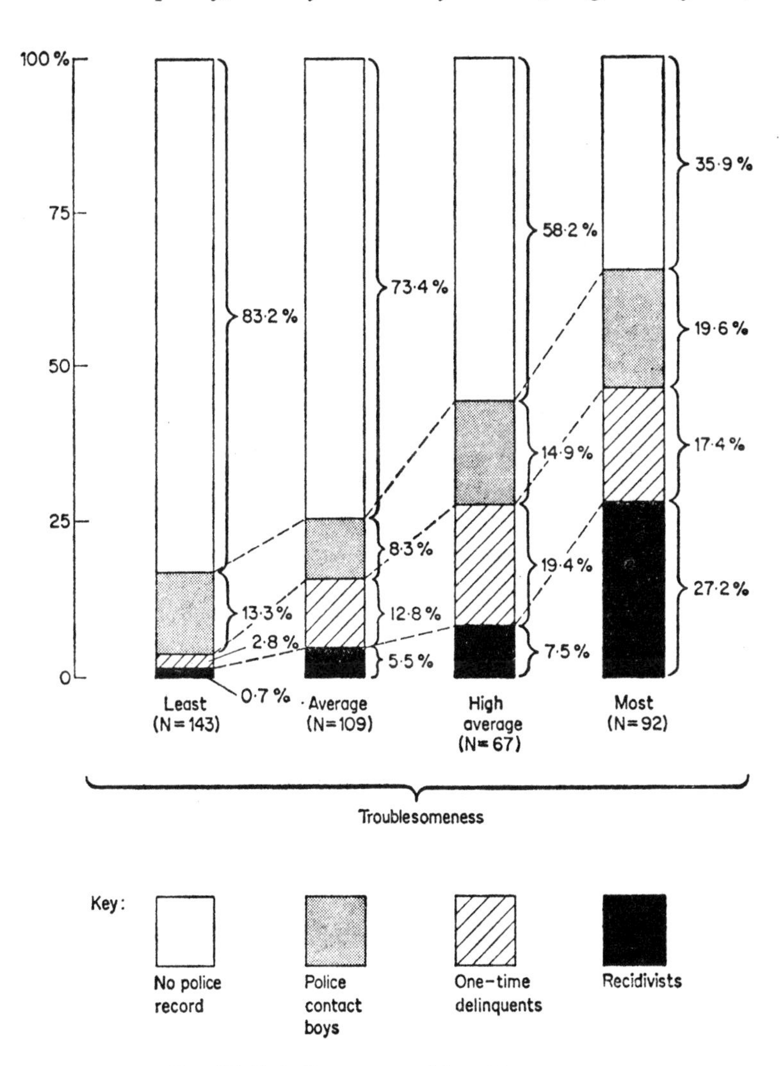

FIG. VI (I) Delinquency and Troublesomeness
(Combined Ratings of Teachers and Peers)

poor parental behaviour, parental criminality and low intelligence. Every one of these factors was also very significantly related to troublesomeness (see Appendix C), but delinquents were still more troublesome than non-delinquents even after matching for any of them (see Appendix B). Moreover, as will be demonstrated in Chapter VIII, troublesomeness alone was a better predictor of delinquency than a combination of the five background factors. It therefore appears that misconduct at an early age was a key factor in determining future delinquency convictions, and that it was important independently of a boy's social and intellectual background.

2. *Daring*

A composite rating of 'daring' was obtained by combining the opinions of peers and parents. In the course of their initial interviews with parents, when the boys were aged 8–9, the PSWs made inquiries about each boy's behaviour and temperament. One of the questions concerned the boy's adventurousness. The PSWs tried to find out whether he was the kind of boy who took risks, for instance in climbing, exploring and crossing the road, or whether he was noticeably cautious or physically timid. On the basis of the impressions gained in talking with parents, the PSWs categorized the boys as 'daring', 'average' or 'cautious'. The boys assessed as 'daring' were significantly delinquent-prone (37·3 per cent of 75, as opposed to 15·8 per cent of 304: $\chi^2 = 16{\cdot}1$, $p < {\cdot}001$). The peer rating of daring was also associated with delinquency (38·0 per cent of 100, as opposed to 11·9 per cent of 253: $\chi^2 = 29{\cdot}8$, $p < {\cdot}001$).

The two measures of daring were very closely related, and were therefore combined in the same way as the assessments of troublesomeness by peers and teachers. As might have been expected, boys identified as daring by this combined rating frequently became delinquents (38·8 per cent of 121, as opposed to 12·9 per cent of 287: $\chi^2 = 33{\cdot}5$, $p < {\cdot}001$). (See also note 4.)

Why should daring be predictive of delinquency? To the PSWs, daring meant taking risks, and risk-taking is said to be an attribute of the delinquent personality (Cohen, 1972). On the other hand, impressions gained from conversations with the boys indicated that, to them, daring meant defiant and bold, the opposite of meek. Overt aggression and rash defiance were probably major elements in this assessment.

The matching analyses indicated that troublesomeness and daring were, at least to some extent, independent precursors of juvenile delinquency. It would seem that both aspects of behaviour contributed to the likelihood of being labelled an official delinquent. The background features most characteristic of the troublesome boys (e.g. low IQ, criminal parents, large families) were much the same as those of the delinquents, but this was not true of daring boys. It may be that daring reflected an element of individual aggressiveness that was independent of other components of delinquency potential. It has been suggested elsewhere (Farrington and West, 1971) that there is an important connection between aggressiveness and delinquency. This topic will be explored further in Chapter X.

3. *Dishonesty*

The psychologist who gave the tests reported that the boys used the word 'honest' to refer to those who refrained from stealing, rather than those who did not lie. Not surprisingly, therefore, the boys rated by their peers as 'least honest' at age 10 were very significantly likely to become delinquents (37·5 per cent of 88, as opposed to 13·2 per cent of 265 : $\chi^2 = 23{\cdot}5$, $p < {\cdot}001$). Recidivists were over-represented among the dishonest boys (13·6 per cent as opposed to 5·7 per cent), as were one-time delinquents (23·9 per cent as opposed to 7·6 per cent), but police contact boys were not to any great extent (15·9 per cent as opposed to 12·5 per cent).

Dishonesty was very closely related to troublesomeness, and the dishonest boys tended to have the same background features as the troublesome boys, although to a lesser degree (see Appendix C). Delinquents were more dishonest than non-delinquents once they were matched for troublesomeness. After matching for dishonesty, however, delinquents were still significantly more troublesome (see Appendix B). These results suggest that dishonesty is only important as a predictor of delinquency because of its association with troublesomeness.

4. *Popularity among Peers*

Several investigators have reported that troublesome boys tend to be unpopular. Croft and Grygier (1956) and Sugarman (1968) found that boys identified as badly behaved by their teachers were rated unpopular by their peers in London schools. Lunzer (1960) showed that boys said to be aggressive by teachers in Manchester schools tended to be unpopular with their peers. In the United States, Teele *et al.* (1966) demonstrated that boys diagnosed as anti-social by psychiatrists were unpopular, and Kraft (1966) reported that boys judged as habitually rebellious by teachers were disliked by their peers. The work of Hargreaves (1967), showing the coexistence of academic and delinquent subcultures in a Northern secondary modern school, suggests that anti-social boys might be popular in the lower streams and unpopular in the higher. However, Sugarman (1968) found that badly behaved boys were unpopular both in high-achieving and in low-achieving groups.

In the present Study, the peer rating test at age 10 showed that the least popular boys were more prone to delinquency than average (Table VI (1)). The boys had also been given a sociometric measure of popularity at age 8, when they were handed lists of names of all boys in their class and asked to mark in order of preference the four classmates they liked best (West, 1969, p. 52; see also Note 5). Based upon the number of times each was selected by others, boys were ranked within each class in order of popularity. Those ranked in the bottom quarter of their class were categorized as 'unpopular', and those in the top quarter as 'popular'.

Boys identified as unpopular at age 8 tended to be similarly rated at 10 (34 of the 84 unpopular boys at 8 being among the 75 unpopular at 10: $\chi^2 = 21{\cdot}1$, $p < {\cdot}001$). A final assessment of unpopularity was obtained by combining, in the usual way, the measures taken at 8 and 10. Unpopular boys were found to be slightly more likely to become delinquents, but the difference did not reach statistical significance (24·6 per cent of 126 unpopular boys becoming delinquents, as opposed to 17·1 per cent of the 269 boys otherwise rated: $\chi^2 = 2{\cdot}62$, not significant). Recidivists, in particular, were over-represented among the unpopular boys (11·9 per cent as opposed to 6·0 per cent).

In this research, therefore, boys who were popular with their classmates did not so often become delinquents as their less popular schoolfellows. The difference was not very substantial, but at least it showed that primary schoolboys in this neighbourhood did not admire social rebels. The association of popularity with conformity was confirmed by the observation that popularity was positively correlated with being rated honest by other boys and negatively with being identified as troublesome or daring.

It might be expected that potential delinquents would choose as friends boys similar to themselves. In order to investigate this, each boy was coded according to the number of future delinquents he 'liked as a friend' in the peer rating test at age 8. Of the 38 boys who selected two or three future delinquents as friends, 31·6 per cent became delinquents. This was a relatively high proportion, but was not statistically significant. The figures can be contrasted with 21·9 per cent of 128 boys naming one delinquent, and 17·1 per cent of 210 boys naming none. The boys were coded again on the results of the peer rating test at age 10. Of the 31 boys who named two or three future delinquents as friends, the percentage who became delinquents (22·6 per cent) was just about the same as among boys who chose one delinquent or none. It must be concluded that having future delinquents among his friends in class was not a good index of a boy's likelihood of becoming delinquent himself. Different results might have been obtained if the boys had been asked to name those who were their friends rather than those who they would like to have as friends.

NOTES

[1] *Boys Convicted before the Ratings were Completed*

The assessments discussed in this Chapter were based in whole or in part on test results or reports from teachers obtained when the boys were already 10 years of age. In fact, six boys had had a finding of guilt by the time they were tested or reported upon. Since the risk that a measure might be contaminated by possible knowledge of a boy's delinquency applied to so few cases, it was decided that this disadvantage was outweighed by the gain in reliability of information resulting from the inclusion of data collected at age 10. In relation to teachers' ratings of troublesomeness, this source of bias was demonstrably negligible. The boys identified as troublesome at age 8 included just as high a proportion who were future delinquents (41 out of 100) as those rated troublesome at 10.

[2] *The Teachers' Questionnaires at Ages 8 and 10*

The questions on which the teachers' ratings were based (with the points contributed by each item given in brackets) were as follows:

Question 1: Is he a very hard worker (0), a hard worker (1), an average worker (2), a poor worker (3) or lazy (4)?

Question 3 (a): Is there any subject(s) . . . in which his performance is outstandingly GOOD?
Yes (0), No (1).

Question 4 (a): Is there any subject(s) . . . in which his performance is outstandingly BAD?
Yes (1), No (0).

Question 5: Do you think he tries to be a credit to his parents? Is very concerned (0), about average (2), just doesn't care (5).

Question 6: Does he lack concentration, or is he restless in a way that seriously hinders his learning?
Yes (2), No (0).

Question 7: Does he have difficulties in his relations with other children in his class?
Yes (2), No (0).

Question 8: When he comes to school in the morning, is he a clean and tidy boy (compared with others in his class)? Noticeably clean and tidy (0), about average (2), noticeably below average (5).

Question 9: Is he difficult to discipline?
Yes (5), No (0).

Question 10: Attendance: considering his record for the past year, what does it show? Very regular attendance, fair regularity, rather a lot of absence, very poor attendance. What is the reason for most of his absence (e.g. ill-health)? [This question was scored 0, 2 or 5 according to a judgment of the absence or severity of truancy.]

At each age level, the boys were divided into three groups, most troublesome, average and least troublesome, according to whether their scores fell into the worst quarter, the middle range or the best quarter of their particular school class. An overall teachers' rating of troublesomeness on a three-point scale was then obtained by combining the assessments at the two ages. In effect, 134 boys were categorized 'most troublesome', because their scores were in the worst quarter at both ages, or in the worst quarter at one age and in the average range at the other. Correspondingly, 123 boys were categorized 'least troublesome', because they were in the best quarter at both ages, or in the best quarter at one age and in the average range at the other.

[3] *The Association between Teachers' and Peer Ratings of Troublesomeness*

In order to compare the ratings of peers with those of teachers, the boys were grouped into three approximately equally sized categories of peer ratings, labelled most troublesome, average and least troublesome. The two assessments were very closely linked. Setting aside the 58 boys for whom peer ratings were not available, 67 of the 109 identified as most troublesome by teachers were among the 123 correspondingly identified by peers ($\chi^2 = 47{\cdot}6$, $p < {\cdot}001$). In producing the composite measure of troublesomeness, the 58 boys not assessed by peers had to be classified on teachers' ratings alone.

[4] *Further Details of the Combined Rating of Daring*

Eliminating those not rated on one or both measures, 26 of the 60 labelled 'daring' by the PSWs were among the 71 identified as 'daring' by peers. The two assessments were closely linked (Comparing daring boys with the remainder on each measure, $\chi^2 = 18{\cdot}2$, $p < {\cdot}001$.)

Among the 121 most daring boys on the combined rating of PSWs and peers, recidivists and one-time delinquents were both very significantly over-represented (19·0 per cent as opposed to 4·9 per cent, and 19·8 per cent as opposed to 8·0 per cent, respectively). Police contact cases, however, were not unusually prevalent in the daring group (14·9 per cent as opposed to 12·9 per cent).

Daring was very closely related to troublesomeness. Setting aside boys not rated on daring, 55 of the 90 most troublesome boys were among the 121 rated most daring. Nevertheless, the matching analyses showed that daring and troublesomeness were independently important as predictors of delinquency. Delinquents were more often daring than non-delinquents, even after matching for troublesomeness, and vice versa (see Appendix B). Moreover, daring was not related to the five background factors in the same way as troublesomeness. For instance, the daring boys showed no tendency to be less intelligent than their peers, and were much less likely than the troublesome boys to have criminal parents and to come from large families.

VII

Miscellaneous Factors of Doubtful Importance

In this Chapter several lines of enquiry are described, none of which yielded clear results of relevance to the development of juvenile delinquency. This point is made at the outset so that readers uninterested in negative findings can move to the next Chapter. For the investigator, however, such findings are as interesting as positive ones, for they suggest that previous researchers may have been mistaken in attributing importance to the features in question. Although the factors discussed were apparently less important than others, it is difficult to establish with certainty that a given item has no relevance. The possibility remains that, with more refined methods of measurement and a larger sample, more positive results might have emerged.

1. *Clumsiness*

Although delinquents probably possess normal muscular coordination and manual dexterity, they are said to perform poorly on tasks involving a combination of thought and movement or requiring an optimal balance between speed and accuracy (Anthony, 1960; Bize *et al.*, 1964, 1965). Some authorities believe that delinquents do badly on psychomotor tests, not through any physiological defect, but because they are impulsive (Doctor and Winder, 1954; Roberts and Erikson, 1968).

The best known psychomotor test in criminology is the Porteus Maze (Porteus, 1965). This consists of a series of paper and pencil mazes of increasing difficulty. It was originally devised as an intelligence test (see p. 85), but many years ago Porteus found that delinquents characteristically disregarded instructions, cut corners, crossed boundary lines and made impulsive changes of direction

(Porteus, 1942). By noting which of these errors of execution discriminated most significantly between delinquent and non-delinquent groups, Porteus developed a system of penalty scores, the total of these being known as the qualitative or Q score. Many investigators (e.g. Doctor and Winder, 1954; Fooks and Thomas, 1957; Gibbens, 1958) have since confirmed the ability of the Q score to identify delinquents. The present Study found, additionally, that the qualitative score predicts delinquency.

At each of three ages (8, 10 and 14), the boys were given three different tests of psychomotor performance, the Gibson Spiral Maze, the Porteus Maze and the Tapping test. A fourth measure, the Body Sway test, was given only at age 8. This has been described previously (West, 1969, p. 50), but was discarded for present purposes because it appeared to have little in common with the other three, which were all paper and pencil tests, and because the body sway scores did not correlate significantly with the scores on any of the other psychomotor measures.

A clumsiness score obtained by combining the results of the three psychomotor measures (see Note 1) proved to be very significantly predictive of future delinquency ($r_{bis} = 0{\cdot}23$, $p < {\cdot}001$). Dividing the sample into four quarters, delinquents were over-represented among the clumsiest boys (31·7 per cent of 104, as opposed to 16·6 per cent of 307 : $\chi^2 = 10{\cdot}01$, $p < {\cdot}005$). The prevalence of recidivists among the clumsiest boys was especially striking (17·3 per cent as opposed to 6·2 per cent).

Clumsiness was closely related to low intelligence (46·6 per cent of the least intelligent boys being among the 104 clumsy boys, as opposed to only 18·2 per cent of the boys of average or superior IQ: $\chi^2 = 31{\cdot}5$, $p < {\cdot}001$). After matching for intelligence, delinquents and non-delinquents ceased to differ significantly in psychomotor clumsiness (see Appendix B). Conversely, after matching for clumsiness, delinquents and non-delinquents ceased to differ in intelligence, although they still differed in the other basic factors of family size, parental criminality and parental behaviour. It might perhaps be concluded that clumsiness, although significantly predictive of delinquency, was of importance only because of its association with low intelligence.

This conclusion was not altogether surprising in the light of other research. Of the three psychomotor measures used here, only the Porteus Q score has previously been compared with intelligence.

Gibbens (1958), with his sample of Borstal boys, reported that the Q score was closely linked (r = 0·42) with low IQ on the Progressive Matrices. The corresponding Study figure was slightly lower (r = 0·30). Correlations of this order have also been obtained with IQ tests other than the Matrices (Tizard, 1951), confirming that poor psychomotor performance is characteristic of less intelligent boys. An exception to this is the recent work by Anthony (1972), who found no relationship between the Matrices and her psychomotor measure. She was, however, using a purely mechanical test, not a paper and pencil one.

2. Physique

According to a number of empirical investigations (Glueck and Glueck, 1956; Gibbens, 1963), delinquents tend to have a mesomorphic (i.e. sturdy, muscular, athletic) type of body build. Accepted methods of classifying physique require elaborate measurements by trained personnel or standardized photographs taken in the nude which can be analysed subsequently. It was not possible to arrange such methods in the present Study. However, the ratio of height to weight provides a crude indication of body build, and 139 boys were identified on this basis as being heavily built (see Note 2). They did not prove to be particularly delinquent-prone (21·6 per cent of 139 becoming delinquents, as opposed to 19·6 per cent of 270). This negative result could have been due to the crudity of the measure of physique, or perhaps to the inclusion among the heavily built of two contrasting physical types, the muscular 'mesomorphs' and the fat, rotund 'endomorphic' boys. On the assumption that true mesomorphs would have more powerful hands, 91 heavily built boys were classified as probable mesomorphs using the strength of their grip, registered on a dynamometer. These boys, however, included rather fewer delinquents than the remainder of the sample (14·3 per cent as opposed to 22·4 per cent).

3. Neurotic Extraversion and 'Lying'

Some predictions derived from social learning theory about the connection between child-rearing practices and delinquency were mentioned earlier (p. 51). The well-known version of this theory developed by Eysenck (1970) emphasizes another aspect, namely the

role of the two personality dimensions called extraversion an
neuroticism. According to Eysenck, extraverts are relatively les
susceptible to Pavlovian conditioning, so that, other things bein
equal, they are less able to develop the association between fear an
delinquent temptation which is the basis of conforming behaviour
Eysenck also claims that, among extraverts, those who are neuroti
are particularly likely to become delinquents. He reasons as follows
The nervous tension which accompanies neuroticism has the effec
of amplifying the individual's natural drives. Of the two opposin
drives, hedonism and fear, which respectively promote and restrai
criminal behaviour, the former predominates in the extravert
Among extraverts, an increase in their drives, due to neuroticism
causes hedonism to predominate still further, and will thereb
increase the likelihood of delinquent development (but see als
Note 3).

Eysenck and his collaborators at the Maudsley Hospital hav
developed personality inventories which purport to measure th
traits of neuroticism and extraversion. It is possible to test th
Eysenck theory by applying these to delinquent groups. Mos
previous workers (e.g. Bartholomew, 1959; Fitch, 1962; Little, 1963
Blackler, 1968) have tested subjects taken from penal institutions
and have demonstrated that, compared with the normal population
institutionalized criminals have higher neuroticism scores, but th
same extraversion scores. Black (1972) concluded that 'a norma
level of extraversion, together with a high level of neuroticisn
(anxiety), is reported for 19 different groups of offenders'.

Hoghughi and Forrest (1970), reviewing four studies of boys i
approved schools, found that in three of these surveys the delinquent
scored higher on neuroticism and lower on extraversion than th
normal population. In the fourth, no significant differences emerged
Moreover, the group of boys identified as neurotic-extraverts wer
less delinquent than the group of neurotic-introverts. Burgess (1972
reviewed three investigations of prisoners. In one of these, th
prisoners were relatively extraverted, in another relatively intro
verted, and in the third not different in this respect from a contro
group. In two of the tests the prisoners were higher on neuroticisn
than the controls, but in the third there was no significant difference

In opposition to Hoghughi and Forrest, Burgess was able to shov
that in all three studies the prisoners were more likely than th
controls to belong to the neurotic-extravert group. Finally, i

comparisons of prisoners and controls by Eysenck and Eysenck (1970), no significant differences in either extraversion or neuroticism were found.

It can be seen that previous research fails to confirm the prediction that criminals should be extraverts. Tests of this deduction have yielded contradictory results. Regarding neuroticism, a majority of reports showed that criminals and delinquents were relatively more neurotic than the normal population. The findings are, however, open to objections that the neurotic responses may have been due to the subjects being in penal detention, and that, due to processes of selection, institutionalized delinquents may be untypical of delinquents in general.

The present Study afforded a unique opportunity in this country to examine neuroticism and extraversion among pre-delinquents and non-institutionalized delinquents. Since the retrospective bias of knowing who is delinquent is not particularly relevant to the responses the boys themselves make to personality inventories, discussion will include the findings of tests at later ages as well as those at ages 8 and 10. The three measures used were the 'Cards' test, developed by Gibson (West, 1969, pp. 44–5 and Gibson, 1965b) and given at age 8, the New Junior Maudsley Personality Inventory (Furneaux and Gibson, 1966) given at ages 10 and 14, and the Eysenck Personality Inventory (Eysenck and Eysenck, 1964) given at age 16 (see Note 4).

The results obtained did not provide much support for Eysenck's theory. Extraversion was significantly correlated with delinquency only at age 16 (at ages 8, 10, 14 and 16, r_{bis} = ·12, ·07, ·09 and ·19 respectively). The only measure of neuroticism significantly associated with delinquency was the NJMI at age 10 (at ages 8, 10, 14 and 16, r_{bis} = ·06, ·14, ·05 and ·01 respectively). Furthermore, the only two significant results were caused by a lack of delinquents among those with the lowest scores (least extraverted or least neurotic), rather than by an excess among those with the highest scores. Every test showed that neither the most neurotic nor the most extraverted boys were more delinquent than the remainder of the sample (see Appendix A, factors 126–35 and 148–50).

Finally, the boys who were above average on both neuroticism and extraversion—the true neurotic-extraverts—were examined at each age. The results were remarkably consistent, and did not favour Eysenck's theory. On each occasion of testing, the neurotic-extraverts included a slightly higher percentage who were delinquents than the remainder of the sample, but in no instance was the excess statistically significant.

Two personality inventories applied to our boys, the NJMI and EPI, both include items which contribute to a lie score. These consist of statements implying an implausible degree of moral rectitude. Children who endorse a high proportion of such statements as applicable to themselves are presumed to be lying, in order to present a socially approved façade. However, high 'lie' scores could be produced by unusually well-behaved children reporting honestly, just as much as by normal or 'bad' boys denying their true natures (Gibson, 1964a, 1964b, 1969d). In view of the doubt about the correct interpretation of lie scores, high scorers were not excluded from the analyses just reported. Instead, it was interesting to discover the association between delinquency and 'lying'.

High lie scores at age 10 were negatively correlated with future delinquency to a significant degree ($r_{bis} = -\cdot15$), but at ages 14 and at 16 they were positively though insignificantly related to delinquency ($r_{bis} = \cdot03$ and $\cdot07$ respectively). The significant result at age 10 was due to an excess of delinquents among the lowest scorers on the scale. Presumably, at this age, the potential delinquents tended to respond honestly by confessing their own shortcomings, thereby producing very low lie scores. At later ages, they probably became more circumspect. This result reproduced the findings of Hoghughi and Forrest (1970) using the Junior Eysenck Personality Inventory. They showed that, among boys at approved schools, 11-year-olds produced significantly low lie scores, but 12- to 14-year-olds gained average scores. High lie scores do not seem to be linked with delinquency, and among younger boys the potential delinquents are more likely to obtain low lie scores.

4. *Nervous Boys*

Stressful conditions of upbringing have been blamed for both juvenile delinquency and nervous disorder among children. There is some difference of opinion, however, as to whether these responses to stress are likely to occur in the same individual (perhaps at different stages of development) or whether they are to some extent mutually exclusive. The present results lend no support to either notion. The PSWs attempted to identify boys showing nervous disturbances at age 8 to 9. They enquired about the presence or absence of some 17 symptoms, such as tics, sleep disturbances, speech disorder and enuresis (West, 1969, pp. 45–8). The 41 boys considered severely nervous (see Note 5) became delinquents with the same frequency as those rated otherwise (19·5 per cent of 41, as opposed to 19·4 per cent of 341).

Unlike most of the adverse assessments made by the PSWs, nervous disorder was not particularly prevalent among boys from poor or large families, or among those with criminal parents. On the other hand, there was a significant tendency for boys rated nervous to have experienced poor parental behaviour (22·5 per cent of 96, as opposed to 7·2 per cent of 300: $\chi^2 = 15{\cdot}0$. $p < {\cdot}001$). This result is what would be expected if nervous disturbance is provoked by parental mishandling rather than by poor social conditions. Delinquency, in contrast, appears to arise from either circumstance.

Since the questionnaire tests of neuroticism used with the boys were originally validated by their ability to distinguish between neurotics and normals, one would expect an association between the PSWs' assessments of nervous disorder and high scoring on these tests. In fact, there were no significant relationships between the PSWs' ratings and any of the neuroticism scores. This certainly casts doubt upon the validity of the measures. Probably neither was very satisfactory. The PSWs were dependent upon secondhand reports from mothers, and the neuroticism questionnaires may have been completed carelessly by our working class schoolboys. The neuroticism scores at ages 10 and 14 were correlated significantly but not very highly ($r = {\cdot}33$).

The PSWs also assessed each boy's temperament, classifying him as 'outgoing', 'average' or 'withdrawn' (see Note 5). A combined measure of 'nervous-withdrawn' identified 95 boys, fewer of whom became delinquents than of those otherwise rated (14·7 per cent as opposed to 21·1 per cent). In general, nervous-withdrawn boys experienced poor parental behaviour. After matching for parental behaviour, the tendency for nervous-withdrawn boys to be non-delinquents rather than delinquents became more definite (see Appendix B). Other things being equal, it seems that a shy, timid temperament tended to prevent a boy becoming a delinquent. This was one of the very few examples in which an apparently unfavourable feature was associated with not becoming a delinquent.

5. *Obstetric Abnormalities*

Complications of pregnancy, premature birth and difficulties in delivery may cause damage to the brain of the new-born baby. It has been found (e.g. by Pasamanick *et al.*, 1956) that even where such damage is too slight to cause paralysis or other obvious physical signs, or to result in mental subnormality, it may still be sufficient to affect personality development, and may show itself in behaviour disorder as the child grows up. Pasamanick suggested that relatively minor obstetric complications were significantly more common among children with behaviour problems. He pointed out that one or more complications might be expected in a quarter of all births of white children. Among children with behaviour problems, the prevalence was higher, about one in three. The theory of sub-clinical brain damage as a potent factor in delinquency was taken up in England by Stott (1962), who claimed that the histories of juvenile offenders were characterized by a high incidence, not only of obstetric abnormalities, but of other medical conditions affecting infant development.

The topic of obstetric abnormality will be mentioned here only briefly, since it has been discussed previously at some length (West, 1969, pp. 108–15). It was reported then that no connection could be discovered between obstetric complications and teachers' or PSWs' ratings of conduct when the boys were aged 8–9.

It was decided to investigate only the 272 boys born in hospital and with medical records available. Of these, about a half (138) were reported to have had one or more obstetric complications, but this group was, if anything, rather less delinquent-prone than the 134 boys with no complications (18·1 per cent as opposed to 19·4 per cent). The prevalence of obstetric complications was higher than that reported by Pasamanick for white births, but was comparable with his figure of 50·5 per cent for births of coloured children.

The high Study prevalence was partly due to the inclusive criteria of abnormality adopted, and partly to the fact that the likelihood of complications was one of the reasons for births taking place in hospital. The abnormalities were made up as follows: Twelve boys had an abnormal birth weight (5 lb. 8 oz. or less, or over 10 lb.), of whom two (16·7 per cent) became delinquents. Fifty-three boys had a severely abnormal confinement (e.g. haemorrhage, mal-presentation or severe asphyxia of the baby), and 20·8 per cent became delinquents, while 56 had a moderately abnormal confinement (e.g. breech deliveries and slight degrees of foetal distress or asphyxia), and 16·1 per cent became delinquents. Finally, 17 boys were the products of abnormal pregnancies (e.g. severe toxaemia or pre-eclampsia) and 17·7 per cent became delinquents, while 38 were from moderately abnormal pregnancies (e.g. early bleeding or mild toxaemia) and 18·4 per cent became delinquents. It can be seen that none of these categories or degrees of obstetric abnormality resulted in a significantly raised likelihood of delinquency.

The effects of obstetric factors could have been masked if different groups, with different delinquency potentials, also had different expectations of obstetric complications. For instance, first born boys, who tended to belong to small families and to have a low delinquency rate, also had a greater expectation of obstetric abnormality. First and later born boys were therefore considered separately, but no relationship between delinquency and obstetric complications emerged. Masking of the obstetric factor by family income or family size did not occur, because obstetric complications were unrelated to these variables. This was rather curious, since obstetric complications, like other medical adversities, are generally commoner among the poor. However, as we were dealing with a neighbourhood sample, and most of the families shared the same hospital facilities, this may have reduced the expected differences between income groups.

It may be concluded from these results that minor obstetric abnormalities among a normal working-class sample are not important as precursors of delinquency. Of course, a single negative finding from a small sample such as this cannot establish that there is no relationship whatsoever, especially since other evidence suggests the possibility of a connection. For instance, the National Child Development Study, a longitudinal survey of a birth cohort of 16,000 children, established that deviation from the norm on either birth weight or duration of pregnancy was associated with subsequent educational subnormality, especially in the case of younger children in large families of the manual classes (Davie *et al.*, 1972). Furthermore, after carefully controlling for other relevant factors, notably birth order and social class, abnormal duration of pregnancy was significantly linked with poor social adjustment subsequently—as measured by Bristol Guides (cf. p. 98) filled in by teachers. A much larger sample than the present one, taken from all social classes, might have yielded some positive correlations between obstetric variables and delinquency. It would then have been possible to assess separately the effects of different kinds of abnormality, and of more extreme cases, and to consider special groups of delinquents, such as those who were also educationally retarded or maladjusted.

6. *Physical Health*

In past generations delinquents may have had poor physical health, but Wootton (1959), reviewing the question as one of her 12 criminological hypotheses, found that the evidence was inconclusive. More recently, Eilenberg (1961) discovered that London remand home boys had a high incidence of minor physical ailments, such as skin complaints, visual defects, skeletal deformities, ear discharges and deafness. In contrast, Scott (1966) concluded that approved school boys were an extremely healthy group. Nevertheless, Gibbens (1963) found that the rate of physical disease or defect among his sample of Borstal boys was high, especially in view of the fact that the courts are compelled to ascertain that candidates are physically fit before they can be sent for Borstal training.

Most of the information about the health of our boys in their early years came from the PSWs' interviews with mothers. For a large section of the sample, however, access to abstracts from school medical notes was permitted, and in the case of some boys who had been in hospital medical records were seen. Time did not permit more extensive enquiries, for instance from general practitioners or the Department of Health and Social Security.

Health at age 8 was assessed by the PSWs on the basis of all the information available. About a quarter of the sample were considered to have a significant history of ill health. Minor accidents and injuries without sequelae, and the usual childhood infections, were discounted, but repeated or persistent illness, such as recurrent bronchitis or asthma, were counted even if not actually present at the time of interview. A history of illness in early life proved to have no significant association with later juvenile delinquency (21·4 per cent of 112 unhealthy boys, compared with 17·9 per cent of 273 rated healthy).

Another attempt to identify boys with medical problems was made during the interviews at 16 years of age. The boys were asked about any accidents or illnesses that had occurred after their fifteenth birthdays, but no relationship with delinquency was discovered

(20·3 per cent delinquents among 69, as opposed to 20·6 per cent among 330 who reported no recent illness or injury).

On the whole, severe health problems were a rarity in our survey. All the boys survived to the age of 18, with the exception of one who died accidentally while making an escape from a penal institution. Only two of the boys interviewed at 18 were chronically unemployable for health reasons, and in one instance this was due to a recent accident.

7. *Place of Residence Within the Neighbourhood*

Michael Power and his collaborators (1972) demonstrated marked variations in juvenile delinquency rates among different areas within a single London borough, Tower Hamlets. The greatest differences were seen when the smallest areas were studied, namely the 300 census enumeration districts. However, considerable variations were also found among the 33 census wards. The annual average number of first court appearances per 100 boys in the years 1964–8 varied among these wards from 2·2 to 5·7. These results suggest that the immediate neighbourhood in which a boy lives, as indicated by the ward in which he resides, may have an important bearing on whether or not he becomes a juvenile delinquent.

When the Study boys were first contacted at the age of 8–9, the vast majority (355, or 86 per cent) were living in one of five adjacent census wards. The delinquency rates in these five wards were respectively 1·1, 2·3, 2·3, 3·1 and 3·2 (see Note 6). Among the Study boys living in these wards, the percentages who became delinquents were 16·8, 20·2, 20·7, 22·7 and 24·5 respectively. It can be seen at a glance that delinquency in our sample reflected the overall rates of the wards, suggesting that our boys followed the same trend as their neighbours. The contrasts within the sample, however, were not so great as expected, and the differences were not statistically significant.

It seemed that the location of a boy's home in one or other of the wards had a minimal effect upon his likelihood of delinquency. One reason for this may have been that the Study boys were concentrated in unrepresentative sections of the wards. Since the sections in question were located close together, they were probably less different from each other than were the wards as a whole.

8. *The Influence of Primary and Secondary Schools*

In principle, the Study boys represented a complete and unselected generation from six neighbouring primary schools. As reported earlier, these schools did not differ from others in the neighbourhood in such factors as social class composition and incidence of pupils appearing before juvenile courts (West, 1969, pp. 26–7). In addition, they did not appear to vary in the character of their pupils, since the distributions of family size, family income, parental criminality and IQ scores of boys in the Study sample were similar in all six schools.

The primary schools varied greatly in the way they were run. The headmasters had different outlooks, and there were considerable differences of policy on such important matters as discipline, streaming and contacts with parents. These influences might have been expected to produce corresponding variations in the boys' scholastic performances and subsequent behaviour. In fact, the schools did not differ to any great extent in educational achievement, as measured by arithmetic, English and verbal reasoning (see p. 84), and they did not vary significantly in the percentages of boys becoming delinquents (see Note 7). One must conclude, therefore, that the different regimes in these primary schools were not major determinants of future delinquency.

Secondary school experience might have more relevance to the risk of becoming delinquent, since this is the time of life when most juvenile convictions occur. On leaving primary school, the Study boys were immediately scattered over a large number of secondary schools, but a majority (283) went to one of only seven different schools—six of these being comprehensives and one a grammar school. Unlike the primary schools, which were dealing with substantially similar populations, the secondary schools tended to receive differently selected pupils. As Table VII (1) shows, School A, the grammar school, tended to receive the best behaved boys (only 5 per cent rated troublesome), the more intelligent boys (average IQ 111), those from small families (average sibship 2·8) and those who generally stayed on after the minimum age (average school leaving age 16 years 7 months). At the opposite extreme, School G received the worst behaved boys (35 per cent troublesome), the dullest boys (IQ 94), those from large families (average sibship 4·1) and those who left early (age 15 years 8 months). The seven secondary schools were ranked in much the same order on a large number of indices, with School G having the worst of the boys and School A receiving the best.

Apart from the grammar school, with entry largely governed by the outcome of the educational assessments at age 11, it is not entirely clear how the schools came to have such contrasting populations. Education authorities vary in their methods of allocation of children. For instance, in selecting children for grammar schools or comprehensives, some authorities rely on formal tests, while others use teachers' assessments or qualitative impressions. In different areas, teachers are instructed either to take home background into

TABLE VII (1)

Characteristics of Study Boys Attending Different Secondary Schools

*Ranked in ascending order of delinquency rate**	*Number of study boys attending*	*Study boys rated trouble-some* (%)	*Becoming delinquents* (%)	*Average family size of study boys*	*Average Matrices IQ†*	*Average school leaving age of study boys Years*	*Months*
A (0·6)	19	5	10·5	2·8	111	16	7
B (2·6)	19	5	15·8	3·3	102	16	3
C (3·0)	46	11	15·2	3·1	100	16	1
D (5·4)	28	21	17·9	3·2	100	15	7
E (5·6)	63	17	20·6	3·6	102	16	2
F (5·6)	68	22	26·5	3·9	98	15	8
G (9·0)	40	35	27·5	4·1	94	15	8

* The figures in brackets represent, for the year 1967, the number of court appearances of boys aged 11–14 per 100 such boys at the school.

† Average of ages 8 and 10.

account, or alternatively not to do so (National Foundation for Educational Research, 1964). If parents can make a real choice, the more favoured schools are likely to be filled up quickly by pupils whose parents are keen to see them obtain the best available place.

A helpful note from a local education officer explained that the methods of allocation used in the Study area were different in 1964 and 1965, when the older and younger cohorts of our boys passed through the system. In 1964 there was a formal examination, but the 1965 assessments were based on primary school performance supplemented by a confidential report by the headmaster on each pupil's abilities, aptitudes and interests. In both years, parents were supplied with the names of secondary schools considered suitable for their child, and were allowed to name two choices. They could discuss the selection with primary school headmasters.

Heads of the secondary schools interviewed applicants and considered the reports received from the primary schools. They were instructed to select a balanced intake in terms of ability. In practice, the less popular schools had difficulty in obtaining pupils from the higher grades, and found themselves with larger proportions of lower grade pupils than they wanted. Furthermore, according to the education officer, there was some evidence that pupils were refused admission to certain schools because of the background social information given in the school report, so that the under-subscribed schools tended to receive socially deprived pupils as well as the less able scholastically.

Elizabeth Goodacre (1967), reporting on parents' experiences of the allocation procedures, notes great variation depending on the conscientiousness of primary school headmasters in their consultations with parents. One London parent described: 'interviews of not more than 10 minutes in the first instance. . . . The head . . . appears to adopt a policy of first come first served. . . . "Lucky you didn't choose X, I already have my quota there." ' Informal contacts with the Study primary schools also gave the impression of considerable variability. One headmaster devised a special questionnaire, and made great efforts to get all parents to complete it and to discuss with him the most appropriate secondary school for their children. Many parents were dilatory or reluctant to visit the schools and exercise their choice. Among those who did express preferences, one particular comprehensive school was especially popular.

Table VII (1) shows that the percentages of Study boys who became delinquents varied among the secondary schools in much the same way as other factors. The contrasts were marked, with only 10·5 per cent becoming delinquents at School A compared with 27·5 per cent at School G. The trend followed roughly the order of the delinquency rates for the total populations of the schools. These rates, displayed in the first column of Table VII (1), were based on information supplied by the Education Authority for the year 1967. They represent the number of court appearances of boys aged 11–14 per 100 such boys attending each school. The grammar school (A) had a conspicuously low rate, less than one court appearance per 100 boys, while the best of the comprehensives (B and C) had rates of 2·6 and 3·0, and the worst schools, D to G, all had rates of 5·4 or more.

These differing delinquency rates reproduce one of the findings of Power *et al.* (1972) in Tower Hamlets, namely that schools within the same London borough vary dramatically in the incidence of court appearances.

Are the differing delinquency rates of secondary schools due to variations present at intake, or does the school itself exert some influence? It would be reasonable to suppose that experiences at a high delinquency school might amplify a boy's pre-existing delinquency potential. Using the information supplied by the Education Authority, the 13 secondary schools which accommodated most of the Study boys were divided into high delinquency schools (three in number, with rates from 9·0 to 20·9) and others (10 schools, with rates from 0·3 to 5·6). Of the 56 boys in high delinquency schools, 37·5 per cent had been rated 'troublesome' by peers and teachers at primary school, in comparison with only 15·8 per cent of the 279 boys at other secondary schools. However, the proportion of troublesome boys who became delinquents was similar in the two types of schools (57·1 per cent in the delinquent schools, 50·0 per cent in the others). Comparisons of the actual percentages of delinquents with those expected on the basis of troublesomeness at primary school also yielded small differences (Farrington, 1972). It seems, therefore, that attendance at different secondary schools made no substantial difference to the boys' pre-existing delinquency potentials.

This conclusion is at variance with the findings of the Tower Hamlets survey. Power *et al.* were of the opinion that schools with a very similar intake (judged by the catchment area served, and by other criteria) differed considerably in the incidence of court appearances among their pupils. This conflict of research results could be accounted for in several ways. Being situated in a different area, and perhaps having different policies, the schools in Tower Hamlets might have exercised a greater influence than the particular schools involved in our Study. Alternatively, it may be that the Tower Hamlets investigators failed to detect some of the antecedent differences that we measured, and therefore exaggerated the effect of the schools. Whatever the explanation, the topic obviously has practical importance, and deserves further exploration.

Attendance at a less favoured secondary school might stunt intellectual growth, even if it has little effect on delinquent development. At schools where the mean IQ was low and the home backgrounds of the pupils (as reflected in family size) were not so good, one might expect boys to lack intellectual stimulation, and hence to fall further below the norm. In fact, the mean Matrices IQs of Study boys going to the seven secondary schools A–G were almost the same at age 14 as they had been at ages 8 and 10 (averaged). The slight differences which did occur were not in the expected direction. Among boys attending school G, the 'worst' of the 7, the mean IQ rose from 94 to 96. Among those attending school C, one of the 'better' comprehensives, it fell from 100 to 96. On the vocabulary test (Mill Hill synonyms) the boys at all seven schools improved their average score by at least three points. The boys at the two 'best' schools, A and B, increased by 6 and 5 points respectively, but this improvement was little greater than that of boys attending the other five schools. Even in respect to vocabulary, which should be particularly sensitive to environment, it did not seem to make much difference to the boys which secondary school they attended.

NOTES

[1] *Details of Psychomotor Tests*

In the Tapping test (Gibson, 1969a), each boy was given a pencil and told to tap with it on a blank piece of paper as fast as possible for 10 seconds. The diameter of the smallest circle which enclosed all the dots was taken as the score. Potential delinquents were expected to show less restraint and to produce a wider scatter of dots. In the Spiral Maze test (Gibson, 1965a, 1969b), using a pencil or a ballpoint pen, the boys were asked to trace a continuous line along a spiral pathway which was printed on a large card. Obstacles, each represented by the letter O in large type, were scattered along the path. The boy was told to go outwards from the centre, anti-clockwise, as quickly as possible, but not to let his pencil track touch the printed borders or cut across the obstacles. The performance was timed, and an error score was obtained by summing penalty points for each occasion the pencil track touched or penetrated one of the printed lines. The error score was adjusted according to the time taken, each boy being rated in comparison with those who took a similar length of time to complete the test. The adjustment was made according to a linear regression equation (see Gibson, 1965a).

The administration and scoring of the Porteus Maze at age 8 followed the method of Porteus (1942), but at ages 10 and 14 the test was varied. At these ages the boys were given only six mazes, and were required to continue tracing their way through each until they reached the end point. In the Porteus method, a longer series of mazes of increasing difficulty was presented, and when a subject traced into a blind alley in a maze for the first time, the maze was removed uncompleted. In the present Study, at ages 10 and 14, a modified Q score was obtained, by counting only one of the components of the Porteus Q, namely the number of cut lines.

A further complication arose because the tests were on some occasions administered individually and at other times given as group tests to the whole class. The scores under the two conditions were not directly comparable. Boys in groups tended to produce a wider scatter of dots in the Tapping test and to take longer and make fewer errors in the Spiral Maze. To allow for this, each boy's score was converted into a percentile rank within either the group scores or the individual scores, according to the condition under which he was tested.

In order to carry out a predictive analysis, only the tests at ages 8 and 10 were considered. On all three tests, the percentile scores at the two ages were significantly correlated (Tapping $r = \cdot 32$; Spiral $r = \cdot 37$; Porteus $r = \cdot 35$). It was therefore decided to use the averages of the scores at 8 and 10 as the most accurate available measures. All three psychomotor scores were related to future delinquency (Tapping $r_{bis} = \cdot 15$; Spiral $r_{bis} = \cdot 19$; Porteus $r_{bis} = \cdot 15$; see also Appendix A, factors 98–108).

The three psychomotor measures were positively intercorrelated (Spiral and Porteus $r = \cdot 40$; Porteus and Tapping $r = \cdot 19$; Spiral and Tapping $r = \cdot 07$). A combined rating of psychomotor clumsiness was derived from each boy by averaging his percentile placings on the three individual measures.

[2] *Measuring Height, Weight, and Strength of Grip*

Height and weight were measured on the three occasions the boys were seen in their schools, at ages 8, 10 and 14. The methods of measurement used, and the corrections for the slightly differing ages at interview, have been described by West (1969, p. 33). Heights and weights were separately scored on 8-point scales at age 8 and on 12-point scales at age 10, according to the boys' percentile rankings in relation to a frequency distribution obtained from a normal sample. At age 14, the raw heights and weights were used in the analysis. At all three ages, heights and weights proved to have slight but significant negative correlations with delinquency, the shorter and lighter boys tending to become delinquents. (For height and weight respectively, the correlations were: at age 8, $r_{bis} = -\cdot 13, -\cdot 15$; at age 10, $r_{bis} = -\cdot 12, -\cdot 14$; at age 14, $r_{bis} = -\cdot 13, -\cdot 14$; see also Appendix A, factors 112–115).

In order to investigate the predictive value of the measurements of height and weight taken at ages 8 and 10, the boys were grouped into heavily built, balanced and lightly built categories. At age 8, 159 boys were classified as heavily built, because their height scores were below their weight scores, while 81 were lightly built on opposite grounds. More boys were heavily built because the Study sample tended to be shorter than, but just as heavy as, the normal schoolboy population (West, 1969, p. 34). The preponderance of heavily built boys was still evident at age 10 (181 as opposed to 122). At neither age level was there any significant excess of future delinquents among the heavily built boys.

The final categorization of 139 'heavily built' boys was a combined estimate from the two age levels, but there was still no association between delinquency and a heavy physique. Furthermore, this measure of physique was not significantly related to any of the major factors of income, family size, parental criminality, parental behaviour or intelligence, and delinquents and non-delinquents did not differ in physique when matched on any of these factors.

At age 10, using a dynamometer supplied by Stanley Cox, Ltd. of London, each boy's strength of grip was measured. The boy was told to grasp the gadget without touching the dial or resting his arm on the table, and to squeeze as hard as he could. No practice was permitted, since a rapid fatigue effect is normal. The result was recorded first for the right hand and then for the left, and the average of the two readings was taken as the boy's strength. The score was coded on an 8-point scale, to express each boy's strength of grip in relation to that of other boys of similar size. The sum of each boy's quartile placings on height and weight was used as a rough index of size. These grip strength scores were not correlated with delinquency ($r_{bis} = \cdot 05$). From among the 181 heavily built boys at age 10, 91 were identified as probable mesomorphs, on the grounds that they had above average grip scores.

At age 14, the ponderal index (i.e. height divided by the cube root of weight) was used as a measure of physique. No significant relationship with delinquency emerged when those with above and below average ponderal indices were compared (18·9 per cent of 191, as opposed to 22·5 per cent of 191; $\chi^2 = \cdot 58$).

[3] *A Comment on Eysenck's Theory*

Eysenck considered two separate fear drives in his theory. The fear drive aroused by aversive conditioning was supposed to add to the fear associated with an anxious neurotic personality. It would be simpler to postulate only one fear drive, and to suggest that punishment would arouse more fear in neurotics than in normals. On this assumption, it would follow that neurotics, whether extraverts or introverts, would be relatively less likely to become criminals. Eysenck chose more complicated assumptions leading to different predictions.

[4] *Reliability of the Personality Measures*

All three personality tests measured neuroticism and extraversion, but the 'Cards' test was the least satisfactory. It was constructed especially for the present Study, and has not been used elsewhere. It proved too difficult for the comprehension of many of the 8-year-olds. The other two tests were well standardized instruments. The NJMI was merely the Junior Maudsley Personality Inventory (Furneaux and Gibson, 1961) with a lie scale added. It was scored according to published norms at age 14, and on the slightly shortened scales derived by Gibson (1967b) at age 10.

Despite the inconsistency of the results for different ages concerning the 'lying' of delinquents (see p. 114), the various lie scores were more closely correlated than either the extraversion scores or the neuroticism scores. The test–retest correlations for the NJMI between ages 10 and 14 were rather small (for neuroticism, $r = \cdot 33$; for extraversion, $r = \cdot 28$; for the lie score, $r = \cdot 44$). It may be that whatever is being measured by the NJMI over the four-year period of development does not remain stable, or alternatively the test may be unreliable.

[5] *Evaluation of Nervousness in Boys*

The PSWs made their assessments by questioning mothers, although in some cases the mothers' accounts were supplemented by information from medical records. In their ratings of minimal or moderate degrees of nervous disorder, there were indications that problems of communication had led to some confusion and bias. For instance, although reading difficulties might be expected to be more prevalent among nervous boys, those rated moderately or minimally nervous included a smaller proportion of poor readers than those said to be symptom-free (West, 1969, p. 169). The category of severely nervous was less ambiguous, because it applied to boys with a multiplicity of obvious symptoms. The analysis was therefore limited to the 41 severely nervous boys. They certainly included a high proportion of poor readers, and boys in the lowest quarter on Matrices IQ were also over-represented ($\chi^2 = 9 \cdot 76$, $p < \cdot 005$).

There was some consistency in the social workers' assessments of nervousness, because ratings by PSWs at age 8–9 were significantly correlated with later reports by other social workers at ages 10 and 14. Nervous boys also tended to have nervous mothers (as measured by questionnaire and interview combined: see p. 76).

Nervousness in boys was closely associated with another of the PSWs' assessments, a classification of the boys into 'outgoing' 'average' or 'withdrawn' personalities. The 95 outgoing boys were aggressively outgoing, cheeky, at ease or not rattled in social situations, while the 83 withdrawn boys were shy, easily embarrassed, ill at ease in social situations, standoffish, withdrawn or living in fantasy. The boys identified as withdrawn tended also to be identified as nervous.

Setting aside boys not rated on one or both factors, 37 of the 83 withdrawn boys were among the 91 moderately or severely nervous. The assessment 'nervous-withdrawn' was a combination of these two measures.

[6] *Delinquency Rates in Different Wards*

The delinquency rates were expressed as the annual number of first offenders per 100 boys in each ward. The numbers of Study boys residing in the five wards were 143, 94, 29, 44 and 45 respectively. We did not obtain delinquency rates for these wards when the boys were first contacted. However, we were able to make a good estimate later through the courtesy of a local Community Project, who supplied information on the number of boys living in each ward who were first convicted during 1968. We computed the rate for each ward by comparing these figures with the ward populations, as given in the 1966 Census. There was no reason to suppose that the wards had changed their position in the delinquency league in the years that had elapsed since our boys were initially contacted.

[7] *Primary Schools and Subsequent Delinquency*

In comparing the six primary schools, we discounted the 22 boys of the pilot group who came from the first school, since they were all taken from a high stream within the school, and were therefore untypical in many respects. Only one of the 22 became a juvenile delinquent. With this adjustment, the numbers of boys in the six schools (labelled A–F by West, 1969, p. 157), and the percentages who became delinquents, were 13·8 per cent of 80, 18·3 per cent of 93, 25·7 per cent of 70, 19·7 per cent of 61, 26·1 per cent of 46 and 29·6 per cent of 27 respectively. The first school contributed a rather low percentage of delinquents, but, owing to the small numbers involved, it was not significantly different from any other.

The above figures do not include the 12 boys recruited from an ESN school (see p. 1), five of whom became delinquents.

VIII

The Prediction of Delinquency

1. *Prediction from Data Obtained at Age 8 to 10*

True prediction involves taking measurements before the onset of delinquency. We actually did this, but many researches loosely called predictive, including that of the Gluecks (p. 134), have not been truly prospective. True prediction also means deciding in advance which factors are important, and making forecasts before the event. Even in prospective studies, investigators sometimes wait for the delinquents to emerge, and then decide what weights to assign to different factors, or what combinations of factors to use, in working out their 'predictions'. Such retrospective exercises are not true predictions. They do, however, give a useful estimate of the maximum possible predictive efficiency that might have been attained if the researchers had been able to decide in advance on the relative importance of their measures.

The first six entries in Table VIII (1) consist of true predictive measures which were actually worked out, or could in principle have been worked out, before the official delinquency records were known. The first four groups of boys were defined and discussed in a previous publication (West, 1969). They consisted of 93 boys from low income families, 55 from socially handicapped backgrounds (i.e. a combination of low income, poor housing and similar factors; see p. 30), 83 rated poor in conduct at age 8–10 (on the combined assessments of teachers and PSWs) and 77 'acting out' boys. This last group was identified by taking into account poor conduct ratings, unpopularity among peers, personality test scores indicative of 'neurotic-extraversion' and attendance at an ESN school (see West, 1969, p. 54).

All four measures proved predictive to a statistically significant degree, in so far as they identified groups containing twice as many delinquents as in the rest of the sample. However, since the proportion of delinquents in a vulnerable group never reached 50 per cent, it was not possible to forecast with confidence that any particular individual would become a delinquent. Taking into account the varying sizes of the groups, no measure was clearly superior. This is hardly surprising, because the four groups overlapped considerably.

Of the predictors so far mentioned, conduct disorder was an index of behaviour, while income and social handicap were measures of social circumstances. These aspects represent two theoretically distinct methods of prediction (Toby, 1961). The first method should be more accurate, for 'nothing predicts behaviour like behaviour'

TABLE VIII (1)

Effectiveness of Predictive Measures

Predictive Measures:	*'Worst' category*		*Remainder of sample*		*Significance test*	
	Becoming delinquents (%)	*Total in category*	*Becoming delinquents* (%)	*Total in category*	χ^1	p<
Combined conduct disorder	39·8	83	15·6	328	22·4	·001
Acting out	39·0	77	16·2	334	18·6	·001
Social handicap	43·6	55	16·9	356	19·4	·001
Low income	33·3	93	16·7	318	11·3	·001
Troublesomeness	44·6	92	13·5	319	40·5	·001
Troublesomeness + 8 factors	46·3	95	12·7	316	48·8	·001
5 Background factors	49·2	63	15·2	348	35·8	·001
Troublesomeness + 5 factors	44·9	89	13·7	322	40·1	·001

(Kvaraceus, 1966, p. 108). However, conduct disorder was not clearly more efficient as a predictor than social handicap. This may have been due to the inaccuracy of the PSWs' assessments of conduct, which depended on secondhand reports by mothers. Even though in some instances they may be less efficient, predictions from background circumstances are more relevant to explanations of delinquency than are predictions from incipient delinquent conduct.

The fifth entry in Table VIII (1) shows the best single predictor of delinquency. This was the rating of troublesomeness, described in Chapter VI, which was based upon the judgments of classmates at age 10, and of teachers at both 8 and 10. Of the 92 'troublesome' boys, 41 became delinquents, including 25 juvenile recidivists.

Due to delays in transcribing and analysing the information, the troublesomeness ratings were not available when the previous book was written, but the data on which they were based were all in existence when the boys were aged 10, and the method of calculating the scores owed nothing to subsequent events. It seems reasonable, therefore, to regard these assessments as truly predictive, since they could in principle have been produced at the same time as the other measures. The superiority of troublesomeness as a predictor was not unexpected. If it had been calculated earlier, it would almost certainly have been earmarked as the most promising predictor of future delinquency. Troublesomeness reflected behaviour which could be regarded as an incipient form of delinquency, and the ratings incorporated the views of two sets of teachers, as well as those of peers. Furthermore, troublesomeness did not depend upon the PSWs' assessments of conduct, which were thought to be inaccurate.

Still considering the possibility of a 'true' prediction, it is reasonable to see whether troublesomeness could have been combined with other measures in an effort to improve its predictive value. In deriving a combination, it is necessary to ignore the results which are now known, and to consider the data as it was at age 10. Given that troublesomeness reflects incipient delinquency, it would have been plausible to assume that the background factors most closely related to troublesomeness would also be related to future delinquency. Eight factors were very significantly related to troublesomeness ($p < \cdot 001$: see Appendix C), namely (1) daring, (2) dishonesty, (3) poor parental supervision, (4) low family income, (5) large family size, (6) criminal parents, (7) clumsiness and (8) low intelligence. Since, at the time, there would have been no way of knowing whether some of these might prove better predictors than others, the only practical method of deriving a combined measure would have been to give equal weight to each. A combined score was therefore obtained by counting the total number of these adverse characteristics (including troublesomeness) possessed by each boy. The delinquent-prone group consisted of 95 boys who were given at least 4 adverse ratings out of 9 (or the equivalent percentage if less than 9 factors were rated).

In spite of the fact that each of the individual factors in the combination proved to be significantly associated with future delinquency, it was no better as a predictor than troublesomeness by itself

(46·3 per cent of the 95 became delinquents: see Table VIII (1)). The combined score and the single troublesomeness score correlated with delinquency to much the same extent (r_{bis} = ·55 and ·54 respectively). This result is in keeping with the view that bad behaviour is the best predictor of delinquency, and that additionally taking into account individual characteristics and background circumstances adds virtually nothing to the statistical efficiency of the prediction.

Finally, we decided to do some retrospective exercises. With the benefit of hindsight, we could choose a combination of just those factors which had proved most closely, and to some extent independently, related to future delinquency. Apart from the troublesomeness rating, there were five early background factors that stood out. These were (1) criminal parents, (2) low family income, (3) large family size, (4) poor parental behaviour and (5) low intelligence. A combined score based on troublesomeness and these five background factors was worked out, giving all six measures equal weight. The numbers were too small for an attempt to assign optimal weights (see Note 1). This combination, shown as the last entry in Table VIII (1), was again no more effective than troublesomeness on its own. The implication seems to be that for the purpose of predicting delinquency, there is little point in measuring anything other than pre-delinquent behaviour.

From the point of view of explaining delinquency, pre-delinquent behaviour is of little interest. However, if background factors existing before pre-delinquent behaviour are predictive, this is an important clue to possible causes. The five background factors mentioned in the previous paragraph were therefore amalgamated into yet another combined score, with troublesomeness ignored. As shown by the penultimate entry in Table VIII (1), this combination was about as accurate a predictor as the others. Of the 63 boys with adverse ratings on three of these factors, 31 (49·2 per cent) became delinquents, 20 of them juvenile recidivists. This proved that early background factors, some of which might be susceptible to alteration by social action, had a very important influence upon the likelihood of a boy becoming delinquent. The possession of three or more out of five easily identified unfavourable features more than trebled the chance of becoming a juvenile delinquent.

2. *The Accuracy of Delinquency Prediction*

The importance of the five background features as precursors (and possibly causes) of delinquency is the kind of result that cannot be ignored in the construction of theories about delinquency. It does not mean, however, that any individual boy is inevitably predestined from an early age to go one way or the other. Such a conclusion would hardly be credible, in view of the many influences which operate at later ages. There is also an element of chance. A substantial proportion of one-time delinquents are no worse in behaviour, and presumably no worse in background, than many of their peers who have been lucky enough to escape conviction.

The predictive factors isolated in this Study still leave a large measure of indeterminacy. Only about half the vulnerable group (31 out of 63) actually became delinquents, and most of the future delinquents (53 out of 84) did not belong to it. For the sake of correctly identifying 31 future delinquents, 32 boys would be incorrectly labelled, and 53 delinquents would be missed. This severely limits the use of prediction for practical, administrative purposes. If potential delinquents are being identified in order to apply some preventive treatment, it might be preferable, so as to avoid wasting limited resources, to concentrate on a small group of extremely delinquent-prone boys, such as those who possessed all five adverse background factors.

Figure VIII (1) illustrates graphically the importance of some of these background factors as determinants of juvenile delinquency, the extent of the overlap between factors and the rapidly cumulative effect of one or more adversities. Only three of the five background factors are shown, because it is difficult to include more on a flat diagram. Whichever three are taken, the results are much the same. The total area of the square figure represents the entire sample of 411 boys, of whom 84 (20·4 per cent) became delinquents. Within this square, the areas enclosed in shaded circles represent the numbers of boys affected by each of three adversities, parental criminality, poor parental behaviour and low family income. Within each of these circles, about a third of the boys became delinquents.

There were 209 boys outside the circles who did not possess any of the three adversities, and only 12·0 per cent of them became delinquents. Of 38 boys from poor families who were free from the other unfavourable influences, 21·1 per cent became delinquents. Of

34 boys from poor families who were also subjected to poor parental behaviour, 53·0 per cent became delinquents. Only 14 boys suffered all three adversities, but a substantial majority of them (71·4 per cent) became delinquents.

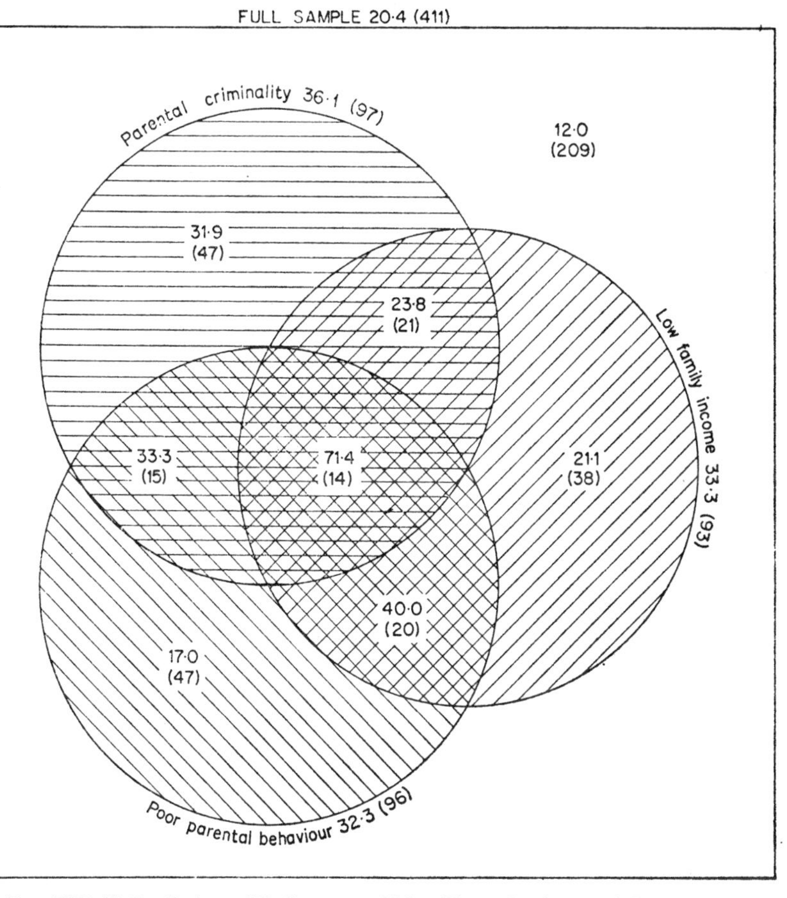

FIG. VIII (I) Prediction of Delinquency Using Home Background Factors

This cumulative effect of undesirable features is reminiscent of the findings of Robins and Hill (1966), who studied delinquency in a cohort of 296 coloured American boys born in St. Louis in 1930–4. They showed that educational retardation, truancy and low socio-economic status (assessed on the occupation of the boy's guardian) were all associated with delinquency before age 15. Where none of these factors was present, only 3 per cent became delinquents, in comparison with 36 per cent in the presence of all three.

At first sight, the limited predictive efficiency of the home background factors compares poorly with claims made for the Glueck prediction system. However, a closer examination of the figures suggests that the Glueck Social Prediction Table (Glueck and Glueck, 1950) is not really more effective. The Glueck predictions

TABLE VIII (2)

The Gluecks' Predictive Measure

	Number of delinquents	*Number of non-delinquents*	*Total boys*	*Delinquents (%)*
(a) *Gluecks' Sample*				
Low score*	24	269	293	8·2
Medium score†	162	138	300	54·0
High Score‡	265	32	297	89·2
Total boys	451	439	890	50·7
(b) *Hypothetical Sample§*				
Low score*	24	1,076	1,100	2·2
Medium score†	162	552	714	22·7
High score‡	265	128	393	67·4
Total boys	451	1,756	2,207	20·4
(c) *Validation Sample¶*				
Low score*	7	119	126	5·6
Medium score†	19	78	97	19·6
High score‡	14	3	17	82·4
Total boys	40	200	240	16·7

* Less than 200 on the Gluecks' scale.
† Between 200 and 299 on the Gluecks' scale.
‡ 300 or more on the Gluecks' scale.
§ Derived from the Gluecks' sample by multiplying the number of non-delinquents by 4 to change the percentage of delinquents from 50 to 20.
¶ Craig and Glick (1963).

were based on five family background factors, namely discipline of boy by father, supervision of boy by mother, affection of mother for boy, affection of father for boy and cohesiveness of family. Their results, comparing 451 delinquents and 439 non-delinquents, are shown in Table VIII (2) (a). Dividing their sample into three, the worst third had roughly a 90 per cent chance of delinquency, the middle third a 50 per cent chance and the best third only a 10 per cent chance.

This appears to be a much better prediction than that obtained with the five factors we identified. It must, however, be realized that the Gluecks were dealing with an artificially enriched sample containing 50 per cent delinquents. Their probable results with a sample comprising only 20 per cent delinquents can be estimated by multiplying all their figures for non-delinquents by four. The outcome is shown in Table VIII (2) (b). In a hypothetical sample with a 20 per cent delinquency rate, only 67 per cent of the Gluecks' 'vulnerable' group would have been delinquents, a result little better than ours. Furthermore, it must be borne in mind that the Gluecks' delinquents were rather extreme cases, taken from penal institutions. It is safe to assume that if they had studied, as we did, all delinquents (even those with only one conviction), the contrasts between their 'vulnerable' and 'non-vulnerable' groups would have been less. Again, in devising their scores, the Gluecks capitalized rather heavily on chance, by weighting their categories according to the proportion of delinquents in each. Finally, since their survey was not prospective, their ratings might have been biased by knowing who were delinquents.

The true efficiency of the Glueck predictors should be evaluated by applying their Social Prediction Table prospectively in a longitudinal survey. This was done by the New York City Youth Board (Craig and Glick, 1963), using the same definition of delinquency as the Gluecks. Their results are displayed in Table VIII (2) (c). Only a small minority of their sample (7 per cent) fell into the 'high score' group, although 82 per cent of them did become persistent delinquents. These figures indicate that it is possible to pin-point a small minority of highly delinquent-prone boys. However, the majority of the delinquents could not be identified without also identifying a substantial number of non-delinquents. Craig and Glick's results showed that, in order to identify correctly 60 per cent of the delinquents (24), it was necessary to mis-label as potential delinquents 33 boys who were in fact non-delinquents. This is almost the same degree of accuracy as the prediction from our own five background factors.

The Glueck Social Prediction Table has been tested in another longitudinal study (see Appendix H), the Maximum Benefits Project in Washington (Tait and Hodges, 1971). Unlike the New York survey, the results cannot be directly compared with our own, because the children followed up were nominated by their teachers as potential delinquents. As it turned out, there were 81 boys who became juvenile delinquents, 77 of whom were correctly predicted by the Glueck Table. On the other hand, of 35 boys in the sample who did not become juvenile delinquents, 26 were predicted to be delinquents. Thus, there was a substantial error in the direction of over-prediction of delinquency.

3. *Delinquents without Background Handicaps?*

A study of individual case histories might reveal why certain boys became delinquents unexpectedly. As described earlier (p. 131), a combined score, based upon the five criminogenic factors of low income, large family size, criminal parents, poor parental behaviour and low intelligence, served to identify 63 boys as potential delinquents. A substantial proportion of those found guilty as juveniles (31 out of 84), including a majority of the recidivists (20 out of 37), came from the group of 63. This still left 53 delinquents (including 17 recidivists) who did not appear to have the background handicaps commonly associated with delinquency. Why did these boys become delinquents?

The 53 boys who became juvenile delinquents against prediction were in fact a less seriously delinquent group than the 31 who were correctly identified. They were, on average, convicted only half as often (89 convictions, or 1·68 per boy, as opposed to 102 convictions, or 3·29 per boy), and fewer of them had convictions as adults (34·0 per cent of 53, compared with 58·1 per cent of 31).

Of the 53 unexpected delinquents, the most anomalous were a small group of five, who became juvenile recidivists in spite of the fact that none of them had been rated badly on any of the five factors associated with delinquency. Nevertheless, their offence histories seemed quite typical of recidivists in general, and four of them had been assessed as troublesome at an early age by classmates and teachers (see pp. 99–100).

Looking back through the case records of these five recidivists, it became apparent that in some instances their backgrounds had escaped adverse comment largely because information was lacking, rather than because they were thought to be particularly favoured. In four of the five cases, the parents were unsatisfactory informants; indeed, two cases belonged to the small minority (of 22) whose parents totally refused to cooperate with the PSWs. In at least three of the five cases, information came to light subsequently which, if it had been known at the time, would probably have made the assessments more adverse, at least in regard to parental attitudes and performance. Here are some examples:

Case 932
The PSW reported 'great difficulty' in securing this mother's cooperation and many attempts to see her failed. She was thought to be a reluctant and unreliable informant who contradicted herself. At the time she was first seen, when the boy was 8 years old, all her attention was focussed on his backwardness in reading, and she would talk of little else. She was thought to be a neurotic woman with 'many problems', loving towards the boy, but 'anxious, over-protective, guilty and defensive'. She mentioned that the boy had some phobias and other nervous symptoms, but not until two years later did she admit that he had had attention at a child guidance clinic and that he was suffering from enuresis, which was continuous every night. She reported that she had had to bring up the boy without the help of a husband. She said the father had become unfaithful to her and she had divorced him when her son was only a year old. The boy was largely looked after by his maternal grandmother in his early years, but she died when he was aged 7.

Subsequent information suggested that this was a disturbed boy from a stressful home. At age 13, he was admitted to a psychiatric treatment unit on account of continuous bed-wetting and various compulsions. At that time, mother was assessed as anxious and nagging, and was advised to take a tranquilliser. She had re-married a year earlier. At age 15, the boy was again admitted to hospital 'as an emergency in view of mother's deteriorating psychiatric condition and his worsening behaviour, e.g. frequent truanting and refusal to return home'. He was still bed-wetting nightly. He was observed to be tense and demanding when in his parents' company, but more relaxed at other times, though ready to throw a temper if thwarted.

Seen at age 18, this boy was superficially more settled, and still living with mother and step-father, of whom he spoke warmly: 'They are both terrific. . . . I get on with mother all right really. She's a bit highly strung. . . .'. He was a recidivist delinquent, and had taken part in a substantial sequence of housebreakings, but he claimed to be a reformed character. He admitted defrauding his employers of several pounds every week, but maintained that this was traditional in his type of work.

Case 290
After two years of contact with this boy's home, the PSW noted: 'Mother is always very friendly and welcoming when I do see her, but there is always some difficulty about making appointments. . . . Why there is this pattern remains a mystery. I think there is more hostility and resistance from mother than one reckoned on.'

The PSW considered mother mildly neurotic, suffering from depression and insomnia. Father was reticent, and the PSW found him difficult to assess. Mother thought he over-indulged the boy, giving him everything he wanted. The PSW thought that mother was also very fond of the boy, but over-anxious and protective. Her marriage was thought to be 'very united and happy'. The home was spacious, well kept and furnished, and reported family income was adequate.

Some years later, when the boy was aged 15 and was on probation for stealing, a less favourable picture of his home background emerged from a discussion with his probation officer. Father was thought to be a rather diffident, inadequate, meek man, and the probation officer was struck by the total lack of closeness between father and son despite a lot of time spent together. Mother was thought to be over-anxious, pushing and controlling, while the boy was polite but reserved and defensive. Well aware of his parents' investment in his education and the social prestige it gave them, the boy seemed to be using truanting and work evasion as a means of manipulating and punishing his parents.

When the boy was 16¾, a social worker re-interviewed the mother and noted that, following her son's delinquency, mother showed a 'sense of shame and depression so great that she had scarcely been out of the house for four weeks. . . . Her immediate response to the crisis seems to have been to give up her job; she was unable to face the sympathy and concern of her colleagues. She had spent the greater part of the intervening weeks sitting brooding in a darkened room'. The PSW thought that 'mother's retreat is an indirect and effective method of punishing her son'. 'She is an extremely controlling woman, and there are marked elements of rejection in her response. Other people's opinions are enormously important to her, and she tries to shape his behaviour to meet their expectations. . . . In many ways she is very rejecting and belittling. For example, his major interest and activity at the moment is [military training], but mother dismisses this because 'it will get him nowhere'. . . . Her reaction to his friendship with [a girl] was far from positive; indeed, she was clearly rather shocked. . . .'

At age 18, having experienced two periods in penal institutions, this boy commented as follows upon his parents' past attitudes: 'Mother has got more of a Victorian attitude towards me and I think to my generation in particular. . . . [With father I] used to get on really lousy. We were always at each other's throats. I would walk out 9 times out of 10 slamming the door . . . and come back late paralytic drunk.' Regarding his parents' reaction to his first conviction, he said: 'They were very shocked, very disappointed. We didn't speak to each other for a while. My father stands up for me as much as he can, but he doesn't want to offend my mother.' He then went on to recall how his father used to slip him money for drink or cigarettes, telling him not to tell his mother or let her see them. 'He used to play both sides of the fiddle.'

The next two cases (690 and 541) were totally uncooperative families in which parental behaviour had been rated 'not known'.

Case 690
The parents persistently rejected all approaches and refused to have any dealings with the Study. The boy's headmaster thought the parents had a 'chip on the shoulder', and he was uneasy about their children, but he could not be more specific. Father and mother were both working, and were living in adequate, self-contained accommodation.

More information became available when the boy was aged 14 and was sent to a remand home following his third conviction. The probation officer who made inquiries thought that he was a listless lad whose apathy towards his parents and tendency to shrug off difficulties might be due to emotional deprivation. His offences apparently commenced after the loss of a special friend, who left the area, and following the death of an aunt to whom he was attached. At the remand home he was considered an easily influenced, weak-willed boy who was nervous, immature and poor in educational attainment compared with his satisfactory IQ rating. The psychiatrist felt that he might have been overshadowed by his elder brother, who had never given any trouble, and who possibly received more attention from the mother than he did. The PSW at the remand home found the mother 'difficult to assess from the point of view of warmth and depth of emotion. She obviously found her elder son easier to understand, but then he was quiet, well-behaved and evidently a steady type. . . .' Mother described herself as 'more highly strung and quick tempered than father'. Mother was vague and forgetful about the boy's early development. She said he used to wet the bed up to 12 years of age and she scolded him a lot for that. She thought the boy's father was placid and too permissive with his son. She and her husband got on well together, although they had disagreements, often over disciplining the children, but they never kept up the quarrels.

This picture of somewhat cool, unconcerned parents was to some extent confirmed by the boy's comments when he was interviewed at age 18. Asked if he liked living at home with his parents, he commented, 'It's cheaper.' Asked how he got on with them, he replied laconically 'All right [with mum]—we have a couple of rows. OK [with dad] . . . Dad's at work most of the time and I don't see him that much apart from Sunday.' Asked about his parent's reactions to his convictions, he said the first time they both 'just had a right go at me. A couple of wallopings you know'. The second time 'They just had a go at me again. Kept me in again for a week.' The third time 'They never said hardly anything. They just said "serve you right if you get put away".' When later on he was convicted for drunkenness 'They just laughed about it.'

The parents in this case were classed as non-criminal because no convictions were recorded up to the boy's tenth birthday, but the following year father was convicted for stealing. At the age of 16, the elder brother, who was said to be so well-behaved, was convicted for fare avoidance.

In this second example of a totally uncooperative family, detailed information about the home was never forthcoming. However, unlike the cases so far quoted, the few facts that came to light suggested no very adverse circumstances, save for an over-anxious neurotic mother.

Case 541
Mother was an anxious, nervous woman. Both parents worked, but otherwise mother was largely house-bound, with neurotic phobias. She had her own mother tell the PSW that questions got her confused and worked up, so that she worried herself sick at the thought of an impending interview. This was the reason given at the outset for a total refusal to cooperate. The home was seen to be nicely kept and furnished, and there was a family car. In her brief contact with the PSW, mother commented that her husband was 'Too slow and thorough and more fussy than I am.'

When the boy was aged 15, and following his first trouble with the police for stealing, mother was visited by a social worker. Her nervousness persisted, and she said that, for several days after the police called about her son's delinquency, she had not been able to eat or sleep properly. Both parents were very shocked and upset, and the father was extremely angry. He had felt he could not trust the boy since, and had restricted him in various ways, like cancelling a camping holiday. Mother felt this to be a mistake. However, she thought the boy got on well with his father and talked with his father about a lot of things.

Seen at age 18, the boy was somewhat reticent. He was still living with his parents, with whom he said he got on all right. 'I couldn't live on me own at the moment.'

He was, in fact, a recidivist delinquent. At age 17, when he was on probation, his probation officer noted that, in spite of persistent denials of any family problems, some dramatic facts came to the surface after a remand for a stealing offence. 'There was tremendous unrest between the parents, though neither expressed this particularly forcibly. Father admitted to compulsive gambling. . . . Mother seemed bored and cooped up at home, and was constantly anxious and nervy. . . . The parents have probably been griping at each other for years, unable to stop doing this, but frequently each very unhappy as a result.' The boy left home to live with his girlfriend's family. Her father was co-defendant when he was convicted.

The last of the five examples of recidivists without background handicaps was a truly anomalous and puzzling case. The parents were cooperative from the outset, the information available was apparently full and reliable, the boy seemed to have a good home in all important respects, and yet he was persistently in trouble:

Case 763

Both parents were 'helpful and cooperative' with the PSW. Their financial and housing situation was 'very secure'. The house was spotless —'like a museum piece'. The parents were thought to 'get on very well' together. Father was assessed as well-meaning and very indulgent in his attitude to the children, being convinced that giving them all the things he missed himself was the best he could do for them. Mother was thought to be concerned about her son and over-protective, but also critical of him. At different interviews, she was variously described as using 'a lot of abuse and threats' and being 'now full of praise, all trouble disappeared'. The boy had one elder sister, a placid, trouble-free girl working successfully, and very attached to and generous with her parents.

Mother reported many problems with this boy. She was anxious during pregnancy because the baby was lying abnormally, and a Caesarean section was needed. A few years previously, she had had a malformed still-birth. She feared she had fussed and spoiled him as an infant and let him cling too much. At six months, he had a severe febrile illness, and meningitis was suspected but disproved. As a young child, he was restless, disliked sleeping alone, and had some phobias. As a schoolboy, he was 'always in scraps', inclined to wander and truant, and was at first most unwilling to leave his mother to attend school. Later he settled down, and was said to like school and to be very active and successful at sports.

The family was revisited when the boy was nearing 13 years of age. He was reported at that time to have turned against school, and to be working badly. He had become defiant and rebellious towards his mother, and his previously indulgent father was now having to be quite strict. The following year, his fighting and rebelliousness at school were so bad that he was expelled. He acquired convictions for both aggressive and stealing offences.

Interviewed at 18, he was rather off-hand about the information he gave, but maintained that he was all right living at home: 'I think it's easier to have your mum cook for you. There are no rows, nothing serious.' He admitted, however, that following a second conviction for stealing his father was 'a bit choked—he hit me like—the first time he ever did'. A more recent conviction for theft (which he described as 'receiving from a relative') did not disturb his father so much. 'My old man gets a lot of nicked gear. It could easily happen to him.'

In addition to the five recidivists quoted above, there were 14 one-time juvenile delinquents who appeared to have none of the five critical background handicaps. Looking through these cases, it again became apparent that, in spite of the absence of the usual predictive criteria, some of the boys had been exposed to unsettling home circumstances. For example, five of the 14 boys (070, 080, 590, 811, 904) were from homes broken by parental separation or desertion. In two other cases (891, 980), parental behaviour was not rated because the PSWs could not persuade the parents to give the necessary information. Here are three examples from this group:

Case 891
Mother granted a door-step interview only and asserted that all was well with the family, but was manifestly hostile to enquiries and unwilling to enter into any discussion. Subsequently she was always 'out' whenever a social worker tried to call. This proved one of the most elusive families in the whole Study. Both at 16 years and at 18 years of age, despite repeated requests, the boy was one of the very few who refused to be interviewed.

Although, when the boy was aged 10, the parents were correctly classed as non-criminal, mother was subsequently convicted on several charges of larceny.

The most noticeable feature was the family's reluctance to open the door to callers. During enquiries at age 16 and 18, the boy was actually seen by prospective interviewers on only two occasions, although over 30 calls were made to the home. The family had a special 'spy hole' constructed in their door. The boy was described by a workmate as 'shy and withdrawn'.

Case 080
This boy had only one official juvenile conviction at age 16, for allowing himself to be driven in a vehicle that had been taken without consent. His involvement in delinquency was nevertheless quite considerable. He had received a police caution at age 15 for trying to gain entry to a cinema with tickets that had been stolen the night before. At age 13, he had been brought to court for persistent truancy and was put under a fit person order. At age 11, he had been warned by the police for stealing a comic from a stall. Again, at 13 he was warned for carrying an airgun in the street. He was also convicted at 16 for a motoring offence, namely aiding and abetting another person to drive while disqualified. On the self-reported delinquency test at 16, he admitted over 6 of the more serious offences.

His home background was less favourable than the predictive rating suggested. The score on parental behaviour was just one point below that necessary to bring the case into the poor behaviour category. The PSW, on initial visits when the boy was aged 8–9, noted that discipline was erratic, mother being highly strung and quick-tempered and alternating between praise and punishment. There were also rows between the parents, some of which were associated with the presence in the home of an interfering paternal grandmother. Moreover, father had been treated in a psychiatric hospital for a paranoid illness with delusions of jealousy centred on his wife.

Subsequently the father had further breakdowns and the parents separated. At first, father took the boy to the paternal grandparents' home, but later he was placed in a hostel by the local authority and then returned to his mother.

At age 14, a social worker visited the mother and noted 'She still seems to be making the boy pay for having chosen to go with his father. . . .' The boy was still living in a hostel and asking to be allowed to come home to her, but she was refusing, fearing that she might not be able to cope with the boy on her own if he proved difficult.

At age 18, when a prospective interviewer called, he found the family atmosphere still very tense. Although members of his family kept calling him, the boy was reluctant to come to the door. His mother said he spent most of his time alone in his room and mentioned that he was under hospital treatment for a nervous disorder.

Case 811

This boy had only one conviction at age 15, for attempted storebreaking. At age 12, however, his foster mother told a social worker that he was stealing money from home continuously and had been caught red-handed on many occasions. In order to frighten him, she had taken him to the local police to complain about it, but she had not charged him. She said he was truanting, and had forged a note from her pretending he was not well.

The boy's mother deserted when he was two, and he was taken over by elderly foster parents, who initially declined to cooperate with the Study, but were eventually won over. The foster mother suffered from chronic depression, and had been treated at a psychiatric hospital. Foster father was relatively placid and tolerant, but the foster mother reported that the boy was moody, wilful, defiant and stubborn, and that 'nothing short of a good hiding does any good'. Although not rated troublesome on the combined assessments of teachers and peers, the headmaster had told the foster father that the boy was unruly and unmanageable at school.

At age 12 the boy was referred to a child guidance clinic, where he was thought to be 'markedly insecure, dependent, with aggressive and fearful traits. However, he is unlikely to benefit from treatment here [because] his foster parents are against it'.

Interviewed at age 18, this youth appeared to have settled down considerably. He was working in a job he liked, and still living with his foster father, now a widower. He said 'I'd prefer to live somewhere else, but I've got to live with my dad . . . out of duty I have to stay.' He denied continued involvement in delinquent activities apart from the usual 'buying cheap' of things suspected stolen, such as whisky and motor cycle parts. The last misdemeanour he recalled was 'doing a cigarette machine about two years ago'.

The boys in the last two examples, like most of those with apparent background adversities, were substantially involved in delinquency in spite of having only one conviction. However, the majority of the 4 boys in this group were only marginally delinquent. In at least 6 cases (243, 492, 612, 632, 993 and 980), the delinquency conviction was rather trivial, and there was no evidence of persistent involvement. Only one of these (980) had been rated troublesome by peers and teachers. Here are some case histories:

Case 612
One criminal conviction only, at age 14, for taking and driving away a moped. His mother said it was not serious, he had just 'borrowed' the motor scooter for a ride. He said he and his friends decided to have a ride—'the main thing was the urge to drive'.

When he was 15, mother reported to the social worker that she and her husband were now pleased with the boy. Although he had truanted in the past, he had now settled down and was doing well at school. She thought there was no fear he would get into trouble again.

Seen at age 19, he was in regular work which he liked very much, and happily married. Apart from buying records cheaply from a questionable source, he denied any further involvement in delinquency.

Case 492
One conviction only at age 16, for allowing himself to be driven in a stolen car, for which he was given a conditional discharge. He said he was offered a lift by a friend and (as his friend had told the police) he did not know at the time that the car was stolen.

When this boy was 15, a social worker visited the home and noted that he 'certainly gives the impression of being a very happy and contented well-adjusted boy, fully occupied and very enthusiastic, with clear-cut ambitions, who finds school work easy and generally enjoys life'.

Interviewed at 18, he was in regular work, which he 'liked a lot' and he denied any involvement in delinquent acts.

Case 632
One conviction only at age 14 for larceny. He and some others climbed into the yard of some derelict premises and stole crates of empty beer bottles. The boy admitted subsequently that he and his school-friends used to steal bottles of mineral waters from the back of lorries.

Mother told the social worker she thought this episode was an isolated incident, but she felt it important the boy should see that both his parents would stand by him in this trouble. She was concerned because he had been truanting and fooling about in class, but she felt he would settle down as soon as he got into work.

Seen at age 18, the boy was in regular work, which he liked. He was spending most of his spare time with a steady girlfriend. Apart from 'buying cheap' articles suspected to have been stolen (a very common habit in the district), he denied any recent involvement in criminal activities.

The outcome of this examination of 19 anomalous cases was in some ways disappointing. When scrutinized closely, very few seemed really anomalous. Most of the boys whose delinquency was substantial did not seem to have such good parental backgrounds as the prediction ratings suggested. Unfavourable aspects of parental attitudes and behaviour or conflictual family relationships had apparently been missed. This was hardly surprising, in view of the difficulty of assessing intimate family matters, especially where (as in a number of these cases) the parents were reluctant or uncooperative informants. Of course, the suggestion that some adverse factors had been missed was a retrospective judgment, possibly influenced by the knowledge that the boys in question had become delinquents. It is easy to convince oneself that almost any family has some imperfections, but in these cases some of the family troubles that eventually came to light were clearly serious.

Where the prediction ratings faithfully reflected a good background, then the boy's delinquency tended to be trivial or short-lived. The very few cases that went against this rule (e.g. Case 763, p. 141) revealed no particular features that might explain the exceptions.

4. *Non-Delinquents from Bad Backgrounds*

The boys from adverse backgrounds who did not become delinquents were another group of anomalous cases. Of 63 boys identified as delinquent-prone, on the basis of having at least three out of five of the predictive factors adversely rated, 32 had no juvenile convictions. Not all of these were genuinely free from delinquent habits, since eight were convicted as young adults, and a further eight had contact with the police as juveniles.

There were, however, eight boys among the 32 from adverse backgrounds who were in the positively delinquent-resistant category. This was defined by the absence of any conviction or police contact, as well as by a low score on the self-reported delinquency tests (see pp. 163–5). These eight, being unusually good boys from unusually bad backgrounds, merit further examination. Their histories are summarized below:

Case 004

The family was first seen when the boy was 9. Mother was thought to be an extremely apathetic woman, who seemed to have no emotional rapport with her children and to know very little about the boy. She said he was a timid boy, who always came home from school on his own and never visited other children. He had recently been in hospital for a serious illness. He was very backward, and never seemed interested in anything or able to occupy himself. He had been treated for a speech defect. Father was away in the regular army, and was said to take no interest in his children, who hardly knew him. The family were very poorly housed. Mother had formed a relationship with another man. A few years later, the parents were divorced. The boy had three older brothers, one treated at a psychiatric clinic and all delinquents.

After transfer to a special school, the boy ceased to be any trouble in the classroom. He was quiet and easily controlled, but often absent due to illnesses. Interviewed at 18, he was thought to be very shy and backward, introverted and unresponding. He had few interests in life and little enthusiasm about anything, doing nothing other than his work. He was obsessed with the idea that he was going to die, and worried each night about going to sleep in case he did not wake up again. He denied any delinquency involvement, with the exception of failing to pay his bus fare a couple of times.

Case 031

The parents were reluctant informants, and gave the PSW little information. Mother said she didn't want her family made into a peep-show. Most of the information, therefore, came from outside agencies.

When our boy was aged 9, a probation officer's report said the father was an aggressive man and a strict disciplinarian, who described his marriage as a disastrous one. Mother, who had been deserted by a previous husband, was over-burdened with a large family that included several delinquents. Father wanted to be rid of some of the older children whose behaviour he found intolerable.

At age 11 the boy was classified as 'troublesome' on the opinions of peers and teachers. A note from a teacher at that time said 'There is some deep emotional trouble in this boy which brings on fits of temper. . . . He becomes defiant and can only be controlled by physical force.' At age 12, a teachers' report noted his continued untidy appearance and stated that 'his mother works, leaving home early, so that the boy must get up very early and sometimes cares for the younger children. . . . Slackness and inefficiency at home spoil things for this boy. . . . The parents would not cooperate with the junior school head by attending an interview. . . . This was typical.' At age 14, the psychologist who tested the boy at school described him as 'quiet in the suspicious non-cooperative sense. . . . Somewhat evasive and probably only truthful if he thinks it necessary.'

In spite of these unpromising beginnings, the boy improved in performance and behaviour at his secondary school. The final teacher's report, at age 15, although still noting 'clothing in constant need of repair', 'poor diction' and 'persistently late' also noted that he was 'average' on most of the attitude and behaviour items and that he had 'a well developed sense of humour and often shows a mature attitude towards life'. Seen at age 16, he was in regular work that he liked, and was attending youth clubs.

Case 180

This was obviously a very disturbed family. Father had had psychiatric treatment for a paranoid illness with morbid jealousy, and had served a term of imprisonment for attacking his wife. Both parents complained that the boy had rages in which he would hit out at anyone. In addition, he had a speech defect, for which he had been treated since the age of 5, as well as nightmares and obsessive-compulsive washing rituals. At age 11, he was psychiatrically investigated in hospital, on account of his violent behaviour. At school, he was said to be insolent, spiteful to other children, extremely mistrustful and backward in lessons. Epilepsy was suspected but not confirmed.

At age 13, following removal to a school where the head took a special interest in him, the boy's health and behaviour improved dramatically. At age 18, he denied any involvement in delinquent activities. He was still a rather inarticulate person, with difficulty in reading, but he was working very long hours, had completed an apprenticeship and was obviously interested in what he was doing.

Case 312

This was a problem family known to many social agencies. When the boy was aged 7, he was removed temporarily to a children's home on a fit person order. A woman police officer had given evidence before the juvenile court that she had found seven children in the house, all in a filthy state and badly clothed.

At age 10, when the PSW finally achieved a visit after several attempts, she found the home to be still dirty and smelling. Both parents were thought to be kind and loving, but completely permissive and lax. Mother was a hopeless manager. The boy's school attendance was very poor, and it was suspected that she was keeping him at home.

The boy was reported to be highly strung and very fearful. He was teased by other children at school. He was dull and scholastically very backward. At age 15, when the social worker visited the family for the last time, he was reported to be less nervous, but extremely shy and withdrawn. Mother had no fear that he would get into trouble with the police, because he had never been one to mix with other boys and spent his evenings at home watching television.

Interviewed at age 18, he was again thought to be very shy and withdrawn. He took a long time to answer questions and had difficulty in reading. He appeared to be a solitary person with no friends other than his brothers. The employment office had not been able to find him a job since leaving school, and this depressed him. He claimed he had never been involved in any delinquent activities, and seemed to be telling the truth. His only outdoor activities were walks and the cinema.

Case 491

This was a large, poor family living in unsatisfactory accommodation. When the boy was aged 10, the visiting PSW assessed the mother as very dull, exceedingly permissive and loving, but unable to control the children. Father was thought to be a much harsher, disciplinarian character. Subsequently, father decided to withdraw his cooperation and wrote asking for no further visits.

Mother was interviewed for the last time by a social worker when the boy was 16. It was noted that: 'All the children are very dependent on her, and as a result of this she is never free of them. She spoke of how worn out she gets with their continued demands, and her losing battle to try to control them. . . . She is so weak and ineffectual with the children that she was asking [her daughter aged 12] to stop the younger ones going out when she had failed to stop them herself.'

At the same interview, mother reported that the boy was very nervous. He bit his nails continually, and was so afraid of the dark that he often went to sleep with one of the other children. He still walked in his sleep frequently.

Interviewed at age 18, the boy denied any involvement in delinquent activities. He was still living with his parents and siblings and commented 'If I left home I wouldn't know where to turn. I would miss them.' He had changed jobs frequently, and was currently unemployed. He had been dismissed after a row with his foreman.

Case 802

This boy was one of a large, poor family. When he was 8 years of age, his father was fined because none of the seven children were attending school. Mother told the court that she could not afford to clothe the children and could not send them to school naked. Father said that since coming out of prison he had nothing but debts.

Mother told the PSW that this boy was 'a funny little thing—not like the others. . . . He runs into a corner if anyone calls. He is terribly nervous. . . . He's dead frightened to open his mouth. . . . He screams with fear when you take him to school. . . . Afraid of the dark and ghosts. . . . Petrified of fires'. A probation officer described him as looking very frightened, sitting crouched in the corner—rather girlish.

When the boy was 11, mother told the PSW that father would do nothing to help the children and was currently under psychiatric treatment for depression. Three of the boy's older siblings were recidivist delinquents.

After transfer to a special school, the boy's attendance temporarily improved. Interviewed at age 16, he was unemployed, but said he was quite happy at home. However, he expressed fears of the police. He felt he was being continually persecuted by them, being stopped in the street and questioned even though he had not done anything.

At age 18, when he was interviewed again, his life was still dominated by a phobia of the police. He said he always stayed close to home, and never went out without one of his brothers. He was still chronically unemployed, having walked out of several jobs because of his fears.

Case 830

At age 6 this boy and his brother were described as the dirtiest children in the school. They had to be sent to wash each day before lessons. At age 8, the Citizens' Advice Bureau had a complaint from a neighbour that her children were terrified of these brothers, who had threatened them with a knife. At age 8, when interviewed by a PSW, the parents denied any problems with their children. The parents were thought to be good natured but dull, and the home was poor and unkempt. Revisited at age 10, mother admitted to the PSW that the boys were getting out of hand, and that father was unwilling to discipline them.

She also reported that this boy was very sensitive, easily upset, quieter than his brother, and more attached to his mother. At age 10, the boy was placed in the 'troublesome' category, according to the opinions of peers and teachers. The teachers' reports revealed that he was untidy, dirty, backward and poor in application to work, but did not suggest that he was particularly unruly. Later teachers' reports, at age 12 and 14, suggested considerable improvement. At age 14, his teacher reported that he was a regular attender, a hard worker, never late, very concerned to be a credit to his parents and timid rather than quarrelsome or aggressive. At the same period, mother told the visiting social worker that he was now a good boy who was never in trouble and gave her no worry. He was spending a lot of his time with a youth organization. He seemed to have taken to heart his parents' warnings not to hang about with boys from the rough street in which they were living.

This boy stayed on at school until 18 years of age, although he had little success in examinations and his parents thought he should have left earlier. Interviewed soon after leaving school, he denied any involvement in delinquent acts. He was critical of his parents for the rather lax way they looked after him when he was young. He said he thought he had learned discipline at the youth organization which he attended regularly, and that this had kept him out of trouble.

Case 982

This boy's parents were described by the PSW as 'utterly unstable'. They had both been diagnosed at a psychiatric hospital as inadequate psychopaths. They were subject to frequent evictions and changes of address. Both parents were thought to use the boy to play each other up. The boy was periodically placed 'in care', where he would receive no visits or letters from his parents. He pretended indifference when other children were visited, but when finally his parents made contact he became very excitable, talked incessantly about them, and was quite desperate to return home.

When the boy was 9, mother told the PSW that he still soiled and wet himself sometimes. She said, 'He is sensitive, often in a daydream. . . . He gets very frightened by the TV, but he will go on looking.' It was noted that the boy had no friends and that mother hardly ever let him out of her sight.

By the time the family were seen again, when the boy was 14, his school attendance and overt emotional difficulties had subsided. He had formed a better contact with his father, but the social worker considered that he kept his thoughts to himself for fear of punishment. Seen at 16, the boy was still at school and said he was worried about his future and about what would happen to him if he failed his exams.

The histories show that all eight boys displayed other forms of disturbance than delinquency. Thus, six out of eight were ranked in the 'troublesome' quarter by teachers and peers, and the remaining two (004 and 982) were both above average in troublesomeness. The eight boys were variously described as anxious, nervous, highly strung, obsessional, timid, quiet, sensitive, suspicious, inhibited or apathetic. This suggests that boys from deprived homes who are not assertive enough to react in a delinquent fashion tend to be difficult in other ways or to suffer emotionally. Some of these boys (e.g. 031, 180, 830) improved considerably as they grew older, but others (e.g. 004, 312, 982) remained somewhat withdrawn, unhappy individuals. Timidity and social isolation were the factors that may have prevented these boys from becoming delinquents. Be that as it may, their siblings were certainly not shielded from delinquency. The eight boys had a total of 19 older siblings, of whom nine were convicted delinquents.

NOTES

[1] *The Assignment of Optimal Weights to Predictive Factors by means of Multiple Regression*

An obvious step was to see if prediction could be improved by assigning optimal weights to the five predictive factors, instead of giving each an arbitrary score of one. One standard statistical procedure for calculating such weights is a multiple regression analysis. In order not to capitalize unfairly on chance variations, the weights had to be calculated from one half of the sample and then applied to the other half to test the predictive value.

Unfortunately, the sample was too small for this procedure to be applied successfully. Using the weights obtained from the even-numbered cases (·203, ·025, —·004, ·104 and zero respectively for the five factors set out on p. 131), the correlation with delinquency in the odd-numbered section of the sample was lower than that obtained when the factors were given equal weights (r_{bis} = ·38 and ·57 respectively). Moreover, when the odd-numbered half was used for a recalculation of the weightings, a quite different set of figures was obtained (respectively ·125, ·120, ·138, ·168 and ·133). This confirmed that the sample was too small, and the weights insufficiently stable, for such an analysis.

The program used for this analysis was kindly supplied by Mr Irvin Waller of the University of Toronto Center of Criminology.

IX

Self-Reported Delinquency

1. *An Alternative Measure of Delinquent Behaviour*

Fortunately for the reputations of adults, youthful delinquencies do not necessarily lead to criminal convictions. Crimes which are brought to the notice of the courts represent the tip of a large iceberg of crimes committed. In recent years, criminologists have tried to explore the hidden part of the iceberg, by making use of questionnaires intended to persuade young people to reveal their true offence histories. The results suggest that delinquency is much more widespread than official records indicate, so much so that boys who have never committed certain common offences are in a small, deviant minority. Hood and Sparks (1970) have summarized much of the evidence from these self-report studies.

It can be argued that the characteristics of officially convicted delinquents which we have found (e.g. tending to come from poorer homes, from larger sized families, to have criminal parents, and to be less intelligent than their peers) are likely to attract the notice of the police and the courts. Boys who do not share these characteristics may be just as delinquent in behaviour, but more successful in avoiding official convictions. For instance, Gold (1963) found that boys apprehended for delinquent acts in an American town were five times as likely to appear subsequently in some official record if they lived in poor rather than wealthy neighbourhoods. Similarly, in Finland, Jaakkola (1966) found that, even after matching for numbers of self-reported delinquent acts, youths who were poorly educated and of lower class were more likely to come into conflict with the police.

The Study boys were given a self-reported delinquency questionnaire, to see if this measure of delinquency would give results differing from those obtained when official records were used. The boys were asked to report delinquent or fringe-delinquent acts

TABLE IX (1)

Self-Reported Delinquency Admission Rates

Item	Act	*Per cent admit, age 14–15* ($N = 405$)	*Per cent admit, age 16–17* ($N = 397$)	*Per cent admit at either age* ($N = 409$)
1.	Riding a bicycle without lights (or with with no rear light) after dark	77·0	78·8	88·3
2.	Driving a car, motor bike or motor scooter under the age of 16	20·3	40·1	43·5
3.	Belonging to a group (of ten or more people) who go around together, making a row, and sometimes get into fights or cause a disturbance	16·8	23·4	31·1
4.	Playing truant from school	54·3	80·9	82·2
5.	Deliberately travelling without a ticket or paying the wrong fare	71·6	84·4	89·5
6.	Letting off fireworks in the street	84·2	86·7	93·2
7.	Taking money from home—with no intention of returning it	9·4	11·3	17·1
8.	Taking an unknown person's car or motor bike for joyriding (with no intention of keeping it for good)	7·4	15·6	18·3
9.	Smashing, slashing or damaging things in public places—in streets, cinemas, dance halls, railway carriages, buses	11·9	18·1	25·4
10.	Annoying, insulting or fighting other people (strangers) in the street	23·0	23·4	35·9
11.	Breaking into a big store, garage, warehouse, pavilion, etc.	4·0	7·3	9·5
12.	Breaking into a small shop (private tradesman) (whether or not anything was stolen)	6·4	8·6	12·7
13.	Stealing things out of cars	8·9	9·6	14·2
14.	Carrying some kind of weapon like a knife or cosh in case it is needed in a fight	20·7	25·4	35·0
15.	Attacking an enemy or someone in a rival gang (without using any sort of weapon) in a public place	18·8	24·4	32·8
16.	Breaking the windows of empty houses	68·9	66·8	82·2
17.	Using any kind of weapon in a fight—knife, cosh, razor, broken bottle, etc.	12·1	17·1	22·0
18.	Drinking alcoholic drinks in pubs under the age of 18	26·4	79·1	79·0
19.	Going into pub bars under the age of 16	51·4	74·6	80·7
20.	Stealing things from big stores, supermarkets, multiple shops (while shop open)	19·3	28·2	36·2
21.	Stealing things from small shops or private tradesmen (shop open)	36·8	39·8	53·3

Item	*Act*	*Per cent admit, age* 14–15 (N = 405)	*Per cent admit, age* 16–17 (N = 397)	*Per cent admit at either age* (N = 409)
22.	Deliberately littering the street or pavement by smashing bottles, tipping dustbins, etc.	24·2	27·0	38·9
23.	Buying cheap, or accepting as a present, anything known or suspected of being stolen	36·3	57·4	64·6
24.	Planning well in advance to get into a house, flat, etc. and steal valuables (and carrying the plan through)	4·7	5·5	7·1
25.	Getting into a house, flat, etc., and stealing things. (Don't count cases here where stealing results from planning well in advance)	5·4	7·3	9·3
26.	Taking a pedal cycle belonging to an unknown person, and keeping it	8·4	10·6	14·7
27.	Struggling or fighting to get away from a policeman	6·9	12·9	15·9
28.	Attacking or fighting a policeman who is trying to arrest someone else	1·7	5·0	5·6
29.	Stealing school property worth more than about 5p	29·1	53·2	58·7
30.	Stealing tools, materials or any other goods worth more than 50p from employers (all in one go) (in working hours —don't count breaking in here)	2·2	12·6	14·2
31.	Trespassing anywhere you are not supposed to go, e.g. railway lines, goods yards, private gardens, empty houses	63·5	66·8	80·9
32.	Going to 'X' films under age	64·0	89·7	91·7
33.	Often spending £1 or more a week on gambling under the age of 16	7·9	19·7	22·0
34.	Regularly smoking cigarettes under the age of 15	31·9	41·8	47·9
35.	Stealing goods or money from slot machines, juke boxes, telephones, etc.	14·6	17·9	25·2
36.	Stealing from people's clothes hanging up anywhere	3·5	5·8	8·1
37.	Obtaining money by false pretences	10·4	9·8	17·4
38.	Taking illegal drugs like purple hearts or smoking reefers	0·5	6·3	6·1
	All acts	25·4	34·0	39·7

which they had committed but which had not necessarily come to the notice of the police. The questionnaire was developed by Gibson (1967a) on the basis of unpublished work by H. D. Willcock of the Government Social Survey. It consisted of 38 descriptions of acts, each one set out on a separate card. In the test, the cards were shuffled into a random order, and the boys were required to sort them into four piles to indicate whether they had frequently, sometimes, once or twice, or never at any time committed each act. The questionnaire was completed by 405 boys at age 14–15, and by 397 at age 16–17. In all, 409 boys completed it at one or both ages.

Table IX (1) displays the 38 acts, together with the percentages of boys admitting each act at the two ages. As might have been expected, almost every act was admitted by more boys at age 16–17. Spectacular increases were registered in some offences which were more easily committed by older boys; for instance item 38 (Taking illegal drugs: up from 0·5 per cent to 6·3 per cent), item 28 (Attacking a policeman: up from 1·7 per cent to 5·0 per cent), item 18 (Drinking under age: up from 26·4 per cent to 79·1 per cent) and item 30 (Stealing from employers: up from 2·2 per cent to 12·6 per cent). In connection with the last item, it should be remembered that the majority of boys left school and started work in between completing the two questionnaires. The acts admitted at 16 should have included all those admitted at 14, with the addition of those committed in the meantime. For this reason, it was thought that the best estimate of the prevalence of each type of delinquent act would be obtained by taking the percentage of boys who admitted the act at either or both ages (see Note 1).

These percentages, given in the last column of Table IX (1), show that the overwhelming majority of our boys had committed the more trivial acts such as letting off fireworks in the street (93·2 per cent), going to 'X' films under age (91·7 per cent), travelling without a ticket (89·5 per cent) and riding a bicycle without lights (88·3 per cent). On the other hand, only a small minority claimed to have indulged in the more seriously delinquent acts such as planned housebreaking (7·1 per cent), unplanned housebreaking (9·3 per cent), store-breaking (9·5 per cent) and shop-breaking (12·7 per cent).

In order to rank the boys on self-reported delinquent behaviour, each boy was scored according to the total number of different acts he admitted at either or both ages. The scores varied from zero to 38, the maximum possible. For ease of comparison with the 84 official delinquents, the 80 boys with the highest self-report scores, all of whom admitted at least 21 acts, were grouped together and referred to as the self-reported delinquents. The use of a single scale of self-reported delinquency, rather than an attempt to isolate different varieties, was justified by the substantial mean intercorrelation between the different items. The use of a scale based on simple admission or denial, rather than one based on the admitted frequency of each act, was justified by the fact that the simpler system produced scores that correlated slightly better with official delinquency (r_{bis} = ·54 as opposed to ·51). Finally, the validity of the scale was confirmed by the fact that the self-report scores were predictive, being significantly related to the likelihood of future delinquency convictions (see Note 1).

2. *Delinquent Acts of Friends and Acquaintances*

The well-known theory of differential association (Sutherland and Cressey, 1970) suggests that a person's own delinquent behaviour develops according to the extent of his exposure to other people's delinquent behaviour and attitudes. It follows from this theory that the boys with the most delinquent friends and acquaintances should be most likely to be delinquent themselves. Short (1957, 1958) and Voss (1964) confirmed this empirically. They found that juveniles who claimed that their friends were delinquents tended to admit more delinquent behaviour than those who did not. It has also been argued, by Hardt and Peterson (1968), that the official delinquency records of a boy's friends may provide a useful index of his commitment to a delinquent style of life, especially if he has successfully avoided a police record. They found that boys without police records, but with friends who were officially delinquent, were likely to have high delinquency commitments themselves, at least according to their own self-reports and to their responses on an attitudinal index.

We did not have access to the identities and criminal records of each boy's friends, but in the course of the self-reported delinquency enquiry the boys were asked about the delinquent behaviour of their acquaintances and friends. At the two ages (14–15 and 16–17), when the boys were given a set of cards bearing descriptions of 38 deviant acts, they were asked to sort them three times. The first sorting indicated whether or not each act had been committed by boys known to them (their acquaintances), and the second whether or not each act had been committed by their own personal friends. It was made clear to all the boys that, by definition, 'acquaintances' included 'friends' Consequently, any acts committed by friends must also have been committed by acquaintances. The third card sort, showing whether or not they themselves had committed each act, was used as the basis for the self-reported delinquency assessment, and has already been discussed.

The first two card sorts served a further purpose (Gibson, 1967a), since they enabled the boy to become familiar with each act before being asked whether or not he himself had done it. This was important in view of the number of poor readers in the Study, and served to lessen the shock effect that some of the questions might have had.

On both occasions of testing, each boy was scored according to the number of acts committed by his acquaintances, and the number committed by his friends. In addition, for both delinquency of acquaintances and that of friends, combined scores were derived for each boy, corresponding to the number of acts endorsed at either age 14–15 or age 16–17. Every one of these scores was significantly related to juvenile delinquency. The combined scores were particularly closely related, especially the one derived from delinquent acts of friends (47·5 per cent of 101 boys whose friends had committed 28 or more acts being delinquents themselves, in comparison with 11·7 per cent of the remaining 308: $\chi^2 = 57{\cdot}7$, $p < {\cdot}001$).

The delinquent acts attributed to friends were about as closely related to official delinquency as were the boys' own (the comparable figures for the self-reported delinquency measure being 50·0 per cent of 96, as opposed to 11·5 per cent of 313: $\chi^2 = 64{\cdot}4$, $p < {\cdot}001$). This result reflects a remarkable correspondence between the reported acts of a boy's friends and those of himself. No less than 70 of the 101 boys with the most delinquent friends were among the 96 highest on the combined self-reported delinquency scale. It appears that a good estimate of a boy's own misbehaviour can be obtained merely by asking him about the misconduct of his friends.

The number of acts committed by a boy's friends and acquaintances was predictive of his own future convictions. Nearly half (44·4 per cent) of the boys who became juvenile delinquents after being questioned at age 14–15 reported that their friends had committed 22 or more of the acts, in comparison with only 18·3 per cent of those who remained non-delinquents ($\chi^2 = 11{\cdot}8$, $p < {\cdot}001$). When convictions as young adults were taken into account, the statistical significance of this comparison increased slightly (39·3 per cent of 61 boys becoming delinquents reporting 22 or more acts by friends, in comparison with 17·2 per cent of 297 boys remaining non-delinquents: $\chi^2 = 13{\cdot}7$, $p < {\cdot}001$.) All these findings are in agreement with the theory of differential association, and with the contention that delinquency of friends provides a good index of a boy's own delinquency potential.

3. *The Characteristics of Self-Reported Delinquents*

Returning to the main self-report measure based on boys' admissions of their own misbehaviour, it can be said that, with few exceptions, the self-reported delinquents possessed much the same characteristics as the official delinquents, but to a somewhat lesser degree. This was partly due to the fact that the self-report technique picked out many of the same boys as the official records (41 of the 80 self-reported delinquents also being among the 84 official delinquents: $\chi^2 = 55{\cdot}2$, $p < {\cdot}001$). This type of result has been obtained by most previous workers, for instance Belson (1968) in England, Short and Nye (1958) in America, and Christie *et al.* (1965) in Norway.

The similarities between the characteristics of self-reported and official delinquents are displayed in Table IX (2), which shows the percentages of self-reported delinquents among boys with 15 important adverse features. For example, 34·1 per cent of those rated troublesome by peers and teachers at age 10 were self-reported delinquents, as opposed to only 15·4 per cent of the remaining boys, a very significant difference ($\chi^2 = 14{\cdot}5$, $p < {\cdot}001$). On the other hand, the association was less close than that obtained with official delinquency. The percentage of the most troublesome boys who were official delinquents (given in the penultimate column of Table IX (2)) was even higher (44·6 per cent). Corresponding differences were apparent in relation to almost all the adverse factors included in the table, the official delinquents being slightly worse than the self-reported delinquents, but not fundamentally dissimilar. (The final column in Table IX (2) will be discussed later: see pp. 162 ff.)

These results were not unexpected in the light of previous work. For example, the finding that self-reported delinquents were over-represented among boys from poor homes is in line with several American researches (e.g. Erickson and Empey, 1965; Slocum and Stone, 1963) which showed a positive correlation between low social class and self-reported delinquency. Gold (1967) has suggested that other investigators (e.g. Nye *et al.*, 1958; Akers, 1964) who failed to demonstrate this relationship would have obtained positive results if they had used interviews instead of anonymous questionnaires. Two self-report investigations in England (Belson, 1968; McDonald, 1969) used personal interviews, and found that self-reported delinquency was more prevalent among the lower classes.

TABLE IX (2)

The Backgrounds of Self-Reported Delinquents

Factor	*Per cent self-reported delinquents* (*N* = 80)				*Per cent official delinquents* (*N* = 84)	*Per cent combined delinquents* (*N* = 83)
	Worst quarter of sample (*N*)	*Rest* (*N*)	χ^2	p <	*Worst quarter* (χ^2)	*Worst quarter* (χ^2)
Daring	34·7 (121)	13·3 (285)	23·2	·001	38·8 (33·5)	40·5 (40·9)
Poor parental supervision	37·0 (73)	15·6 (308)	15·8	·001	31·1 (7·23)	32·9 (9·90)
Troublesomeness	34·1 (91)	15·4 (318)	14·5	·001	44·6 (40·5)	47·3 (50·5)
Parental criminality	32·0 (97)	15·7 (312)	11·4	·001	36·1 (17·9)	33·0 (11·7)
Dishonesty	30·7 (88)	15·2 (264)	9·35	·005	37·5 (23·5)	37·5 (23·4)
Separations	30·0 (90)	16·6 (319)	7·17	·01	32·2 (8·94)	31·1 (7·51)
Low intelligence	28·4 (102)	16·6 (307)	6·07	·025	31·1 (8·70)	31·4 (9·42)
Unsatisfactory parental behaviour	28·4 (95)	17·1 (299)	5·17	·025	32·3 (12·3)	31·6 (10·6)
'Catholic' families	28·8 (73)	16·3 (277)	5·13	·025	28·8 (5·27)	28·8 (6·35)
Low family income	28·0 (93)	17·1 (316)	4·73	·05	33·3 (11·3)	33·3 (11·6)
Large family size	27·3 (99)	17·1 (310)	4·31	·05	32·3 (10·4)	31·3 (8·93)
Clumsiness	26·2 (103)	17·3 (306)	3·33	·10	31·7 (10·0)	33·0 (12·7)
Delinquent older brothers	35·1 (37)	19·9 (136)	3·01	·10	40·5 (4·25)	35·1 (2·01)
Parental authoritarianism	21·9 (73)	16·5 (224)	0·76	N.S.	27·4 (4·89)	27·4 (5·68)
Parental uncooperativeness	25·6 (43)	18·9 (366)	0·72	N.S.	39·5 (9·50)	37·2 (7·37)

N.S. = Not significant.

Nye (1958) found that a large family size was associated with self-reported delinquency, but Slocum and Stone (1963) did not obtain a significant result in this case. Table IX (2) shows that our results support Nye's findings. Nye agreed with Slocum and Stone in finding broken homes related to self-reported delinquency, but Dentler and Monroe (1961) did not obtain statistical significance. In our sample, the factor 'separations' (which included broken homes) was associated with self-reported delinquency.

Table IX (2) also demonstrates that a low non-verbal IQ was characteristic of the self-reported delinquents (cf. p. 93). No other researcher has specifically investigated this point, but Kulik *et al.* (1968) found that some types of self-reported delinquency were related to verbal intelligence, and Slocum and Stone (1963) and Gibson (1967a) discovered an association with low educational attainment. Although they are not displayed in Table IX (2), our own measures also showed that self-reported delinquents tended to be retarded in verbal intelligence and in educational attainment.

Self-reported delinquency was also linked to poor parental behaviour. This result agrees with previous research showing that self-reported delinquents tend to experience unfair discipline and to have unaffectionate families (Nye, 1958; Slocum and Stone, 1963), and that they perceive their parents as unloving (Dentler and Monroe, 1961).

To sum up, our own self-report findings, in conformity with most previous work, indicate that officially convicted boys are not substantially different from those identified as delinquents on the basis of their own confidential admissions.

4. *Is there a Selective Bias in the Official Delinquency Records?*

It seems reasonable to assume that conviction records and self-report scores were both effectively measuring the same thing, namely delinquent behaviour. Since they did not always pick out the same boys, the two measures were probably subject to different types of distortion. In spite of the general similarity between self-reported and official delinquents, the processes of apprehension and conviction might still have been biased to some extent. Table IX (3) explores this possibility further, by examining the characteristics of boys who were classified differently according to self-report and official criteria.

The table subdivides the population into four groups, A, B, C and D, shown in the four columns from left to right. Group A consists of the 41 boys who were delinquents on both the official and self-report criteria. Group B comprises the 39 who were self-reported but not official delinquents, while C comprises the 43 official but not self-reported delinquents. Finally, group D is made up of the 286 boys who were not delinquents on either criterion. The figures given in each cell of the table show the percentages of boys in each group falling into the 'worst' category of a number of factors. The 'worst' category was generally defined to include approximately one quarter of the sample.

Looking at the first row of the table, 56·1 per cent of group A and 41·9 per cent of group C were in the troublesome category. In groups

TABLE IX (3)

Differences between Official and Self-Reported Delinquents

Factor	A *Official and self-reported* (*N* = 41)	B *Not official, self-reported* (*N* = 39)	C *Official, not self-reported* (*N* = 43)	D *Not official, not self-reported* (*N* = 286)
Troublesomeness	56·1	20·5	41·9	14·7
Daring	34·2	20·5	23·3	6·7
Dishonesty	54·8	27·8	43·2	18·2
Parental criminality	53·7	23·1	30·2	18·5
Poor parental behaviour	47·5	21·1	32·4	20·1
Low family income	48·8	15·4	25·6	19·6
Large family size	48·8	18·0	27·9	21·0
Clumsiness	43·9	23·1	34·9	21·3
Parental uncooperativeness	17·1	10·3	23·3	7·7
Separations	39·0	28·2	30·2	17·5
Low intelligence	48·8	23·1	27·9	21·3
Poor parental supervision	36·8	35·1	25·0	13·7
'Catholic' families	38·7	25·7	25·7	17·3
Parental authoritarianism	44·4	15·4	29·6	22·6
Delinquent older brothers	42·9	21·1	25·0	16·5

The figures in each cell represent the percentage of each group falling in the 'worst' category on each factor.

B and D, however, the percentages of troublesome boys were much lower, 20·5 per cent and 14·7 per cent respectively. A similar trend is to be seen in most rows of the table. Group A has the highest proportion of boys in the adverse category, group C has rather less, and groups B and D have much less. Group B, the boys who are self-reported delinquents but who do not have official juvenile convictions, are akin to group D, the non-delinquents. They do not possess to any great extent the characteristics we have come to associate with official delinquents.

This finding suggests two opposite interpretations, according to whether one accepts self-report or official records as the more accurate measure of delinquent behaviour. If one accepts official records, then it could be argued that the self-reported delinquents include a group of boys (the group B cases) who have exaggerated their delinquency. They are not true delinquents, and so are properly excluded from official records. On the other hand, if one has more faith in self-reports, it could be argued that the group B boys are genuine delinquents, but, because the official processes are selectively biased towards labelling as delinquents those who possess the characteristics of the delinquent stereotype, the group B boys tend to get left out.

The different forms of bias assumed in these explanations are not mutually exclusive, and it is difficult to discover evidence as to which type predominates. However, a clue to which explanation is the more correct was found in the number of group B boys who acquired official convictions for the first time as young adults. At the time of the latest search, there were only 26 boys in the whole sample first convicted as adults, but 9 of them were among the 39 group B boys (some three times chance expectation). There was also, among the group B boys, a disproportionate number (13, about double chance expectation) who belonged to what we have called the police contact category (i.e. dealt with by the police as juveniles but not convicted of a juvenile criminal offence). In all, out of the 39 group B boys, 19 were either police contact cases or had an adult conviction.

These figures strongly suggest that the group B boys were in reality a delinquent-prone group, despite having no juvenile conviction records, and that their high scores on the self-report questionnaire correctly reflected this. The conclusion might have been anticipated from the evidence that self-reports tend to minimize rather than exaggerate misconduct (see Note 1). The fact that so many of group B had police contacts short of conviction, or convictions after they had turned 17, suggested that in some instances their misconduct was probably known to the police, but that prosecutions were avoided or delayed. Since their background characteristics did not fit the stereotype of a juvenile delinquent, it is tempting to speculate that this could be the reason why official processes worked in their favour.

The group B boys may have been viewed favourably by the police, but they certainly did not return the compliment. At age 14–15, all the boys were given a questionnaire concerned with their opinions of the police. Of the 39 boys in group B, 33 were among the half of the sample who gave the most adverse comments. Indeed, the police questionnaire scores of group B showed that their attitudes to the police were just as unfavourable as those of group A, the self-reported delinquents who were convicted as juveniles. These results provide further evidence of the delinquent attitudes of the group B boys. It would seem that some of them were at least as delinquent in behaviour and attitude as the official delinquents (see also Note 2.)

Having discovered and reported this evidence for a certain amount of biased selection in the official labelling of juvenile delinquents, it must be pointed out once again that the effect was not sufficient to give a totally false picture. To a considerable extent, the self-reported delinquents still possessed the adverse features characteristic of official delinquents.

5. *A Scale of Delinquency using both Official Records and Self-Report Scores*

From the discussion in the earlier sections of this Chapter, it seems probable that official records and self-reported delinquency are both valid measures of delinquent behaviour. However, they are subject to different forms of bias, and neither is completely efficient. This being the case, a more accurate index of delinquent behaviour might be obtained by amalgamating the two measures into a single combined scale. The inadequacies of the two components might then balance out. The official delinquency scale (pp. 21–2) was therefore combined with (slightly modified) self-report scores in order to produce a new combined scale of delinquency (see Note 3).

Eighty-three boys, being the most delinquent fifth of the sample when both official records and self-admissions were taken into account, were termed the 'combined delinquents'. At the opposite extreme, 86 boys identified as being the least delinquent, with no police contacts or convictions and no admissions of serious offences on the self-report schedule, were termed the 'delinquent-resistant' boys.

This 'combined delinquency' categorization probably identified the boys who were the most delinquent in behaviour more accurately than either self-report or official conviction records. It is of some interest, therefore, to see what background features characterize the combined delinquents. The answer is shown in the right-hand column of Table IX (2). It can be seen that the combined delinquents more frequently occur among the troublesome boys (47·3 per cent of 91) than do either the official delinquents (44·6 per cent) or the self-reported delinquents (34·1 per cent). These percentages can be directly compared, since the numbers of combined delinquents, self-reported delinquents and official delinquents were similar. (The corresponding values of χ^2 were 50·5, 40·5 and 14·5.) The remaining entries in Table IX (2) demonstrate that most of the background factors listed were at least as closely related to combined delinquency as to official delinquency.

These results confirm that the combined delinquency category was, as intended, a more realistic measure of delinquency than official convictions. More importantly, it shows that this method of modifying the official delinquency category to take self-reports into account did not substantially alter previous conclusions. Troublesomeness, daring and dishonesty still appeared to be the most significant precursors of delinquency, while such background factors as parental criminality, low income and unsatisfactory parental behaviour still had much the same importance as before. It may also be mentioned that none of the factors that previously appeared to have only a slight or insignificant association with official delinquency became important when examined in relation to combined delinquency. In short, the use of the combined delinquency scale yielded no surprises, but gave additional reason for confidence in the validity of previous results.

6. *The 'Delinquent-Resistant' Boys*

So far, this report has emphasized that the most delinquent boys come from the 'worst' categories of a variety of background factors. But do the least delinquent boys come from the 'best' categories? The introduction of the combined delinquency scale, which identified the delinquent-resistant as well as the most delinquent, enabled this question to be investigated. The results are set out in Table IX (4).

The delinquent-resistant boys did indeed tend to come from the 'best' quarter on many factors. They were drawn from the least dishonest, the least troublesome, from those of high intelligence and from those in comparatively small or high-income families. However, they did not come to any notable extent from those with better behaved or non-criminal parents, or from those whose parents exercised good supervision, or from those who performed least

TABLE IX (4)

The Backgrounds of Delinquent-Resistant Boys

	Per cent delinquent-resistant boys ($N = 86$)			
Factor	*Best* (*N*)	*Rest* (*N*)	χ^2	p <
Least daring	40·5 (111)	13·9 (295)	32·7	·001
Least dishonest	41·0 (95)	14·4 (257)	27·6	·001
Least troublesome	34·3 (143)	13·9 (266)	22·0	·001
Small family size	30·1 (146)	16·0 (263)	10·5	·005
High family income	30·4 (125)	16·9 (284)	8·73	·005
High intelligence	28·4 (102)	18·6 (307)	3·91	·05
Absence of separations	22·9 (319)	14·4 (90)	2·52	N.S.
Parents cooperative	22·1 (366)	11·6 (43)	1·96	N.S.
Parents not criminal	22·8 (312)	15·5 (97)	1·95	N.S.
Good parental behaviour	26·4 (125)	19·7 (269)	1·87	N.S.
No delinquent older brother	18·4 (136)	8·1 (37)	1·57	N.S.
Least clumsy	25·0 (104)	19·7 (305)	1·02	N.S.
Least authoritarian parents	25·7 (70)	19·8 (227)	0·79	N.S.
Not 'Catholic' families	21·7 (277)	16·4 (73)	0·67	N.S.
Good parental supervision	25·0 (88)	20·5 (293)	0·57	N.S.

N.S. = Not Significant.

In the case of certain factors displayed in the table, notably absence of parental criminality and parental cooperativeness, the 'best' category included much more than a quarter of the sample. These have been included in the table for the sake of completeness, although the statistics are not properly comparable.

clumsily on psychomotor tests. In other words, measures of behaviour, tests of intelligence and two measures of social class (income and family size) predicted either low or high delinquency potential, according to whether a boy belonged to the favoured or the adverse category. In these respects, delinquent-resistant boys possessed favourable characteristics opposite to the adverse features typical of delinquents. In other respects, such as parental supervision and parental behaviour, the delinquent-resistant boys were not particularly favoured.

In short, delinquency resistance was not just the obverse of delinquency potential. It appeared that good parents had less influence in producing delinquency resistance than had bad parents in producing delinquency potential. It must be remembered, however, that the parents we considered 'good' were those who did not possess obviously undesirable features, rather than those who possessed positively desirable ones. While good parental behaviour was no guarantee of delinquency resistance, being exposed to poor parental behaviour did not necessarily preclude it (19·8 per cent of delinquent-resistant boys experiencing poor parental behaviour, in comparison with 23·2 per cent of the whole sample).

Perhaps the most important result in this analysis was that the least troublesome boys were likely to become delinquent-resistant. Just as bad early conduct predicts high delinquency potential, good early conduct predicts high delinquency resistance.

NOTES

[1] *Validity of Self-Reports*

There is some evidence that boys are more likely to conceal their delinquent acts than to exaggerate them (Clark and Tifft, 1966). Some confirmation of this was obtained in the present Study. The boys who gave high scores on the lie scale of the New Junior Maudsley Personality Inventory (p. 114) tended to admit relatively few acts on the self-report questionnaire (cf. Farrington and West, 1971). Since the lie scale purports to measure a tendency towards concealment, it seems that the presence of some 'liars' served to diminish rather than to increase the numbers of admissions made by our boys. During interviews at age 14–15, when the boys were asked about their appearance at juvenile courts, they showed no tendency to claim spurious convictions. Where a boy had been convicted of an offence, he nearly always admitted the corresponding act on the questionnaire (Gibson *et al.*, 1970).

The validity of the self-reported delinquency scale was confirmed by the fact that the scores had predictive value, being significantly related to future delinquency convictions. Farrington (1973) showed that this was true in our sample, and also that self-report scores predicted delinquency even after allowing for other predictive factors such as low income, large family size, parental criminality and low intelligence. According to our most recent figures, 61 boys who had been non-delinquents when tested at age 14–15 were subsequently convicted, as adults or juveniles. These boys admitted 11·6 acts on average, in comparison with only 8·3 admitted by the 297 non-delinquents. The 47 boys found guilty before taking the test, who admitted 15·5 acts on average, were eliminated from this analysis. There was a highly significant correlation between the number of admissions by non-delinquent boys at age 14–15 and whether or not they were subsequently convicted ($r_{bis} = 0{\cdot}34$, $p < {\cdot}001$). Erickson (1972) also showed that self-report scores predicted delinquency, but did not show specifically that this held true for previously non-delinquent boys.

[2] *Self-Report Scores and Official Convictions*

All self-reported delinquents had self-report scores in excess of 20. The group

A boys (the self-reported delinquents who also had an official juvenile conviction) had an average score of 27. The group B boys (the self-reported delinquents with no convictions) had a significantly smaller average score of 23·9. Only six of the group B boys had self-report scores of 27 or more. It is clear, therefore, that part of the difference between the two groups in relation to background characteristics was due to the fact that the group B boys were less serious delinquents than the group A boys.

[3] *The Construction of a Combined Scale of Delinquency*

The main index of self-reported delinquency was the number of different acts admitted at either age. However, the acts varied considerably in their seriousness. The vast majority of boys admitted the more trivial ones such as letting off fireworks in the street, while only a small minority admitted seriously delinquent

TABLE IX (5)

Official and Self-Reported Delinquency

Self-reported delinquency (acts admitted)	*Official delinquency*				
	No police record	*Police contact boys*	*One-time delinquents*	*Recidivists*	*Total boys*
Up to 11*	86	2	5	0	93
Up to 11†	26	2	3	2	33
12–14	65	18	6	5	94
15–20	66	21	14	8	109
21 or more	26	13	19	22	80‡
Total boys	269	56	47	37	409

* Including no admission of serious offences.
† Including admission of serious offences.
‡ These boys were the 'self-reported delinquents'.

acts such as planned housebreaking. In general, the most serious acts seemed to be those in two groups, 7 aggressive acts (p. 170) and 7 describing 'active theft' (items 8, 11, 12, 13, 24, 25 and 26: see Table IX (1). These groupings were decided upon by taking into account both the content of the acts and the intercorrelations between them (Farrington, 1973). Since the two groupings were themselves fairly closely correlated, they were amalgamated to produce a single set of 14 'serious' acts.

Rather surprisingly, admitting a comparatively large proportion of the serious acts was less closely related to official delinquency than admitting a large number of acts from any part of the schedule. This justified the use of the total score as the main index of self-reported delinquency. It was noted, however, that a low total score was not so closely associated with the absence of official delinquency as was the denial of all the 14 serious acts. In other words, while the total score was the more useful in identifying delinquents, a serious offence score of zero was particularly useful in pin-pointing non-delinquents. It was decided, therefore, to take out of the group with the lowest self-report (total) scores those boys who did not admit any of the 14 serious offences. This produced a group of boys with a very low delinquency potential.

Table IX (5) shows how these slightly modified self-report scores were related to official delinquency. At the lowest end of the scale, among 93 boys with a low total score and no admission of serious offences, there were no recidivists and only five one-time delinquents. In other words, 86 boys had low self-report scores, no admissions of serious offences and no official record of police contacts or convictions. This group, indicated within a square box in the top left-hand cell of the table, seemed to be the least delinquent fifth of the sample, and were called the delinquent-resistant group.

At the opposite extreme, the most delinquent fifth of the sample seem to be in the seven cells at the bottom right of the table (also shown encased by a square box). They consist of three overlapping categories:

(i) All the self-reported delinquents with any police record.
(ii) All the recidivists.
(iii) All one-time delinquents with above average self-report scores.

This group, totalling 83 boys, being the most delinquent when both self-report and official records are taken into account, were termed the 'combined delinquents'. They differ from the 84 official delinquents in excluding 14 one-time delinquents with below average self-report scores and including 13 police contact cases that fell into the self-reported delinquent category.

X

Delinquency and Aggression

Many personality attributes believed to be associated with delinquency, such as impulsiveness or low frustration tolerance, were not investigated in the present Study. This was mainly because of the difficulty of devising appropriate tests that did not take up too much time and could be applied to young boys in school. Among the personality measures that were taken at age 10 or younger, the only one that proved closely related to delinquency was the assessment 'daring'. This was a rating that combined the opinions of peers and parents (see p. 104).

Since there was considerable overlap between boys rated troublesome in behaviour and boys rated daring, it was possible that daring was merely an aspect of incipient delinquent behaviour. On the other hand, the measure may have reflected a definite trait of personality, such as a predilection to take risks, or overt aggressiveness. However that may be, it is important to know if aggressiveness is a characteristic of delinquents, as commentators from widely differing fields have suggested (e.g. Matza and Sykes, 1961; Woodmansey, 1971).

Some indications of the aggressiveness of the delinquents in our sample have already been cited. Their responses to the self-report schedule showed that they were particularly prone to such aggressive behaviour as street fighting and scuffles with the police. This was amply confirmed by further details given in the course of interviews at age 18. In view of this, it may seem odd that few were actually found guilty of offences of violence. It may be that the police only take action in selected circumstances for instance if a victim complains or someone is robbed. An aggressive temperament may possibly contribute to the likelihood of conviction when non-violent offences are committed. Some American research by Piliavin and Briar (1964) indicated that boys questioned for non-aggressive offences were particularly liable to be arrested if they responded aggressively to the police.

In view of the importance of the relationship between aggressiveness and delinquency, we will make an exception in this Chapter, and will draw upon data from later ages in so far as they concern aggressiveness. Some of these measures of aggressiveness were taken while the boys were still relatively young, so it was possible to see whether aggressiveness was both characteristic of boys already delinquents and also predictive of boys destined to become delinquents subsequently. In previous research, aggressiveness has been measured by self-report questionnaires and by projective techniques. Both methods were tried here.

1. *Aggressive Behaviour Measured by Self-Report*

Most of the self-report questionnaires used to measure aggressiveness have been very similar in design to personality questionnaires, including such statements as 'I often feel like picking a fight'. Indeed, one of the most widely used aggressiveness questionnaires, the Manifest Hostility Scale (Siegel, 1956), was actually derived from one of the best known personality questionnaires, the MMPI. Other important American questionnaires designed to measure aggressiveness have been devised by Buss and Durkee (Buss, 1961) and by Zaks and Walters (1959).

Attempts to validate these questionnaires have been made by comparing the responses either with behavioural ratings of aggressiveness or with convictions for aggressive crimes. In a typical test of validity, Walters and Zaks (1959) showed that high self-reported aggressiveness scores were significantly correlated with peer ratings of aggression. However, such attempts have by no means always confirmed the validity of the self-report scores (Shipman, 1965; Murstein and Wiens, 1965).

The major problem with all self-report questionnaires is lying. Perhaps because of this, Zaks and Walters (1959) found that the most valid items were not directly relevant ones like 'I often feel like picking a fight' but more indirect items such as 'I often do things I regret'. The Manifest Hostility Scale is particularly vulnerable to test-faking, according to Shipman and Marquette (1963).

One of the few self-report measures of aggressiveness devised by British investigators is the Hostility and Direction of Hostility Questionnaire (HDHQ). Foulds (1968) showed that scores on this questionnaire discriminated significantly between prisoners and (non-psychotic) patients admitted to mental hospitals, while Warder (1969) showed that they discriminated between extremely assaultive and moderately assaultive prisoners. It will be interesting to see whether, in future validation tests, the HDHQ will prove better than the American questionnaires.

Our self-reported aggressiveness questionnaire differed from those discussed above in seeking factual answers about actual behaviour instead of hypothetical ones about feelings. Instead of saying, for example, whether or not he often feels like starting a fight, the subject has to say whether or not he has actually been involved in fights. Because of this, our questionnaire may be more valid than previous ones, at least in relation to aggressive behaviour.

The questions about aggressiveness formed part of the self-reported delinquency questionnaire described in the last Chapter. Seven of the items referred to actual or potential violence against persons. (These were numbers 3, 10, 14, 15, 17, 27 and 28: see Table IX (1), pp. 152–3). The responses to these items were intercorrelated, so that, if a boy admitted one of these acts, he tended to admit others as well. It seemed reasonable, therefore, to use as an index of a boy's aggressive behaviour the number of these acts he admitted, either at age 14–15 or at age 16–17. This self-reported aggression score was, in effect, a subdivision of the total self-report score, and was almost as closely associated with official delinquency as the total score. Moreover, self-reported aggression scores at age 14–15 predicted delinquency (see Note 1).

Boys convicted of aggressive offences, such as robbery, assault or threatening behaviour, tended to obtain high self-reported aggression scores. 'Carrying an offensive weapon' was not counted as an aggressive offence for this purpose. The self-report enquiry indicated that it was a common practice among youths in the neighbourhood, and descriptions of the circumstances leading to these convictions suggested that the offenders usually came under suspicion for reasons other than violent behaviour. This offence apart, there were 10 boys convicted as juveniles of aggressive offences. These 10 admitted considerably more aggressive acts (average 4·1) than the remaining 74 juvenile delinquents (average 2·9), and many more than the non-delinquents (average 1·4). If convictions as young adults are included, the average self-reported aggression scores became 3·3 among 19 boys convicted of aggression, 2·8 among the other 91 delinquents and 1·4 among 299 non-delinquents.

Two points emerge. First, boys with a potentiality towards criminal violence have high scores on self-reported aggression. Second, compared with non-delinquents, delinquents in general obtain relatively high self-reported aggression scores. These results support the hypothesis that aggressiveness is an important characteristic of the young delinquent.

2. *Verbal Aggression in a Picture Frustration Test*

Projective tests, in which subjects are presented with ambiguous stimuli, are supposedly less susceptible to faking than self-report inventories. In making responses, the subjects are believed to project their own conflicts and needs into the situation, thereby unwittingly revealing personality traits of which they may be unaware. Although the Rorschach test has been used to measure aggressiveness (e.g. Townsend, 1967), the most popular technique for the purpose is the Thematic Apperception Test (TAT).

In the TAT, subjects are shown pictures of situations involving people, and are asked to make up stories to indicate what is happening. They are supposed to identify with one of the characters in the situation, usually the hero. Consequently, stories in which the hero behaves aggressively are said to indicate a similar tendency in the subject himself. Whether subjects who appear to be aggressive in this test actually are more aggressive in real life behaviour is open to doubt. For example, the studies of Mussen and Naylor (1954), Purcell (1956), Shore *et al.* (1967) and Megargee and Cook (1967) are in favour of this contention, whereas those of Gluck (1955), McNeil (1962), Horrocks and Gottfried (1966) and Silber and Courtless (1968) are not.

A more recent, promising device for measuring aggressiveness is the Hand Test (Wagner, 1969). In this test, 10 drawings of a hand are shown to the subject, and he is asked to say what he thinks the owner of each hand is doing. Wagner and Hawkins (1964) and Sarbin *et al.* (1968) found that Hand Test responses discriminated between assaultive and non-assaultive delinquents, the former tending more often to associate the hands with aggressive activities. This test is being given to our boys at age 18, but the results are not yet available.

Another well-known projective technique is the Picture Frustration test (Rosenzweig, 1945; Rosenzweig *et al.*, 1947). Each picture shows a person in a frustrating situation, and subjects are asked to imagine what the person would say. Responses are classified as extrapunitive if external persons or things are blamed, intropunitive if there is self-blame, or impunitive if blame is avoided altogether. Extrapunitive responses are supposed to be particularly characteristic of delinquents (Gatling, 1950).

Earlier attempts to validate this test were not particularly successful (e.g. Albee and Goldman, 1950; Fry, 1952; Holzberg and Hahn, 1952; Vane, 1954). Later investigations, however, do indicate that it has some validity. For example, Beswick and Cox (1958) found that extrapunitive responses were characteristic of boys rated aggressive by their peers, and Kaswan *et al.* (1960) found that they were associated with self-reports of aggressiveness and with a history of anti-social aggressive behaviour.

The Study boys were given a variant of the Picture Frustration test at age 14–15. This was the 'Blamed Boy' test, devised by Ruth Hanson and inspired by the children's version of Rosenzweig's test (Rosenzweig *et al.*, 1948). In order to avoid the problem of subjectivity in classifying responses, which occurs when subjects can make any comment they like, the boys were supplied with alternative responses and asked to choose between them. This method was reminiscent of the multiple-choice version of the TAT devised by Hurley (1955). The material of the 'Blamed Boy' test consisted of a series of 10 drawings, each vividly portraying a difficult, frustrating situation in which a 15-year-old boy finds someone complaining at him. The situations were of a kind likely to be familiar to our boys, such as being told to tidy up when in a hurry to go out. Three of them were taken from the Rosenzweig children's test, and the remaining seven were suggested by psychologists and social workers in the research team. The pictures were drawn by Lewis F. Lupton, an artist who has illustrated a large number of children's books and cartoon-strip stories for children's magazines. The test was intended to identify boys who gave aggressive responses in frustrating situations.

Each of the 10 illustrations was accompanied by a separate typed card bearing five different comments. The boy was asked to choose from among these the one which came closest to what he might have felt like saying if he had been the boy in the picture. It was explained to him that what a boy might feel like saying was not the same as what he might actually say. This instruction was inserted because previous work with the Rosenzweig test had shown that subjects tended to say either what they would feel like saying or what they actually would say (Bernard, 1949), and that these were two different things (Sutcliffe, 1955). The comments used in the test were selected by a panel of judges (psychologists and others with experience of teenagers) from remarks spontaneously made by working-class boys in London who were shown the pictures during pilot work. The judges were asked to choose comments which were unambiguous and represented a variety of attitudes. The full text of the test is given

TABLE X (1)

Verbal and Behavioural Aggression

Verbal aggression picture frustration score at age 14–15	*Behavioural aggression: acts admitted at age 14–15 or age 16–17*								*Total boys*	
	0		1		2–3		4+			
	(%)	(*N*)	(%)	(*N*)	(%)	(*N*)	(%)			
24–38 (Low)	46·4	(45)	25·8	(25)	17·5	(17)	10·3	(10)	100%	(97)
39–47 (Low average)	41·9	(39)	16·1	(15)	24·7	(23)	17·2	(16)	100%	(93)
48–61 (High average)	30·4	(31)	16·7	(17)	28·4	(29)	24·5	(25)	100%	(102)
62–95 (High)	27·4	(26)	15·8	(15)	28·4	(27)	28·4	(27)	100%	(95)
Total boys	36·4	(141)	18·6	(72)	24·8	(96)	20·2	(78)	100%	(387)

Note: Only 387 boys were given the picture frustration test, because it was not fully developed at the time the first boys were tested at age 14–15.

Significance Test: Comparing 197 boys above average on verbal aggression with the remainder, and comparing 174 boys above average on behavioural aggression with the remainder, $\chi^2 = 15{\cdot}0$, $p < {\cdot}001$.

in Appendix D. After the boy had made his first choice for each of the 10 pictures, he was asked to look through them again and to indicate the 10 comments he would least have felt like saying. During this process, the test administrator covered over the comments previously chosen, so that they could not be selected again. The test was scored on a system which provided an index of aggressiveness (see Note 2).

Table X (1) shows that verbal aggression, as measured by picture frustration test scores, and behavioural aggression, as measured by self-report scores, were significantly associated (but see also the last paragraph of Note 2). Unlike behavioural aggression, verbal aggression appeared to be unrelated to general juvenile delinquency (21·1 per cent of the boys with the highest verbal aggression scores being delinquents, in comparison with 19·9 per cent of the remainder, a completely insignificant difference). However, the 10 boys convicted of aggressive juvenile offences did show aggressive responses on the picture test, all 10 of them having above average scores, and 7 having scores in the top quarter. Of the remaining 68 delinquents who were given the picture test, only 33, not quite half, had above average scores. These results suggest that the picture test scores were measuring an aspect of aggressiveness, but not one of much relevance to delinquency in general.

3. *Aggressiveness indicated by Self-Concept*

One of the ways of exploring how a person sees himself is by means of the semantic differential test (Osgood *et al.*, 1957), in which each subject is given a series of descriptions of concepts, such as 'home' or 'other people'. In order to determine the meaning he attaches to these concepts, he is asked to rate each one on scales labelled at opposite ends with antithetical adjectives such as 'good . . . bad' or 'strong . . . weak'. When the concept 'myself' is presented, the subject's ratings are supposed to reveal his conception of himself. Similarly, ratings of the concept 'myself as I would like to be' are meant to reveal the subject's ideal self.

An early example of the use of the semantic differential in criminology was in a survey of delinquent gangs in Chicago (Gordon *et al.*, 1963; Short and Strodtbeck, 1965). It was found that gang members tended to make self-critical ratings like 'bad', 'dirty', 'cruel', 'unfair' and 'unpleasant' to a greater extent than other working class youths, and to a very much greater extent than middle class youths. Gang members also appeared to have the worst concepts of an ideal self, while the middle class youths had the highest ideal selves.

The finding that delinquents have less favourable self-concepts than non-delinquents was confirmed by investigations in other countries. In New Zealand, Masters and Tong (1968) found that recidivist delinquents had worse self-concepts than either non-recidivist delinquents or non-offenders. In Glasgow, Bhagat and Fraser (1970, 1971) showed that, both in a slum area and in a new housing estate, delinquents tended to think of their actual selves and their ideal selves unfavourably. They tended to endorse the adjectives bad, dirty, cruel, dangerous, unpleasant, dishonest and worthless more often than non-delinquents (see Note 3).

In the present Study, differences in aggressiveness between the self-concepts of delinquents and non-delinquents were investigated with a semantic differential test. This test was developed by the Government Social Survey in a study of the smoking habits of adolescent boys (Bynner, 1969; McKennell and Bynner, 1969), and was given to the Study boys at age 14–15. Each boy was asked to locate himself on 19 four-point scales, the extremes of which corresponded to two opposite descriptions such as 'gentle' . . . 'tough'. He was required to place a cross in one of four boxes on the paper, to indicate whether (in this instance) he thought of himself as 'gentle', 'fairly gentle', 'fairly tough' or 'tough'. Each boy completed two questionnaires, one corresponding to 'the kind of boy you really are' (actual self) and the other to 'the kind of boy you would like to be' (ideal self).

Table X (2) sets out the opposing descriptions, and summarizes the results obtained when the four boxes were collapsed into two. It can be seen that in almost every case there was more consensus among the boys about their ideal selves than about their actual selves. For example, nearly all the boys ideally wanted to be good at school work, but only about half of them claimed that this description fitted their actual selves. On the whole, the pattern of responses given by the Study boys was similar to that reported by Bynner (1969), except for some differences due to our boys being older than most of the Government Social Survey sample. For instance, our boys saw themselves as rather more bullying, and as rather more interested in and trying to attract girls.

There were differences between delinquents and non-delinquents. The delinquents tended to see themselves as more interested in girls, tougher and better fighters, more prone to swearing and bullying, worse at school work and as preferring to be with a group rather than by themselves. Their ideal selves differed from those of non-delinquents in being worse at school work, tough, scruffy, prone to swearing, poor at sports and liking to do forbidden things. However, although these differences were in the expected direction, few were statistically significant (see Table X (2)).

Seven of the items (4, 5, 7, 8, 12, 15 and 19) seemed to be measuring some aspect of aggressiveness. In order to obtain a score representing the aggressiveness of each boy's self-concept, he was scored 4, 3, 2 or

TABLE X (2)

Delinquency and Self-Concept at Age 14–15

Item	*Description*	*Actual concept* *N(%D)*	*Ideal concept* *N(%D)*
1	Good at school work	191 (16·2)	393 (19·9)
	Not so good at school work	215 (24·2)	13 (38·5)
2	Interested in girls	329 (22·5)*	348 (21·6)
	Not interested in girls	77 (11·7)	58 (13·8)
3	Good at sports	247 (20·2)	365 (19·5)
	Not good at sports	159 (20·8)	41 (29·3)
4	Gentle	206 (16·5)	193 (21·2)
	Tough	200 (24·5)	213 (19·7)
5	Often disobedient	199 (23·1)	109 (25·7)
	Usually do as I am told	207 (17·9)	297 (18·5)
6	Like to be alone	101 (13·9)	86 (17·4)
	Like to be with a group	305 (22·6)	320 (21·3)
7	Good fighter	212 (25·0)*	322 (19·6)
	Not much of a fighter	194 (15·5)	84 (23·8)
8	Try to act 'big'	68 (25·0)	40 (17·5)
	Act my own age	338 (19·5)	366 (20·8)
9	Plan and think ahead	274 (22·3)	345 (19·7)
	Cannot wait, want everything at once	132 (16·7)	61 (24·6)
10	Have many friends	316 (20·9)	337 (20·8)
	Have one or two friends	90 (18·9)	69 (18·8)
11	Scruffy	56 (19·6)	29 (31·0)
	Neat and clean	350 (20·6)	377 (19·6)
12	Do not bully	206 (17·0)	265 (18·5)
	A bit of a bully	200 (24·0)	141 (24·1)
13	Like to do forbidden things	194 (22·2)	159 (25·2)
	Do not do forbidden things	212 (18·9)	247 (17·4)
14	Want to be grown up	299 (20·4)	314 (20·7)
	Do not yet want to be grown up	107 (20·6)	92 (19·6)
15	Do not swear	80 (13·8)	144 (12·5)*
	Sometimes swear	326 (22·1)	262 (24·8)
16	Spend my money	234 (22·2)	187 (21·4)
	Save my money	172 (18·0)	219 (19·6)
17	Often successful	265 (20·8)	353 (19·6)
	Often a failure	141 (19·9)	53 (26·4)
18	Try to attract girls	287 (20·9)	304 (20·1)
	Do not try to attract girls	119 (19·3)	102 (21·6)
19	A bit of a cissy	43 (16·3)	19 (5·3)
	Tough	363 (20·9)	387 (21·2)

* = Significant (p = ·05) difference between percentages of delinquents (based on the value of χ^2 calculated from a 2 × 2 table).

1 on each of these items, according to whether he selected the aggressive description, one of the middle boxes, or the non-aggressive description. The total scores ranged in theory from 7 to 28. Both actual and ideal aggressive self-concept scores, but particularly the actual scores, were significantly associated with aggressive behaviour according to self-report. For example, 39·7 per cent of the 78 boys with aggression scores of 21 or more on actual self-concept were among the 83 boys admitting four or more aggressive acts at age 14–15 or at age 16–17 ($\chi^2 = 20{\cdot}7$, $p < {\cdot}001$).

Juvenile delinquents tended to have aggressive actual self-concepts (33·3 per cent of 78 boys scoring 21 or more being delinquents, in comparison with 17·4 per cent of 328: $\chi^2 = 8{\cdot}91$, $p < {\cdot}005$). The 10 boys convicted of aggressive offences had particularly aggressive self-concepts, every one obtaining a score in the top third of the sample. In contrast, the ideal self-concept aggression score did not appear to be related to delinquency. Aggressive self-concepts were not good predictors of delinquency (see Note 4).

These results provided still further evidence of the aggressiveness of delinquents. In their own estimation, delinquents, more often than non-delinquents, saw themselves as the kind of boy who had a variety of aggressive characteristics.

4. *Attitudes to the Police*

Convicted persons are known to be antagonistic in their attitudes to the police. For example, Mylonas and Reckless (1968) used an attitude questionnaire and found that, both in Greece and the United States, prisoners expressed more unfavourable attitudes than did civilian workers. In the 'criminal attitude' questionnaire devised by Taylor (1968) one of the statements most typically endorsed by various delinquent and criminal groups in New Zealand was that 'the police hound you if you have a criminal record'. Delinquents probably hold anti-police attitudes even before being officially convicted. Clark and Wenninger (1964) found that a high self-reported delinquency score was significantly related to the expression of attitudes antagonistic to the police and courts. Waldo and Hall (1970) showed that delinquency potential, as rated by teachers, was associated with similarly unfavourable attitudes.

The police attitude questionnaire which we used, like the self-reported delinquency questionnaire, was derived from the work of

H. D. Willcock. In the course of pilot work to test the effectiveness of the questionnaire, Gibson (1967a) applied it to three groups of 15-year-old boys, one in a grammar school, one in a secondary modern school and one in an approved school for delinquents. He found that the approved school boys held the most unfavourable attitudes, and the grammar school boys the most favourable. He also found that boys who made a large number of self-reported delinquency admissions expressed more anti-police attitudes than did other boys.

The Study boys were given this police attitude questionnaire both at age 14–15 and at age 16–17. Each boy was shown 32 cards, each one bearing a different statement about the police. He was asked to sort the cards into two piles, according to whether he considered the statements to be probably true or probably false. He was given an assurance of complete confidentiality, and was reminded that everyone was entitled to his own opinion. The full questionnaire is given in Appendix E.

The juvenile delinquents disagreed with the non-delinquents over almost every statement (see Appendix E), but especially so on five statements (1, 16, 21, 24 and 32). The delinquents were particularly likely to say that they hated the police, and that the police threatened people to make them admit things. The non-delinquents were more likely to assert that they would tell the police if they saw someone breaking into a shop, that they respected the police and that the police ought to get more support from the public.

Delinquents and non-delinquents tended to agree about the police not taking bribes. Although neither group was willing to agree that the police 'never take bribes', the majority of both groups thought that hardly any policemen would take bribes or presents to help people get away with serious crimes, and that the British police were much less corrupt than most police forces in other countries.

Using the results of a principal component analysis carried out during pilot work, 13 statements were identified as a group which, on inspection, appeared to represent critical or aggressive attitudes towards the police. These statements are marked 'X' in Appendix E. Each boy was scored according to the number of these statements he rated 'probably true' and the number of the other 19 statements he rated 'probably false'. It was found that, at both ages, this score of critical attitudes to the police was closely related to delinquency.

A combined score was derived for each boy, by counting the number of critical statements rated true at either age, and the number of other statements rated false at either age. This proved to be particularly associated with delinquency. Table X (3) shows the very significant over-representation of delinquents (42·2 per cent) among boys with unfavourable opinions of the police. There was an even more striking under-representation of both delinquents (3·9 per cent) and boys with a record of police contacts (3·9 per cent) among those with the most favourable attitudes.

A critical attitude to the police was much more likely to follow

TABLE X (3)

Delinquency and Critical Attitudes to the Police (Combined Score at Ages 14–15 and 16–17)

Critical attitudes to the police	*Delinquency* Non-delinquents (%) (*N*)	Police contact boys (%) (*N*)	One-time delinquents (%) (*N*)	Recidivists (%) (*N*)	Total boys
Low (10–)	92·2 (94)	3·9 (4)	2·9 (3)	1·0 (1)	100% (102)
Low average (11–16)	66·0 (70)	17·0 (18)	12·3 (13)	4·7 (5)	100% (106)
High average (17–21)	60·6 (60)	20·2 (20)	10·1 (10)	9·1 (9)	100% (99)
High (22+)	44·1 (45)	13·7 (14)	20·6 (21)	21·6 (22)	100% (102)
Total boys	65·8 (269)	13·7 (56)	11·5 (47)	9·0 (37)	100% (409)

Significance Test: Comparing 102 most critical boys with the remainder, and comparing 84 delinquents with the remainder, $\chi^2 = 37{\cdot}2$, $p < {\cdot}001$.

official convictions than to precede them. More than half of the boys convicted before completing this questionnaire at age 14–15 were among the quarter of the sample with the most critical attitudes at that age (51·1 per cent of 47, as opposed to 18·4 per cent of 358: $\chi^2 = 23{\cdot}7$, $p < {\cdot}001$). Future delinquents were much less critical (30·6 per cent of 36 boys who became juvenile delinquents after the test being among those with the most critical attitudes at age 14–15, in comparison with 17·1 per cent of the 322 boys who remained non-delinquents: $\chi^2 = 3{\cdot}07$, $p < {\cdot}10$). The relationship between critical attitudes and future delinquency did not quite reach statistical significance even when the adult delinquents were included.

The boys convicted before the test at age 14–15 may have been particularly critical because of their experiences of being prosecuted by the police. Alternatively, they may have been more extreme in their views because they were generally more extreme delinquents. The latter explanation seemed unlikely, since there was no evidence that subsequent recidivism was associated with a particularly critical attitude. Of the 36 boys found guilty after the test, the 19 who became recidivists were, if anything, less critical than the 17 who did not (26·3 per cent of the 19 recidivists being among the most critical quarter, compared with 35·3 per cent of the 17 non-recidivist delinquents).

These results suggest that critical attitudes to the police were considerably enhanced by previous experience of being convicted. Nevertheless, they were also associated with future delinquency potential in the absence of previous convictions. This is in agreement with the finding mentioned earlier (p. 162), namely that self-reported delinquents have unfavourable opinions of the police even when they have no official convictions recorded against them.

The boys' critical attitudes were not due to the influence of criminal parents, because those boys with criminal parents were not significantly more critical. Furthermore, the relationship between critical attitudes and delinquency held true at all levels of family income.

In so far as critical and hostile attitudes to the police reflect an aggressively anti-authoritarian outlook, these results fit in with the other aggressive characteristics of the delinquent group.

5. *Secondary School Teachers' Ratings*

When the boys were aged 12–13, and again at 14–15, their secondary school teachers were asked to fill in a questionnaire concerning their general behaviour in and adjustment to school. This was based on the one used in 1959 by Douglas in the National Survey (Douglas *et al.*, 1968, pp. 109–12). The majority of the questions required the teacher to place the boy in one of three categories. These questions are set out in Appendix F, which also gives the number of boys placed in each category at the two ages, and the percentage of them who were delinquents.

At both ages, the delinquents were particularly prevalent among the boys said to be persistently late at school, frequently truanting, quarrelsome and aggressive, frequently disobedient, and frequently difficult to discipline. In addition, at age 14–15, they were especially prevalent among those who were frequently restless in class, frequently cribbing, frequently evading the truth to keep out of trouble, liable to get unduly rough during playtime, showing off and seeking attention, dare-devils, and reacting to criticism or punishment by becoming unduly resentful. It is clear that teachers had a very poor opinion of delinquents. This may have been partly due to negative halo, the tendency to perceive individuals as bad in almost every respect. The worsening characteristics of delinquents in their later years at school could have reflected a worsening of their behaviour at an age when delinquency convictions were particularly frequent. On the other hand, the teacher's opinions may have hardened as a result of knowing which boys had become official delinquents.

Six of the questions from the teachers' form were chosen by inspection as indicators of aggressiveness, and were each scored one, two or three, according to whether the 'best', 'intermediate' or 'worst' description was endorsed. The categories receiving three points were: frequently disobedient, frequently difficult to discipline, liable to get unduly rough during playtime, quarrelsome and aggressive, over-competitive with other children and reacting to criticism or punishment by becoming unduly resentful. A total score for each boy at each age, ranging from 6 to 18, was obtained by adding together his scores on these six questions. Where a teacher answered some, but not all, of the six questions, the boy's total score was increased in proportion. For example, if a teacher only answered five questions, the total score on these would be multiplied by 6/5. These scores were significantly related to delinquency at both ages, but especially at age 14–15 (see Table X (4)). Once again, the results are in agreement with others quoted in this Chapter, showing that delinquents are notable for their aggressive behaviour.

The teachers' ratings of aggression at age 12–13 were predictive of future juvenile delinquency (33·8 per cent of the 68 juvenile delinquents first convicted after the assessment being among the most aggressive, in comparison with only 18·3 per cent of the 323 non-delinquents: $\chi^2 = 7{\cdot}29$, $p < {\cdot}01$). It was not possible to investigate whether the ratings of aggression at age 14–15 were similarly predictive, because such a small number (21) of the juvenile delinquents were first convicted afterwards. However, when the adult delinquents were included, it became clear that these assessments were significantly predictive as well (35·6 per cent of 45 delinquents first convicted afterwards being among the most aggressive, in comparison with 14·8 per cent of the 278 non-delinquents: $\chi^2 = 10{\cdot}15$, $p < {\cdot}005$.) In view of the predictive power of the earlier teachers' ratings (see pp. 100, 107), this result was not surprising.

The fact that reports of aggressive behaviour predicted delinquency seems to provide further evidence that the aggressive traits characteristic of delinquents are not just consequences of conviction experiences. On the other hand, measures of aggression described in this

TABLE X (4)

Delinquency and Aggression (Measured by Teachers' Ratings at Age 14–15)

Teachers' ratings of aggression	*Delinquency*								
	No police record		*Police contact boys*		*One-time delinquents*		*Recidivists*		*Total boys*
	(%)	(*N*)	(%)	(*N*)	(%)	(*N*)	(%)	(*N*)	
Low (9 or less)	74·7	(56)	14·7	(11)	6·7	(5)	4·0	(3)	100% (75)
Average (10–11)	72·0	(154)	14·5	(31)	8·9	(19)	4·7	(10)	100% (214)
High (12 or more)	42·7	(38)	13·5	(12)	20·2	(18)	23·6	(21)	100% (89)
Total boys	65·6	(248)	14·3	(54)	11·1	(42)	9·0	(34)	100% (378)

Note: Teachers' ratings were obtained for only 378 boys at age 14–15.

Significance Test: Comparing 89 most aggressive boys with the remainder, and comparing 76 delinquents with the remainder, $\chi^2 = 38{\cdot}8$, $p < {\cdot}001$.

Chapter may not have been as specific as they appeared. For instance, in the case of the teachers' ratings, the negative halo effect, whereby badly behaved boys tended to be viewed unfavourably in every possible way, may have caused some confusion between aggressiveness and general troublesomeness.

At both ages, teachers' ratings of aggression predicted future self-reported aggression. For example, 35·3 per cent of the 85 most aggressive boys at age 14–15 according to teachers were among the most aggressive according to self-report at age 16–17, in comparison with 15·7 per cent of the remainder rated ($\chi^2 = 14{\cdot}4$, $p < {\cdot}001$.) The fact that these two quite different and independent assessments taken at different ages tended to identify the same group of boys provides some evidence of the validity of each.

6. *Parental Discipline and Boys' Defiant Reactions*

Questions about parental discipline were part of the unstructured interviews with parents when the boys were aged 8–10 (see pp. 50–2). A different team of social workers re-interviewed the parents when the boys were aged 13–14, and this time put to them a schedule of prepared questions relating to discipline. On the latter occasion, there was a determined attempt to make the enquiry more systematic and the assessments less impressionistic.

The questions asked at age 13–14 (see Appendix G) were suggested by the social workers in the light of their past experiences of discussing this topic with mothers. They were meant to identify important aspects of discipline, and covered such matters as the rules made by parents, the main sources of conflict between parents and boys, the ways in which parents handled these conflicts and the reactions of the boys to the disciplinary measures taken by parents.

The schedule contained one set of 13 questions, which were all rated in the same way, by placing the answers into five mutually exclusive categories. The system is best explained with an example. Question 4 (What sort of time do you think he should be in bed by?) was rated 'parents lax' if the parents had no rules about bedtime, or if the boy seemed to be setting standards for himself which were higher than those set by his parents. The assessment 'boy conforms' was recorded if the answer indicated that the boy was so closely identified with his parents' standards that they had no need to make formal rules about bedtime. If a rule was made, and the boy tended to keep to it, a rating of 'always obeys' or 'mostly obeys' was recorded as the case might be. Finally, if it appeared that the boy constantly disregarded, openly flouted or defied the parents' bedtime rules, he was rated 'often defiant'.

A defiance score was derived by noting the percentage of questions rated 'often defiant'. It proved to be only slightly related to delinquency (23·1 per cent of the 91 most defiant boys being delinquents, in comparison with 16·3 per cent of the remaining 251 rated: $\chi^2 = 1{\cdot}62$, not significant). Although this result failed to yield clear evidence that the delinquents were particularly aggressive in their reactions to parental discipline, it would be wrong to attach too much importance to this finding. The discipline schedule as a whole was not a particularly effective instrument for extracting information (see Appendix G). It should be remembered that, apart from verbal aggressiveness on the picture frustration test, which was characteristic only of delinquents convicted of aggressive offences, the other four measures described in this Chapter all showed that delinquents were significantly more aggressive than non-delinquents.

NOTES

[1] *Association between Self-Reported Aggression Scores and Delinquency*

About 42 per cent of delinquents admitted four or more of the seven aggressive acts, in comparison with only about 15 per cent of non-delinquents ($\chi^2 = 28{\cdot}2$, $p < {\cdot}001$). Only 8 boys claimed to have done all seven acts, and six were juvenile delinquents. The association between high self-reported aggression scores and delinquency held true at all three levels of family income.

Considering only the aggression scores obtained from the test given at age 14–15, 36 juvenile delinquents were convicted for the first time after completing the self-report schedule. This does not include the one delinquent who did not take the test at age 14. These 36 boys were much more likely to have admitted three or more of the aggressive acts than the 322 boys who remained non-delinquents (30·6 per cent as opposed to 10·9 per cent: $\chi^2 = 9{\cdot}52$, $p < {\cdot}005$). If young adult convictions are included, 26·2 per cent of 61 'subsequent' delinquents admitted three or more acts, compared with only 10·1 per cent of 297 continued non-delinquents ($\chi^2 = 10{\cdot}36$, $p < {\cdot}005$).

The boys first convicted before completing the questionnaire at age 14–15 did not appear to be more aggressive than those first convicted after (31·9 per cent of 47 previously convicted delinquents admitting three or more aggressive acts, in comparison with 30·6 per cent of 36 subsequently convicted juvenile delinquents). This was somewhat surprising, since the boys convicted at an early age tended to be more extreme delinquents, with a greater tendency towards recidivism. Two-thirds (66·0 per cent) of boys convicted before the test became recidivists as adults or juveniles, in comparison with about half (52·8 per cent) of juvenile delinquents convicted after the test. These results show clearly that aggressive behaviour, as reflected in self-report scores, was not merely a consequence of official delinquency convictions, but also preceded them.

[2] *The Picture Frustration Test Scores*

The method of scoring used for the purposes of this report was not the same as that devised by Ruth Hanson for the 'Blamed Boy' test. The five alternative comments presented after each drawing were ranked according to aggressiveness. The ranking could have been decided by inspection, but was in fact determined on the basis of a principal component analysis. Each of the 50 comments comprising the test was scored 1, 5 or 3 according to whether the boy selected it as first choice, last choice or neither. A 50 × 50 correlation matrix was prepared, relating scores on each comment to scores on all others, and the principal components were extracted from this matrix.

The first and major component, accounting for 14·6 per cent of the variance, appeared to reflect aggressiveness. The comments with the highest loadings appeared to be the most aggressive. This was verified by asking eight members of the Cambridge Institute of Criminology, independently, to inspect the test comments and to rank each set of five in order, from the most aggressive to the most conciliatory. Their orderings agreed closely with the relative magnitudes of the loadings of the comments on the principal component. For purposes of scoring the picture test, the five comments in each set were ranked according to the order of their loadings on the principal component.

Each of a boy's first choice comments were scored from 1 to 5, from the least to the most aggressive. The last choices were scored in reverse order, namely 1 for the most aggressive and 5 for the least. The score on each picture for each boy ranged from 2 to 10, and his score on the whole test from 20 to 100.

The association between the picture frustration measure of verbal aggression and self-reported aggression was much less marked for the self-report scores at age 16–17 than for those at age 14–15, when the picture frustration test was given. The corresponding values of χ^2 were 4·81 and 12·2. The differences may have been due to changes in verbal or behavioural aggressiveness between the two ages, or it may be that features of the test situation at age 14–15 encouraged boys to give similar responses to both tests.

The absence of any relationship between verbal aggression and general delinquency leads one to suspect that its association with self-report aggression could be artefactual, due perhaps to a tendency for verbally aggressive boys to exaggerate their aggressive behaviour on self-report. If this were happening, elimination of the contaminating effect of verbal aggressiveness should improve the self-report measure as an index of actual behaviour. However, after correcting for verbal aggressiveness using a linear regression (see p. 96), the self-reported aggression scores did not become any more closely related to delinquency.

[3] *The Semantic Differential Technique*

It is only fair to point out that delinquency research with the semantic differential is very much in its infancy, and that more extensive investigations may reveal some methodological problems. Already, Walkey and Boshier (1969) have discovered one disadvantage with the usual seven-point bipolar scales, namely that delinquents tend to respond either in the central category or at the extremes. Researchers have tended to use only bipolar scales measuring the factors of evaluation, potency and activity suggested by Osgood *et al.* (1957). They have shown that the self-concepts of delinquents differ from those of non-delinquents on the evaluative dimension (good–bad), but no consistent differences have been found in self-concepts of either potency (strong–weak) or activity (active–passive). It is important to investigate, as we have, whether or not the self-concepts of delinquents and non-delinquents differ on other dimensions. Short and Strodtbeck (1965) made a start in this direction by measuring self-concepts on a 'smartness' scale inspired by the 'focal concerns' of Miller (1958). They found that middle class youths and negro gang members thought of themselves as smarter, luckier and having a more exciting life than lower class youths and white gang members.

[4] *Do Aggressive Self-Concepts Precede the Experience of Being Convicted?*

The juvenile delinquents who were already convicted by the time they took the test were particularly aggressive in their self-concepts. (34·0 per cent of 47 boys convicted before the test scoring 21 or more, in comparison with only 17·3 per cent of the remaining 359 boys.) However, an aggressive self-concept did not significantly predict delinquency, even when adult convictions were included. (23·0 per cent of 61 boys first convicted after the test, as juveniles or adults, scoring 21 or more, compared with 16·1 per cent of the 298 who remained non-delinquents $\chi^2 = 1{\cdot}22$, not significant). These figures suggest that aggressive self-concepts are not present to any great extent in delinquents until after they have been convicted.

XI
Conclusions

1. *Summary of the Main Findings*

In this chapter, an attempt will be made to bring together the most important findings and to draw some general conclusions. Delinquency in this report refers to juvenile delinquency among boys living in an urban, working class neighbourhood. Delinquency in middle class or suburban environments may well have different connotations, but we have not been able to explore this. Since the Study neighbourhood was in no way out of the ordinary, we believe that the conclusions would apply in similar working class areas found in most large towns.

Like so many such places, the Study neighbourhood was relatively under-privileged. For instance, there were no private schools in the area, educational standards were below the national average and there was a relatively high incidence of delinquency. At the time the Study began, many families were living in overcrowded and dilapidated housing, often without bathrooms; but it was not an area of particularly high unemployment or of racial migration.

Such working class neighbourhoods may seem drab and homogeneous, but the inhabitants are not. The Study revealed a surprising amount of variation between families in material standards, in social competence, in attitudes to child-rearing and in life style generally. These differences proved highly relevant to the likelihood of boys becoming delinquents.

The boys defined as delinquents were those found guilty by the courts of offences warranting entries in the Criminal Record Office. It is sometimes argued that official records bear only a distant relationship to actual behaviour. In addition to the accident of being caught, the acquisition of a criminal record depends upon the willingness of neighbours, parents and schools to report children's misdeeds, the amount of time children spend on the streets where their misbehaviour is visible, and the policy of local police regarding the prosecution of juveniles.

Despite these objections, the Study showed that official convictions realistically identified the worst behaved boys. The scale of official delinquency, based on police records and numbers of convictions, correlated satisfactorily with admissions of delinquent acts by the boys themselves. In addition, the official scale was closely related to assessments of troublesome behaviour derived from the observations of teachers and the opinions of classmates. Moreover, when a delinquency scale based solely on the boys' self-reports was substituted for the scale based on official records, the findings concerning the characteristics and backgrounds of delinquents remained substantially unchanged.

Two special circumstances favoured the official conviction statistics in our Study. Firstly, when the research began it was the policy of the police in the area to prosecute as many arrested juveniles as possible, so that all known delinquents acquired conviction records. With the alternatives to prosecution introduced in the Children and Young Persons Act (1969), and with the setting up of the Police Juvenile Bureau system, misconduct by younger juveniles is now less likely to be revealed by criminal records. Secondly, a narrow range of offences against property accounted for the great majority of the convictions of our boys. Special categories of offender, such as drug abusers, were conspicuously absent from the sample. The Study delinquents were a relatively homogeneous group of juvenile thieves, so that the number of their convictions was a fairly realistic index of the extent of their delinquent behaviour. The number of convictions was also a good indicator of the extent of a boy's deviation from the norm of his peer group in many other respects. The contrasts between delinquents and non-delinquents were largely due to the recidivists, who were an extreme group on almost every measure.

In the main, the comparisons set out in this report have been based upon a simple division of the sample into two groups, the juvenile delinquents with an official criminal record and the remainder, called non-delinquents. This crude dichotomy sufficed for most purposes, and satisfactorily revealed the essential characteristics of the delinquent group. It had the great advantage of facilitating comparisons with other researches based on official records. Nevertheless, it meant that the contrasts between delinquents and non-delinquents in the various tabulations were conservative estimates, since the delinquent group included some boys with only an isolated conviction for a trivial offence, while the non-delinquents included some whose behaviour was known to be of a delinquent type and who were subsequently convicted as young adults.

An attempt was made to refine the categorization by means of a scale combining official convictions and self-admissions. This combined delinquency scale was probably a more realistic index of delinquent behaviour than either official convictions or self-reports alone. It yielded two groups, each including about a fifth of the sample, consisting of unusually bad boys and unusually good boys respectively. The behaviour, scholastic performance and background characteristics of these two groups were very markedly contrasted. It seems that normal boys can be ranged along a continuum of delinquent tendency, with the majority in the intermediate categories, and the two extremes of persistent delinquents and delinquent-resistant types almost equally deviant from the norm.

The justification for introducing a combined delinquency scale was the evidence that self-report scores and official convictions were valid indices of delinquent behaviour. To a large extent, the two measures tended to pick out the same bad boys. When self-admissions were used to detect the most delinquent fifth of the sample, half of these self-reported delinquents overlapped with the fifth of the sample who were officially convicted. Furthermore, an unduly large proportion of the self-reported delinquents without juvenile convictions were subsequently convicted as young adults. High self-report scores were significantly predictive of future official delinquency. Considering the boys not yet convicted at the time they took the self-report test at age 14, those who made many admissions were subsequently convicted much more often than those who made few admissions. Many adverse characteristics, including troublesomeness as rated by teachers and peers, were almost as closely associated with self-reported delinquency as with official delinquency.

It should not be supposed that either self-reported delinquency or official conviction is a completely unbiased index of delinquent behaviour, but the two measures will have different kinds of bias. In incidence of certain adversities, such as parental criminality, low family income, low intelligence and poor parental behaviour, the self-reported delinquents who remained free from juvenile convictions were not appreciably worse than the generality of non-delinquents. This suggests that, among boys who indulge in the same delinquent behaviour, those who have adverse background characteristics of a kind noticeable to authorities are more likely to acquire an official juvenile conviction record. Samples of official delinquents are probably biased in the direction of an over-representation of boys with obviously unfavourable backgrounds.

Perhaps the most important result to emerge from this Study was the undramatic and unfashionable conclusion that traditional criminological beliefs about the backgrounds and characteristics of delinquents are true. Impressions gained from retrospective enquiries into the histories of established delinquents have not been so misleading after all. Many of the features that are apparent among older delinquents were demonstrably present by the age of 10 and were significantly predictive of future delinquency. In fact, as the long list in Appendix A bears witness, practically every factor investigated proved to be associated to some extent with future delinquency. The association was often very slight, but virtually without exception in the expected direction. The delinquents were more common among those with adverse characteristics. For example, it was the unpopular boys rather than the popular ones, those with high 'neuroticism' scores rather than those with low, those from broken homes rather than those from intact homes, those with nervous mothers rather than those with more stable mothers, those born illegitimate rather than those born to married parents, who in each instance were the ones more likely to become delinquents.

This was a satisfactory outcome from a research standpoint. Each factor included in the investigation represented some hypothesis or presumption about delinquents. Our findings were at least consistent with the ideas that inspired the enquiry. Since so many different features had been investigated simultaneously, it was possible to take a further step, and to single out from the mass of factors those which proved to have the closest and most important links with delinquency. This was not just a matter of picking out the largest correlations. Most of the factors closely associated with delinquency were themselves interlinked. The analysis of the results consisted largely of a search for factors which had some importance independently of others. For this purpose, every important factor that proved closely associated with delinquency was tested to see if it still differentiated between delinquents and non-delinquents after they had been matched in turn for all the other seemingly important factors.

The necessity for this method of approach was exemplified by the results obtained with psychomotor tests of clumsiness. As expected from previous research, poor performance on such tests proved to be very significantly associated with future delinquency. However, clumsiness was also closely related to low intelligence, and after matching for intelligence the delinquent boys were no longer any clumsier than the non-delinquents. Although other explanations were considered, it was concluded that in all probability the clumsiness of delinquents was merely a feature of their low intelligence.

The analysis yielded five background factors of particular significance, namely low family income, large family size, parental criminality, low intelligence and poor parental behaviour. These features were not necessarily more closely associated with delinquency than some of the others investigated, such as erratic paternal work record, physical neglect of boy or unstable mothers (see Appendix A, factors 10, 14 and 61). They were, however, reasonably well defined and carefully measured, and each one was associated with delinquency to some extent independently of the other four. In other words, each of the five factors remained significantly associated with delinquency after matching in turn for each of the others (with the single exception of family income, which became insignificant after matching for intelligence: see Appendix B). All five were factors that might have been expected, on theoretical grounds, to play a role in the genesis of delinquency, although the importance of low intelligence was not anticipated, because of the scepticism about this factor in recent criminological writings.

Boys affected by these five adverse background features were rendered extremely vulnerable to delinquency. Of the 63 boys who had three or more such adversities, half became juvenile delinquents, and a third became juvenile recidivists. Even so, this degree of predictability did not make it possible to forecast with certainty that any individual boy would become delinquent. The majority of future delinquents did not come from the small group identified as vulnerable.

Allowing for differences in the proportions of delinquents in the two samples, the predictive efficiency of these five background factors was much the same as that of the combination of family factors identified by the Gluecks and used for their famous social prediction table. The content of the factors was different. The Glueck predictors were largely measures of parental attitude and discipline, which in this Study were combined into the single factor of parental behaviour.

Because of the close inter-relationship between the five background factors, it was possible to go a long way towards identifying the vulnerable boys by using only three (any three) of the five. For instance, among boys who had at least two out of the three factors parental criminality, poor parental behaviour and poor family income, 40 per cent out of 70 became delinquents. For purely predictive purposes, however, it appeared hardly necessary to consider background factors at all. The ratings of troublesome behaviour based on the observations of teachers and the opinions of classmates were in themselves as predictive of official delinquency as any combination of background assessments. Moreover, virtually no improvement in prediction was obtained by taking into account background features as well as troublesome behaviour.

A statistical correlation does not necessarily imply a direct causal link, and the statistical importance of these five background factors does not mean that they were the essential causes of delinquency. Each of them stood for a complex situation, and we cannot claim to have identified the particular elements within the situation that brought about the association with delinquency. The predictive value of the factor of low family income, for example, merely confirmed a relationship which had been suggested by many previous surveys, and demonstrated that the association still holds true in contemporary urban conditions. It left the way open for a variety of speculative interpretations.

A simple explanation of the findings would be that boys from poor families are impelled to steal because they lack pocket money and possessions. On the other hand, these boys were deprived in other ways. It was argued in Chapter II that income was an index of the social level of a family, since low income correlated with most of the items which define low social class membership, such as overcrowding, poor housing and large family. Factors indicative of low social class were also associated with a variety of adversities of a more personal kind, such as poor parental supervision, marital disharmony and mothers of unstable personality, all of which in turn were linked with an increased risk of delinquency. No amount of statistical analyses of correlations discovered in social surveys is likely to succeed in showing conclusively which particular elements are most to blame. It seems difficult to get beyond the observation that certain adversities are linked with delinquency, and that an accumulation of these adversities makes a delinquent outcome more probable.

Regarding the role of low income, the Study findings showed a correlation between it and unsatisfactory child-rearing. This raises a question to which the data provide no certain answer. Do parents find themselves in poverty because of their own social incompetence, or is it that external economic pressure turns otherwise good parents into bad ones? The results also showed that low income retained some significance even after matching for parental behaviour or parental supervision. This suggested that financial deprivation had an effect over and above its association with inadequate child-rearing. Unfortunately, this was not a very firm conclusion. Numbers were too small to permit matching for all the relevant child-rearing factors simultaneously.

A scientific answer to some of these questions is more likely to be obtained by experimental research than by further survey work. For example, it would be possible, in principle, by treating similar groups of poor families in different ways, to distinguish the effects of poverty from those of defective child-rearing techniques. One group might receive money, but no other help, a second might receive guidance in child-rearing but no money, while a third group might be left untreated to act as a control with which to compare the relative effectiveness of the different types of intervention.

Returning to the actual findings of the Study, another important feature closely linked to low income was large family size. Boys from large families were significantly delinquent-prone, even after matching for income or parental behaviour. It seems that the bad effects of having to care for too many children were not simply the result of poverty and parental deficiencies, although of course these associated factors greatly aggravated the situation. In the Study sample families were usually poor if they had a large number of children.

It was the actual number of siblings that mattered, not whether they were older or younger, male or female. Being led astray by older brothers did not seem to be the reason why boys from large families became delinquents. More likely, it was the inability of the over-burdened mother to give adequate attention to each child that was the root cause of the difficulty. Large family size was significantly associated with poor (i.e. lax and careless) parental supervision, although not with the global rating of poor parental behaviour (see Appendix C). Boys from large families who were left largely to their own devices would naturally gravitate more towards peers, and for that reason one might expect them to adopt the attitudes and behaviour prevalent in the culture of the streets.

Poor parental behaviour was a particularly important factor, both on account of its statistical significance as a predictor, and because of its theoretical implications. Unfortunately, it was not a very well-defined entity, since it was derived by combining a great variety of assessments made by the PSWs. This was unavoidable, because it was evident that the PSWs had found difficulty in keeping apart their evaluations of different aspects of attitude and behaviour, so that parents rated good in one respect tended to be thought good in all respects, and vice versa. Other reasons why the ratings were insufficiently distinctive were that the descriptive categories employed were not precise enough, and that judgments had to be made in some cases on the basis of information given half-heartedly or with a deliberate intention to conceal. Many points about the families that were not discovered in the PSWs' initial interviews came to light in the course of subsequent inquiries. Even so, it was hard to see how the PSWs could have done better, since the more structured interviews and questionnaires used later failed to yield more positive results.

The poor parental behaviour factor was a global impression of family conflict and generally unsatisfactory parental attitude and discipline, taking into account both the emotional quality and the techniques of child-rearing. Parental behaviour was shown to have an important influence upon the likelihood of delinquency, independently of social factors such as low income and large family. These results lend strong support to the theory that the unsatisfactory attitudes and methods of individual parents play an important part in the genesis of juvenile delinquency, over and above the influence of external social pressures. This conclusion justifies the effort put into this aspect of the enquiry, even though the relevant elements of parental behaviour were not identified with any precision.

Poor parental supervision, which referred to a lack of watchfulness (vigilance) over the boy's activities and a lack of concern with enforcing rules, was another important factor. It was a judgment that the PSWs made with particular frequency in the case of boys from large and poor families, and appeared to reflect a generally low standard of social competence. It was a simpler and more direct observation of parental practice than the evaluation of parental behaviour, which was more interpretative and took into account emotional attitudes and relationships within the family.

Poor parental supervision was as affective a predictor of future delinquency as poor parental behaviour. It was not, however, pinpointed as one of the five major predictive factors, because it was not important independently of others. After matching for family size, or family income, or the boy's intelligence, it ceased to have any clear relationship with delinquency. These three factors might have been precursors of delinquency mainly because of their associations with poor parental supervision. However, this could not have been the only reason, because the three factors in question were each significantly associated with delinquency after matching for parental supervision.

Poor parental supervision and poor parental behaviour often coincided, but they were by no means identical ratings. It is conceivable that poorly supervised boys who were not also subjected to the family disturbances which poor parental behaviour signified were more likely to become delinquents of the socialized than the emotionally maladjusted variety. Unfortunately, the numbers involved were too small for this suggestion to be tested here.

Among the five major background predictors, all but one were particularly closely associated with convictions of early onset, which in turn were linked with the likelihood of juvenile recidivism. Criminality of parents, especially of the father, was a very significant predictive factor, but it was exceptional in being associated primarily with convictions at age 14 or later. Having an older brother with a criminal record was also a significant precursor of delinquency, but it added nothing to the likelihood of becoming delinquent of those boys who also had a convicted parent.

The association between criminal parents and delinquent sons was scarcely ever due to direct indoctrination. It was not unknown for a criminal mother to take her boy along on shoplifting expeditions, but most parents, regardless of their own past misdeeds, were censorious towards the involvement of their own children in delinquent activity. The association was at least as strong in the case of those fathers who had not more than one adult conviction (usually long past) as it was for fathers with two or more adult convictions.

Rather surprisingly, there was no significant tendency for criminal parents to be rated poorly on the global assessment of parental behaviour. There was, however, an association between parental criminality and poor (lax or careless) parental supervision. After matching for parental supervision, there ceased to be a clearly significant relationship between boys' delinquency and parental criminality. This result might be explained by supposing that it was some kind of social irresponsibility in the criminal parents that accounted both for their own past convictions and for the poor supervision which permitted their sons to drift into delinquency at adolescence.

An exception to these generalizations must be made for the small minority of boys from a highly criminal milieu. When several members of the family were recidivists, the incidence of all kinds of social pathology was particularly high, poor parental behaviour was the general rule, and the sons nearly always became recidivists.

The fifth predictive factor, low intelligence, as measured by a non-verbal test, Raven's Progressive Matrices, was just as closely associated with future delinquency as poor verbal or scholastic performance. This appeared to contradict the widely held view that verbal and educational retardation is more characteristic of delinquents than low intelligence. On all three occasions of testing, at 8, 10 and 14, low Matrices scores correlated with delinquency to roughly the same extent as low verbal and attainment scores. These results may have been due to the peculiarities of the Matrices test, which differs from most non-verbal measures in giving scores closely correlated with those from verbal tests.

Since the relationship was unexpected, some care was taken to explore alternative explanations. Another non-verbal measure, the Porteus Maze Test Quotient, gave substantially similar results. An examination of the scoring on the easier and more difficult sections of the Matrices test, and an analysis of the times spent trying to solve the test problems, gave no support to the theory that the delinquent group performed badly because of their poorer motivation.

Although low IQ was very significantly linked with delinquency, the average IQ of the delinquents was only 6 points below that of the non-delinquents. A difference of this magnitude is not very striking, and is similar to that obtained by other researchers. The novel feature of the present results was the demonstration that the slightly depressed average IQ of delinquents sufficed to produce marked contrasts in delinquency potential, according to whether a boy was in the upper or lower range of the IQ distribution. Another important aspect was the demonstration that IQ and delinquency were still associated even after matching for social factors such as family income, family size and parental behaviour. A low IQ was particularly characteristic of boys first convicted at an early age, but, at any given age of first conviction, boys who became recidivists had a lower average IQ than those who did not. These results were in keeping with the general conclusion that most of the unfavourable characteristics of delinquents were particularly evident among those convicted early and among those who became recidivists.

The reasons for the association between low IQ and delinquency are not obvious. Low IQ could be a factor in getting caught. The self-report enquiry suggested that the more intelligent among the badly behaved boys sometimes succeeded in avoiding conviction, at least until they were young adults. Low IQ scores correlated closely with school failure, and school failure may lead to delinquency. School failure, however, has many causes, and does not necessarily result from an innate inferiority of intellectual potential.

Several of the major predictors of delinquency, such as low income, parental criminality and poor parental behaviour, although not measured until the boys were at least 8 years old, were family factors of a kind likely to have been present for a long time. This implies that delinquency is to some extent predetermined from a very early age, perhaps even from birth.

Apart from the five major background factors, many other features were associated with delinquency. Various aspects of family life and parental behaviour that, for one reason or another, had not been included in the main parental behaviour rating were nevertheless linked with an increased likelihood of a boy becoming delinquent. One of these was parental uncooperativeness. Lack of information about some of the worst homes probably led to the importance of poor parental behaviour being somewhat underestimated in the tabulations. This was shown by the outcome of an intensive examination of the few boys who became recidivists despite coming from homes that had been judged satisfactory. The conclusion was that most of these cases were not really as anomalous as they had seemed at first. If the adverse information, which came to light subsequently, had been available at the time, the boys' backgrounds would not have been rated so favourably.

Parents (and especially mothers) who endorsed authoritarian statements on a questionnaire about child-rearing tended to produce delinquent sons. There was no significant association, however, between poor parental behaviour or poor parental supervision, as assessed by PSWs, and the expression of authoritarian opinions on the questionnaire. This agrees with previous investigations, which have found verbal opinions and actual child-rearing behaviour to be substantially unrelated. Since low income and large family size were both very significantly associated with authoritarianism, it is likely that many of the high scores were produced by the less subtle and less intelligent parents. Whatever the reason, boys whose parents endorsed authoritarian views were at some disadvantage.

The boys born illegitimate were singularly delinquent-prone, which is understandable if illegitimacy tends to reflect poor parental standards. An interesting by-product of this aspect of the enquiry was the discovery that many illegitimate births were not officially registered as such. Boys with 'unstable' mothers, so labelled by the PSWs through erratic or psychopathic behaviour, were particularly likely to become delinquents. The same was true for boys with unstable fathers, although not quite to the same degree. Nervousness and physical ill health among mothers were also associated with delinquency, but only to a slight extent. Boys with high educational achievements whose mothers had relatively low aspirations for them regarding jobs in the future were especially vulnerable to delinquent behaviour. Presumably, such boys were being subtly undervalued or rejected. Yet another indirect indication of the importance of parental attitudes came out of the enquiry into boys' leisure pursuits. Boys who spent relatively little time at home, whose parents shared no leisure activities or interests with them, were significantly delinquent-prone. Generally speaking, unsatisfactory maternal influences appeared to be more potent than paternal ones, but that could have been an artefact of measurement, since the social workers had easier access to mothers than fathers.

Some of the less positive results were particularly instructive. 'Broken homes' were not very frequent, and were only significantly associated with delinquency when they were due to parental desertions or divorce rather than to parental death. Temporary separations from parents were more frequent than permanent breaks, but once again were only significantly related to delinquency when cases due to illness were eliminated. These findings suggest that it was the atmosphere of disruption and conflict which promoted delinquency, rather than the physical break. Normal families survive bereavements without the children becoming delinquents, but desertions, because they usually imply an unsatisfactory family situation of long standing, are more likely to lead to delinquency.

Boys of mesomorphic physique, as far as it was possible in the present Study to identify them by measures of height, weight and strength of grip, were not particularly delinquent-prone. Again, boys with a record of some complication during their mother's pregnancy and delivery were not especially likely to become delinquents. Minimal brain damage at birth does not seem to be a plausible explanation for delinquent tendency in the majority of cases. Likewise, we were not able to confirm Eysenck's theory that neurotic-extraversion is related to delinquency. There was no evidence that particular secondary schools fostered juvenile delinquency. Our results suggested that differences between schools were largely a matter of different populations at intake. Attendance at a secondary school with a relatively high incidence of delinquent pupils caused boys to become only marginally more delinquent than would have been expected from their behaviour and characteristics before admission. There were slight but statistically insignificant differences in delinquency rates between Study boys coming from different census wards within the neighbourhood. Had it been possible to subdivide the area into much smaller parts, identifying particular streets and housing estates, much bigger differences would probably have been found.

Some attempt was made to investigate the connection between nervous tendency and delinquency. Boys rated by PSWs as 'nervous-withdrawn' individuals rarely became delinquents, in spite of the fact that this trait was significantly associated with poor parental behaviour, one of the major determinants of juvenile delinquency. The results were consistent with the idea that shyness, timidity and neurotic symptoms on the one hand, and delinquent behaviour on the other, were alternative forms of response to family stress. Some confirmation of this suggestion was obtained in intensive case studies of eight boys from bad family backgrounds who, contrary to expectation, remained well behaved and non-delinquent. Most of them revealed considerable signs of emotional disturbance, being described in such terms as nervous, obsessional and socially withdrawn.

One of the most startling of our findings was the highly significant association between teachers' ratings of bad behaviour in class, when boys were still only 8 years of age, and subsequent official delinquency. The teachers' ratings at age 8 correlated with different teachers' assessments at 10, 12 and 14. They also correlated with the opinions of classmates at primary school as to which boys were 'daring', which ones 'got into trouble', and which ones were NOT 'most honest'. The behavioural traits which, according to teachers, characterized future delinquents (such as laziness, being difficult to discipline, truanting and not being clean and tidy) appear to have little direct connection with stealing or other law-breaking activity. It seems that the typical delinquent is prone to deviate from the norm in a wide range of different aspects of behaviour, many of which are evident from an early age.

In later years, the delinquents were much more aggressive in behaviour and attitude than the non-delinquents. This emerged in their admissions of aggressive acts on the self-reported delinquency schedule, in their aggressive self-concepts in a semantic differential type of questionnaire administered at school when they were 14, in their aggressive attitudes to the police at ages 14 and 16, and in their aggressive behaviour according to teachers' ratings at ages 12 and 14. Aggressiveness seems to be an important characteristic of juvenile delinquents, even though they rarely have any official convictions for violent offences.

The interviews with the boys when they reached the age of 18 years are not part of the subject matter of the present report, but it is worth noting that the results so far confirm that at this age the delinquent group still differs from the rest in various behavioural traits not directly concerned with law-breaking. For instance, in comparison with the non-delinquents, the delinquents smoked more, drank more, gambled more, got into more fights, were more sexually promiscuous and changed their jobs more often. They were also more likely to be of the opinion that 'school did me no good' and that 'police rough people up'.

Altogether, the findings of the present Study strongly support the concept of a typical delinquent, in the sense that most delinquents display a behavioural syndrome which encompasses far more in the way of deviant conduct than the limited range of illegal acts for which they are apt to be convicted. Moreover, this general syndrome of deviancy was apparent from an early age. Apart from general misconduct and IQ, the only personal characteristic of primary schoolboys which proved significantly predictive of delinquency was the assessment of 'daring' by peers and by mothers reporting to PSWs. It seems likely that other predictive characteristics would have been discovered if it had been feasible to devise and apply appropriate tests (e.g. of aggressiveness or impulsiveness) while the boys were still at primary school.

The typical delinquents were not held in much esteem by peers. Judging by the small number of their classmates who wanted them as friends, potential delinquents were unpopular rather than popular. They were not even liked by their fellow delinquents. The future delinquents did not, to any significant extent, select other future delinquents from among their classmates as the boys they would most like to have as friends. On the other hand, in later years, from the high proportion of boys caught offending in company with other members of the Study, it seemed likely that the delinquents tended to mix together. In their responses to the self-report enquiry, delinquents claimed that their friends and acquaintances were as anti-social as themselves. In fact, the number of delinquent acts attributed to his friends was almost as good an index of a boy's commitment to delinquency as his own self-report score.

As this summary shows, our findings have contributed evidence for or against a large number of specific hypotheses about delinquents. They also have some bearing upon one of the major theoretical issues in criminology, namely the controversy between the psychological and sociological orientations. Psychologists are professionally interested in the personal characteristics of delinquent individuals. They are the chief supporters of the notion that delinquency stems from character defects that may be partly innate but are more likely due to inadequate upbringing. Sociologists are professionally interested in the structure of society, and in the balance between relatively deprived and relatively powerful segments of the community. They want to know who defines property rights and property crimes, and whose interests are served by the system. They are concerned with the social interactions which generate crime-prone subcultures. In some sociological models, delinquents appear to be the product of irresistible social forces, and any distinguishing characteristics they may possess are the result of social pressures.

In so far as the present Study concentrated upon individual characteristics, and was based on a working class neighbourhood sample rather than a total population, it could be said to be a predominantly psychological enquiry. Even so, the findings include many items of sociological interest. For instance, the connections between self-reported and official delinquency are relevant to theories about the labelling processes of society. In different sections of the data, it would be possible to find support for either psychological or sociological theories. For example, the importance of low income, and of other indices of low social status, was indisputable, but so too was the importance of the behaviour of individual parents, regardless of their social status. It may be tempting, in the interests of theoretical neatness, to underplay either the psychological or the social factors, but neither one nor the other is adequate on its own to account for all the results. The Cambridge Study in Delinquent Development suggests that delinquency arises from a complex interaction between the individual home atmosphere, the personal qualities of the boy and the circumstances in which the family live. However unfashionable or inconvenient, a multi-causal theoretical approach seems necessary.

2. *Some After-Thoughts on Delinquency Prevention*

The translation of research findings into social action is a task that investigators are apt to find repugnant. It calls for decisions whose full consequences cannot be foreseen. It calls for difficult value judgments, especially when conflicting needs and competing demands on scanty resources have to be weighed against each other. It calls for an appreciation of what is administratively practicable and tolerable to public opinion, as well as what is theoretically desirable. Finally, policy decisions involve a consideration of the welfare of the entire community, whereas research merely provides evidence on the one small aspect under investigation. What is good for delinquency prevention is not necessarily good for society as a whole.

In discussing proposals for preventive action, one must leave behind the safe haven of academic research and enter the arena of social controversy, where testable knowledge is lacking and personal opinions, or prejudices, hold sway. Nevertheless, it would be cowardly to close the report without giving some indication of the views we have developed as a result of this protracted enquiry. These views take into account preliminary data from interviews with delinquents and non-delinquents at age 18, which have not yet been published, as well as impressions gained from seeing delinquents in clinical work and in other settings.

Although a relatively small group within the population, young recidivist delinquents merit first consideration. They comprise a distinctive minority of troublesome and socially disruptive individuals of unfortunate parental backgrounds, difficult personalities and inadequate scholastic and vocational attainments, for whom life is an unrewarding struggle against authority. Their attitudes and habits are such that they tend to be thrown together with others of their kind. Their problems become self-perpetuating, passed on from one generation to the next in what has been referred to as an unending cycle of deprivation. Successful intervention at any point in the cycle would be preventive for future generations as well as ameliorative in the present.

Our research has shown that, at least by the age of 8, and probably even before they begin to go to school, some boys are marked out as potential recidivists. Typically, they are socially and intellectually backward, the product of poor homes with too many children, and reared by parents whose standards of care, supervision and training are woefully inadequate. Perceived by teachers as difficult, resistive children, they fit uncomfortably into the scholastic system. Their parents have little or no contact with the schools, and display minimal concern about their children's scholastic progress or leisure pursuits. Aggressive and impulsive in temperament, these boys resist the constraints of school, learn poorly, attend badly and leave early. Unattracted by organized activities or by training schemes, they spend their time on the streets and gravitate to unskilled, dead-end jobs for the sake of the higher wages offered.

Throughout this sequence of unfortunate developments, the boys and their parents experience points of contact with caring agencies. Ante-natal clinics, health visitors, general practitioners, schools, social security offices, voluntary social services, youth employment offices, and also of course police and childrens' officers, all come into the picture at some stage. None of these agencies seems able to change the course of events. The schools, who have charge of the children's training for a decade, might be expected to exert the greatest influence. In practice, however, it seems that most of those who start off as problem cases in primary schools remain problem cases right through until they leave school and run into difficulties with employers.

Two important reasons for the ineffectuality of social intervention are obvious. First, the worse the problems, the less the members of the family seem able to make proper use of the facilities that are available to them. For instance, the worst parents are as unlikely to take advantage of parent–teacher meetings as they are to cooperate with research workers in a social enquiry. Alienated boys do not join youth clubs or outward bound schemes. A second reason for the failure of remedial measures is that the amount of effort and money and organizational coordination needed to alter the situation is far greater than society is prepared to give. There is a striking disparity between the amounts of money spent on the treatment of medical crises (e.g. intensive care units for renal and cardiac patients) and social emergencies. Both these reasons for failure are amenable to correction, by putting a more realistic effort into remedial schemes, and by organizing existing services to reach those who are in greatest need.

The problem of excessive family size may serve as a practical example. Research has shown with monotonous regularity that overburdened parents, with limited money and perhaps limited skills, cannot cope with many children. Family planning is a basic necessity. This means training in the use of contraceptives, and free distribution of material at readily accessible points in shopping centres. It is not good enough for the agencies to leave the initiative to parents to seek advice. Training for both sexes should start at school. Attention to the progress of family planning arrangements should be as much a routine part of medical and ante-natal consultations as attention to diet and health hazards. If a further pregnancy does occur in a large, poor family, a medical abortion should be the first consideration, followed by an offer of sterilization. The knowledge that large families in poor circumstances make serious difficulties for themselves and for the community should be widely disseminated through all educational channels, including schools, clinics, churches, government information services and the mass media, more especially perhaps in the entertainment serials on television. In that way, a climate of opinion favourably disposed to rational contraceptive practice could be built up, and perhaps in time percolate to the more resistive sections of the community. It seems from our interview findings at age 18 that delinquent youths are both more sexually promiscuous and less likely to consider contraception than their non-delinquent peers. The provision of vasectomy under the National Health Service for fathers over a certain age might also help a little.

Obligatory limitation of family size, backed by the forcible removal of babies from overcrowded homes, and compulsory sterilization of mothers, is unthinkable in a permissive, democratic society. Nevertheless, one cannot but note the strange contrast between the rigorous rules which are applied to ensure the suitability of couples wanting to adopt children, and the complete *laissez-faire* attitude towards irresponsible breeding. Although compulsion in this field is certainly not to be recommended, more realistic inducements might be tried. It could be made easier, financially and otherwise, for parents to release their babies for adoption when it becomes clear that they cannot provide sufficient care.

Poverty, and all the harassment that goes with chronic debts and threatened evictions, weighs heavily upon large families with low earning capacity. The level of minimum wages and family allowances, and the possible introduction of negative taxation, have a direct bearing upon the likelihood of some of these over-burdened parents fulfilling their responsibilities. Economic policies which have the effect of redistributing wealth, and lessening the gap between rich and poor workers, would no doubt help, but such political decisions involve considerations far beyond the scope of delinquency research. Apart from direct financial support, many other forms of assistance could be provided, such as special home helps, child minders, crèches and nursery schools, all of which might spread the load and encourage mothers to take up paid work outside the home. This would provide them with a little financial independence, as well as bringing some variety and interest into their lives. Of course, all of these things are being tried, but to produce practical results they need to be on a generous scale and directed specifically towards the most needy families.

Rational preventive action ought to be based upon aetiological theory. The data of the present Study do not prove, but at least they are consistent with, explanations in terms of modern psychological theories of socialization. For instance, the importance of adequate and consistent parental role models, the need to spend time with children in order to pass on verbal and social attainments, the need to provide for and take an interest in constructive use of leisure, the need for firm and consistent guidance without repressive or rejecting attitudes, and the advantages of harmony between the parents, are all supported by empirical data as well as being predictable theoretically. How can all these desirable parental practices be encouraged?

The education of adolescents of both sexes in the practical skills of parenthood and in the psychological needs of children should be a major part of the school curriculum. Teachers should be as much concerned with these matters of everyday life as they are with the conventional examination syllabus. Furthermore, education for parents should obviously continue after leaving school. At present, youth training schemes and evening classes, like the schools, pay insufficient attention to practical matters, such as raising loans, finding accommodation, negotiating with authorities and exercising civil rights. Guidance on child rearing could fit unobtrusively into practical training in citizenship. At the stage when children are actually on the way, health visitors should concern themselves with the total home environment, not just with hygiene and physical welfare. Their training should fit them to assess family situations and give counselling where required. The integration under one authority of health, mental welfare, housing, social security and children's services should, in theory, allow for smooth liaison between the workers responsible for different but interdependent aspects of family welfare.

Much of this effort will be wasted unless the problem of reluctant clients is solved. There are many reasons for reluctance: fear of the exposure of guilty secrets, resentment at interference with parental rights, distrust of middle class social workers, unwillingness to accept direction from authority figures, anxiety about reprisals from other members of the family if their shortcomings are revealed, and an obstinate adherence to the right of privacy and independence in family matters. In the face of these understandable anxieties, offers of help need to be made more attractive. Clients who have already benefited by cooperation might be enlisted to canvass others. If material assistance is the only need a client can acknowledge, this can be exploited in an attempt to establish trust and rapport. Incompetent parents might be enticed to come with their children to holiday homes, in the hope of bringing helpful and educative influences to bear during their stay.

Influences outside the home assume a special importance in the lives of children deprived of parental care. Theoretically, it should be possible to compensate for shortcomings at home, but, in practice, outside influences all too often confirm deprived children in their anti-social ways. Such children tend to mix with others like themselves—the worst peer group they could choose. The delinquent acts of juveniles occur for the most part when they are in the company of other delinquent-prone companions. The schools seem unable to counteract this. One of our most depressing findings was that delinquency proneness recognizable at primary school age seemed to remain substantially unaltered whatever school a boy subsequently attended.

A different and more aggressive educational policy, directed more towards the needs of the worst pupils, might change this state of affairs. Since the verbal and social retardation of deprived children is evident at school entry, the first line of attack should be earlier than this, through nursery schools. Children whose development has been held back through lack of stimulation at home may be helped considerably by close contact with peers and adults from an early age. Unfortunately, it is usually the children of the better off and more enterprising parents who are taken to such schools, rather than the children whose needs are greatest.

At the primary school stage, the links between intellectual handicap, poor school record and the onset of delinquent behaviour are all too evident. The duller and more troublesome boys, who opt out of school life in social as well as in educational activities, constitute the crux of the problem. They are the boys who so often become the juvenile recidivists of later years, and they warrant special attention. Unless they are seriously subnormal, it is probably not a good policy to segregate troublesome pupils in special schools. Certainly, the schools for the subnormal should not be used for this purpose. There is already an over-representation of boys and of coloured children at these schools, which suggests that subnormality is not the only reason for admission.

The aim should be to bring difficult children back into the fold by making school more attractive to them and more relevant to their needs. Deprived children need to have acceptance and to experience some kind of achievement, otherwise they become confirmed outcasts and rebels. Changes in the curriculum, greater emphasis on practical and social activities, encouragement in self-expression, a playing down of academic competition and above all a positively concerned attitude on the part of teachers to achieve rapport with the more difficult pupils, would be beneficial. In some schools, however, nothing short of a radical reorientation of function would work. One possibility is to draw the school into the life of the adult community, in order to break down the barriers between parents and schools. Teachers, and to some extent pupils themselves, could participate in community projects, such as play centres, clubs, tenants' associations, legal aid, addiction prevention schemes, aftercare services, police liaison work with juveniles, and so on. Until these more venturesome approaches have been tried out on a sufficient scale, it is not fair to conclude that the schools have no power to change the fate of children who seem destined to become third-class citizens.

The retarded and the delinquent tend to leave school at the earliest possible moment. Although they are the ones who are in greatest need of further training, they are the ones least likely to obtain apprenticeships or to take posts where training or day-release schemes are in operation. Instead, they form a reservoir of relatively cheap, low-grade, casual labour. Having no particular commitment to an occupation or a career, their alienation from the mainstream of conforming youth is aggravated still further. They have nothing to lose by drifting about and changing jobs as the impulse takes them.

This situation could be counteracted by stricter control of the employment of young school leavers, to prevent them from being recruited for jobs that have no provision for training. Unfortunately, such a policy could not be put into operation until the general problem of high unemployment among school leavers is solved. This thought leads once again to far-reaching issues of economic organization. Society's most valuable asset is young people. The demands of business competition and the profit motive should not be allowed to take priority over the duty to apply civilized standards to the task of inducting new members into the labour force. Under the present circumstances, the transition from school to work is altogether too abrupt and too haphazard.

Thoughts on prevention are naturally preoccupied with how to counteract the social deprivations that are so frequent among recidivist delinquents. However, deprivation is not the only cause. Some individuals become delinquents for other reasons, perhaps from some aggressive or assertive quality of temperament, or perhaps from casual associations and delinquent opportunities. Such developments are peculiarly difficult to prevent, but on the other hand the individuals concerned may be more easily dissuaded from a criminal career because they are relatively normal and have other options available. If the penal system were able to concentrate on socializing the wayward, rather than having to cope with the casualties of the social system, it might have considerably more success.

Our research confirms that boys found guilty of offences at an early age have a particularly poor prognosis. This means that the agencies concerned with the early identification and processing of delinquents are failing to divert young offenders from their way of life. One discouraging finding of the research was that the critical attitudes to the police characteristic of delinquents were present only to a slight extent before prosecution. Actual experience of police behaviour was the main reason why the delinquents developed hostile attitudes. When describing their experiences of being convicted, boys often complained of unsympathetic handling by the police and of unfairly 'loaded' versions of events presented to the courts. It is important that the law should not be enforced in ways that give the offender an excuse to blame anyone but himself.

No doubt the police have a hard and thankless task, but justice needs to be seen to be fair and scrupulous at every step, not merely at the stage of magisterial deliberation. Delinquents have a tough and aggravating façade, but a greater readiness to listen to them and reason with them might save some ill-feeling, and need not interfere with the course of justice. Parents with a past record of convictions tend to have sons who become delinquents at adolescence. One reason for this could be that they pass on anti-establishment attitudes.

In so far as boys who become delinquents differ from their peers in temperament, they seem to be more venturesome and to like excitement more. Their energy is impulsive, they like taking risks, and they are easily bored. It is important to take this into account in making provisions for the young to use their leisure to better advantage. Unconventional and risky pursuits, in which they can prove their masculinity, may have a particular appeal to delinquents and serve to divert their aggression from more anti-social outlets.

In conclusion, if the aim of delinquency prevention is to be seriously pursued, educational and welfare efforts must be more concentrated on and more relevant to the needs of the groups who are at greatest risk. This means discriminating against the better endowed for the sake of the weaker members of the community.

APPENDIX A

Summarizing all Relationships with Official Juvenile Delinquency

Factor	At age	Description of 'worst' group	N(%D)	Remaining N(%D)	χ^2	p<
1. Family income	8–9	Poor	93 (33·3)	318 (16·7)	11·3	·001
2. Housing of family	8–9	Poor	137 (27·7)	274 (16·8)	6·08	·025
3. Condition of interior of house	8–9	Neglected	50 (32·0)	349 (17·8)	4·77	·05
4. Socio-economic class of family	8–9	Low (V manual)	64 (25·0)	347 (19·6)	·67	N.S.
5. Socio-economic class of family	10–11	Low (V manual)	57 (26·3)	354 (19·5)	1·02	N.S.
6. Support by social agencies	8–9	Family supported	83 (41·0)	328 (15·2)	25·4	·001
7. Social handicap	8–9	Severe	55 (43·6)	356 (16·9)	19·4	·001
8. Family size	10	Large (four or more siblings)	99 (32·3)	312 (16·7)	10·39	·005
9. Ordinal position of boy in family	10	Middle	170 (24·7)	241 (17·4)	2·82	·10
10. Job record of father	8–9	Erratic	82 (34·2)	291 (15·1)	13·7	·001
11. Special training of father	8–9	None	278 (21·6)	84 (10·7)	4·26	·05
12. Job of mother	8–9	Full-time job	88 (14·8)	296 (20·6)	1·13	N.S.
13. Job of mother	10–11	Full-time job	85 (11·8)	281 (22·1)	3·75	·10
14. Physical neglect of boy	8–9	Present	49 (40·8)	349 (17·2)	13·5	·001
15. Criminal father	10	Present	83 (38·6)	318 (15·7)	19·7	·001
16. Criminal mother	10	Present	37 (37·8)	371 (18·6)	6·54	·025
17. Criminal parent	10	Present	97 (36·1)	314 (15·6)	17·9	·001
18. Delinquent older brother	10	Present	37 (40·5)	136 (22·1)	4·25	·05
19. Criminality of parents or siblings	10	Present	122 (36·1)	289 (13·8)	24·7	·001
20. Maternal attitude	8–9	Cruel, passive or neglecting	42 (33·3)	339 (17·4)	5·14	·025
21. Maternal discipline	8–9	Very strict or erratic	135 (26·7)	241 (15·8)	5·83	·025
22. Emotional quality of maternal discipline	8–9	Harsh	43 (37·2)	334 (17·4)	8·29	·005
23. Attitude and discipline of mother (combined)	8–9	Unsatisfactory	62 (38·7)	321 (15·9)	15·7	·001
24. Paternal attitude	8–9	Cruel, passive or neglecting	68 (30·9)	286 (16·1)	6·91	·01
25. Paternal discipline	8–9	Very strict or erratic	83 (27·7)	279 (16·8)	4·17	·05
26. Emotional quality of paternal discipline	8–9	Harsh	41 (36·6)	324 (17·0)	7·81	·01
27. Attitude and discipline of father (combined)	8–9	Unsatisfactory	77 (31·2)	290 (16·2)	7·80	·01

H

Factor	At age	Description of 'worst' group	N(%D)	Remaining N(%D)	χ^2	p<
28. Marital disharmony	8–9	Present	89 (31·5)	284 (14·8)	11·3	·001
29. Parental inconsistency	8–9	Present	100 (26·0)	261 (16·9)	3·30	·10
30. Parental dominance	8–9	Mother dominant	118 (24·6)	232 (15·5)	3·67	·10
31. Parental conflict (combined)	8–9	Present	60 (35·0)	322 (16·2)	10·44	·005
32. Parental behaviour (combined)	8–9	Poor	96 (32·3)	300 (15·3)	12·3	·001
33. Separation from parent	10	Separated for reasons other than death or hospitalization	90 (32·2)	321 (17·1)	8·94	·005
34. Broken homes	10	Due to reasons other than death	31 (38·7)	380 (19·0)	5·72	·025
35. Broken homes	15	Due to reasons other than death	48 (37·5)	363 (18·2)	8·58	·005
36. Illegitimacy	Birth	Illegitimate	25 (40·0)	386 (19·2)	5·05	·025
37. Obstetric abnormality	Birth	Present	138 (18·1)	134 (19·4)	·01	N.S.
38. 'Catholic' parent	8–9	Present	73 (28·8)	279 (16·1)	5·27	·025
39. 'Non-British' parent	8–9	Present	54 (29·6)	357 (19·1)	2·61	N.S.
40. Paternal interest in children	8–9	Absent	43 (30·2)	323 (17·0)	3·55	·10
41. Parental interest in education	8–9	Absent	63 (31·8)	318 (17·3)	6·06	·025
42. Praise by parents	8–9	Boy not praised	44 (25·0)	327 (18·7)	·63	N.S.
43. Vigilance of parents	8–9	Under-vigilant	43 (44·2)	339 (16·2)	17·4	·001
44. Rules of parents	8–9	Lax rules	66 (28·8)	309 (16·8)	4·32	·05
45. Parental supervision (combined)	8–9	Poor	74 (31·1)	309 (16·5)	7·23	·01
46. Maternal authoritarianism	10	High	82 (28·1)	209 (13·9)	7·12	·01
47. Maternal under-concern	10	High	81 (19·8)	210 (17·1)	·12	N.S.
48. Paternal authoritarianism	10	High	57 (17·5)	175 (16·6)	·00	N.S.
49. Parental authoritarianism (combined)	10	High	73 (27·4)	226 (15·0)	4·89	·05
50. Physical health of mother	8–9	Poor	103 (27·2)	280 (16·4)	4·92	·05
51. Physical health of father	8–9	Poor	79 (26·6)	282 (17·4)	2·78	·10
52. Intelligence of mother	8–9	Mother dull	66 (22·7)	329 (19·2)	·25	N.S.
53. Nervousness of mother	8–9	Mother nervous	73 (31·5)	310 (16·5)	7·65	·01
54. Psychiatric treatment of mother	8–9	Mother treated	81 (23·5)	298 (18·1)	·85	N.S.
55. Neuroticism of mother (health questionnaire)	10	Mother neurotic	70 (25·7)	209 (14·8)	3·57	·10
56. (Combined) nervousness of mother	10	Mother nervous	125 (24·8)	262 (16·8)	2·98	·10

Factor	At age	Description of 'worst' group	N(%D)	Remaining N(%D)	χ^2	p<
57. Nervousness of father	8–9	Father nervous	79 (22·8)	290 (18·6)	·45	N.S.
58. Psychiatric treatment of father	8–9	Father treated	42 (31·0)	326 (18·1)	3·13	·10
59. (Combined) nervousness of father	8–9	Father nervous	81 (23·5)	288 (18·4)	·75	N.S.
60. Instability of father	8–9	Present	47 (34·0)	321 (17·5)	6·16	·025
61. Instability of mother	8–9	Present	49 (44·9)	333 (15·3)	22·3	·001
62. Uncooperativeness of parents	8–9	Present	43 (39·5)	368 (18·2)	9·50	·005
63. Interviews with father	8–9	Absent	120 (28·3)	291 (17·2)	5·83	·025
64. Progressive matrices IQ of boy	8–9	Low	86 (31·4)	325 (17·5)	7·20	·01
65. Progressive matrices IQ of boy	10–11	Low	129 (29·5)	279 (16·1)	8·87	·005
66. (Combined) Progressive matrices IQ of boy	10–11	Low	103 (31·1)	308 (16·9)	8·70	·005
67. Progressive matrices IQ of boy	14–15	Low	98 (31·6)	307 (16·9)	8·96	·005
68. Porteus Maze TQ of boy	8–9	Low	108 (34·3)	299 (15·7)	15·5	·001
69. Porteus Maze TQ of boy	10–11	Low	106 (24·5)	300 (19·0)	1·15	N.S.
70. Porteus Maze TQ of boy	14–15	Low	97 (21·7)	309 (20·1)	·04	N.S.
71. Word Comprehension	8–9	Low	96 (30·2)	301 (17·3)	6·72	·01
72. Sentence reading	8–9	Low	133 (24·8)	244 (16·8)	3·01	·10
73. Mechanical reading	8–9	Low	101 (32·7)	302 (16·6)	11·1	·001
74. Mill Hill vocabulary	10–11	Low	124 (32·3)	277 (15·5)	13·6	·001
75. Mill Hill vocabulary	14–15	Low	93 (31·2)	313 (17·3)	7·72	·01
76. Attainments arithmetic	11	Low	83 (33·7)	303 (16·2)	11·5	·001
77. Attainments English	11	Low	88 (31·8)	298 (16·4)	9·12	·005
78. Attainments verbal reasoning	11	Low	136 (29·4)	250 (14·8)	10·9	·001
79. Secondary school allocation	11	Low	121 (29·8)	290 (16·6)	8·36	·005
80. Cleverness (peers)	10–11	Low	85 (25·9)	268 (17·2)	2·62	N.S.
81. Troublesomeness or conduct disorder (teachers)	8–9	High	100 (41·0)	311 (13·8)	32·7	·001
82. Troublesomeness or conduct disorder (teachers)	10–11	High	99 (38·4)	312 (14·7)	24·4	·001
83. Troublesomeness or conduct disorder (teachers) (combined at 8–9 and 10–11)	10–11	High	134 (38·1)	277 (11·9)	36·4	·001
84. Troublesomeness or conduct disorder (PSWs)	8–9	High	60 (38·3)	306 (16·7)	13·3	·001
85. Combined conduct disorder (teachers, PSWs)	8–9	Present	83 (39·8)	328 (15·6)	22·4	·001

Factor	At age	Description of 'worst' group	N(%D)	Remaining N(%D)	χ^2	p<
86. Troublesomeness (peers)	10–11	High	80 (37·5)	273 (13·9)	20·6	·001
87. Troublesomeness (peers and teachers combined)	10–11	High	92 (44·6)	319 (13·5)	40·5	·001
88. Acting out	8–9	Present	77 (39·0)	334 (16·2)	18·6	·001
89. Daring (peers)	10–11	High	100 (38·0)	253 (11·9)	29·8	·001
90. Daring or adventurousness (PSWs)	8–9	High	75 (37·3)	304 (15·8)	16·1	·001
91. Daring (peers and PSWs combined)	10–11	High	121 (38·8)	287 (12·9)	33·5	·001
92. Dishonesty (peers)	10–11	High	88 (37·5)	265 (13·2)	23·5	·001
93. Popularity (peers)	8–9	Low	97 (20·6)	288 (19·8)	·00	N.S.
94. Popularity (peers)	10–11	Low	77 (24·7)	276 (17·8)	1·44	N.S.
95. (Combined) popularity (peers)	10–11	Low	126 (24·6)	269 (17·1)	2·62	N.S.
96. 'Ideal' (peers)	10–11	High	86 (15·1)	267 (20·6)	·93	N.S.
97. 'Like self' (peers)	10–11	High	87 (19·5)	266 (19·2)	·01	N.S.
98. Porteus Q	8–9	High (clumsy)	100 (25·0)	307 (19·2)	1·21	N.S.
99. Porteus Q (cut line)	10–11	High (clumsy)	109 (29·4)	297 (17·2)	6·55	·025
100. (Combined) Porteus Q	10–11	High (clumsy)	104 (26·9)	307 (18·2)	3·09	·10
101. Porteus Q (cut line)	14–15	High (clumsy)	96 (25·0)	310 (19·0)	1·26	N.S.
102. Spiral Maze Errors (corrected)	8–9	High (clumsy)	105 (30·5)	303 (17·2)	7·66	·01
103. Spiral Maze Errors (corrected)	10–11	High (clumsy)	92 (35·9)	283 (16·3)	14·9	·001
104. (Combined) Spiral Maze Errors (corrected)	10–11	High (clumsy)	102 (28·4)	306 (18·0)	4·50	·05
105. Tapping score	8–9	High (clumsy)	96 (21·9)	240 (21·7)	·01	N.S.
106. Tapping score	10–11	High (clumsy)	92 (30·4)	279 (17·6)	6·21	·025
107. (Combined) Tapping score	10–11	High (clumsy)	99 (28·3)	298 (18·1)	4·08	·05
108. Tapping Score	14–15	High (clumsy)	109 (25·7)	298 (18·6)	2·05	N.S.
109. Psychomotor clumsiness (Porteus, Spiral and Tapping combined)	10–11	High (clumsy)	104 (31·7)	307 (16·6)	10·01	·005
110. Body sway	8–9	Erratic	76 (23·7)	298 (19·1)	·53	N.S.
111. Church attendance of boy	8–9	Non-attenders	285 (19·7)	69 (14·5)	·66	N.S.
112. Height of boy	8–9	Small	50 (34·0)	356 (18·5)	5·35	·25
113. Height of boy	10–11	Small	71 (32·4)	331 (17·5)	7·14	·01
114. Weight of boy	8–9	Light	102 (24·5)	303 (18·8)	1·20	N.S.
115. Weight of boy	10–11	Light	87 (26·4)	312 (18·6)	2·13	N.S.
116. Mesomorphy	8–9	High	159 (20·8)	246 (19·9)	·01	N.S.
117. Mesomorphy	10–11	High	181 (18·8)	217 (21·2)	·22	N.S.
118. (Combined) mesomorphy	10–11	High	139 (21·6)	270 (19·6)	·11	N.S.
119. Strength (dynamometer grip)	10–11	High	92 (19·6)	298 (20·8)	·01	N.S.
120. Elbow measurement	10–11	Large	93 (19·4)	295 (20·3)	·00	N.S.
121. Health of boy	8–9	Poor	112 (21·4)	273 (18·0)	·42	N.S.
122. Head injuries and fits of boy	8–9	Present	39 (18·0)	340 (18·5)	·02	N.S.

Factor	At age	Description of 'worst' group	N(% D)	Remaining N(% D)	x^2	p<
23. Nervousness of boy	8–9	High	41 (19·5)	341 (19·4)	·03	N.S.
24. Outgoing or withdrawn boy	8–9	Withdrawn	83 (16·9)	300 (20·0)	·23	N.S.
25. Nervous-withdrawn (combined)	8–9	High	95 (14·7)	294 (21·1)	1·46	N.S.
26. Neuroticism of boy (cards test)	8–9	High	70 (20·0)	230 (17·4)	·10	N.S.
27 Neuroticism of boy (NJMI)	10–11	High	116 (24·1)	279 (18·6)	1·21	N.S.
28. Neuroticism of boy (NJMI)	14–15	High	103 (25·2)	303 (18·8)	1·58	N.S.
29. Extraversion of boy (cards test)	8–9	High	99 (18·2)	201 (17·9)	·01	N.S.
30. Extraversion of boy (NJMI)	10–11	High	115 (21·7)	280 (19·6)	·11	N.S.
31 Extraversion of boy (NJMI)	14–15	High	108 (22·2)	298 (19·8)	·16	N.S.
32. Neurotic extraversion of boy (cards test)	8–9	High	89 (22·5)	211 (16·1)	1·31	N.S.
33. Neurotic extraversion of boy (NJMI)	10–11	High	114 (21·1)	281 (19·9)	·01	N.S.
34. Neurotic extraversion of boy (combined)	10–11	High	178 (21·9)	220 (19·1)	·32	N.S.
35. Neurotic extraversion of boy (NJMI)	14–15	High	91 (26·4	315 (18·7)	2·09	N.S.
36. Lying of boy (NJMI)	10–11	High	86 (15·1)	309 (21·7)	1·41	N.S.
37. Lying of boy (NJMI)	14–15	High	103 (21·4)	303 (20·1)	·02	N.S.
38. Defiance (discipline questionnaire)	13–14	High	91 (23·1)	251 (16·3)	1·62	N.S.
39. Critical attitude to police	14–15	High	108 (34·3)	297 (15·5)	16·0	·001
40. Self-reported delinquency	14–15	High	108 (46·3)	297 (11·1)	58·0	·001
41. Reported delinquency of friends	14–15	High	101 (42·6)	304 (13·2)	38·5	·001
42. Reported delinquency of acquaintances	14–15	High	97 (41·2)	308 (14·0)	32·0	·001
43. Teachers' rating aggressive	12–13	High	86 (31·4)	318 (17·0)	7·90	·005
44. Teachers' rating aggressive	14–15	High	89 (43·8)	289 (12·8)	38·8	·001
45. Verbal aggression (picture frustration test)	14–15	High	97 (24·7)	290 (18·6)	1·33	N.S.
46. Actual aggressive self-concept (Semantic differential)	14–15	High	103 (32·0)	303 (16·5)	10·47	·005
47. Ideal aggressive self-concept (semantic differential)	14–15	High	102 (27·5)	304 (18·1)	3·56	·10

Factor	At age	Description of 'worst' group	N(%D)	Remaining N(%D)	χ^2	p<
148. Neuroticism of boy (EPI)	16–17	High	106 (20·8)	292 (20·6)	·01	N.S.
149. Extraversion of boy (EPI)	16–17	High	89 (25·8)	309 (19·1)	1·53	N.S.
150. Neurotic extraversion of boy (EPI)	16–17	High	118 (24·6)	280 (18·9)	1·29	N.S.
151. Lying of boy (EPI)	16–17	High	123 (24·4)	275 (18·9)	1·24	N.S.

Note: On each factor, the boys were divided, as far as possible, into the worst 'quarter' and the remaining three-quarters. This dichotomy was then compared with the delinquent/non-delinquent dichotomy in a 2 × 2 table. This method made the relationships of the different factors with delinquency directly comparable. The resulting values of χ^2 all have one degree of freedom. They are shown to two decimal places unless they exceed 10·83 (p = ·001), in which case they are shown to one decimal place.

APPENDIX B

The Matching Analyses

Each matching analysis was carried out to investigate whether a factor was important as a precursor of delinquency independently of another factor. For example, delinquents may appear to have larger-sized families than non-delinquents only because delinquents tend to come from poorer families, which tend to be larger in size. If this were so, delinquents and non-delinquents would not differ in family size when matched for family income. The matching analyses were restricted to factors measured at ages 8–10, because only these could be precursors of delinquency.

When carrying out the matching, each delinquent was paired with the non-delinquent nearest to him on the alphabetical name list who had the same rating on the factor to be matched, in this case income. The only exception was that a delinquent could not be matched with the nearest boy on the list if that happened to be his own brother, because brothers were necessarily rated the same on many family factors. Delinquents who were 'not known' on a factor were not included in the analysis, but this did not apply when matching for income, since no boy was rated 'not known' on this. The difference between the ratings of the members of each matched pair was noted, and the statistical significance of the set of differences was tested using the Wilcoxon T statistic. In this example, the differences were significant, indicating that delinquents and non-delinquents still differed in family size even when matched for family income. It was concluded that the association between family size and delinquency held true independently of any association between family income and delinquency.

There were two main reasons for analysing our results by this matching method. First, it was simpler and more easily understandable than many statistical techniques. Second, our sample was too small, and many of our measurements were too crude, for the application of more sophisticated statistics, particularly of the parametric variety. A disadvantage with the matching analysis was that, owing to the fact that there were only 84 delinquents, comparisons had to be based on less than half the sample—a maximum of 168 boys out of 411. It could be argued against the result of each matching test that a different answer might have been obtained if the delinquents had been paired with a different set of non-delinquents. In an attempt to overcome this objection, each matching test was repeated twice, using two further sets of delinquent/non-delinquent pairings. Each additional set was selected as before, by pairing boys closest on the alphabetical list, but excluding, as far as possible, the non-delinquents used in previous matchings. Two more Wilcoxon T tests were then carried out, to evaluate the significance of the additional matching tests.

By carrying out three matching analyses in this way, the comparison could cover more than 80 per cent of the sample (336 boys). However, the three analyses were not independent, because the same delinquents were used in each. If they had been independent, it would have been possible to calculate a final value of p from the three individual p values. As this was not possible, we were left with three values of p, in some instances substantially different, and were obliged to adopt some rules to decide what conclusion to draw from them. This was the main disadvantage of using three matching tests. However, on balance, it was thought preferable to carry out three tests rather than one, as the extra tests did provide additional information.

The rules adopted for interpreting the results of the three Wilcoxon T tests were as follows: Where all three were significant at $p = \cdot 05$ or less, it was obvious that delinquents and non-delinquents differed. It was equally obvious that they did not differ significantly if none of the tests reached the ·05 level. If one of the tests was significant at $p = \cdot 05$ (but not at $p = \cdot 01$) and the other two failed to reach significance, this was taken to suggest that delinquents and non-delinquents did not differ. If, however, one of the tests was significant at $p = \cdot 01$ or less, this was taken as evidence of a difference. These last two rules were decided upon in the light of the fact that one result significant at $p = \cdot 05$ would be expected by chance in only 7 sets of three tests, while one result significant at $p = \cdot 01$ would require 34 sets of three tests to occur by chance. Finally if two out of three tests were significant at $p = \cdot 05$, it was decided to follow the majority result and conclude that a difference did exist.

Table B1 displays the results of analyses in which delinquents and non-delinquents were matched on each of 13 factors and then compared on 20 others. It shows, for example, that delinquents and non-delinquents did differ in family size after matching for family income (one T test being significant at $p = \cdot 01$, although the other two were not significant). They also differed in intelligence when matched for income, since two of the three T tests were statistically significant. A more definite difference was obtained when delinquents and non-delinquents were matched on family income and compared on troublesomeness (all three T tests being significant at $p = \cdot 001$).

In Table B1, the delinquents have been compared on 20 factors, but matched on only 13. The remaining 7 factors were not significantly related to delinquency, and there would have been little point in matching on them, since the absence of a relationship meant that the delinquent and non-delinquent groups were already sufficiently alike in these respects.

On the other hand, it did make sense, after matching for a significant factor, to compare delinquents and non-delinquents on a factor that initially had no significant association with delinquency. An example of a hidden relationship emerging from this comparison occurred in connection with the boys rated 'nervous-withdrawn'. There was initially no significant relationship between this assessment and delinquency. There was, however, a significant positive relationship between poor parental behaviour and the rating, and in turn poor parental behaviour was significantly

TABLE B1

The Matching Analyses

Comparing in	*Matching for:* *Troublesomeness*	*Daring*	*Dishonesty*	*Parental criminality*	*Family income*	*Intelligence*	*Family size*	*Parental behaviour*	*Clumsiness*	*Parental supervision*	*Separations*	*Parental authoritarianism*	*'Catholic' families*
'roublesomeness		S**	S**	S**	S**	S**	S**	S**	S**	S**	S**	S**	S**
)aring	S		S**	S**	S*	S**	S**	S**	S*	S	S**	S**	S*
)ishonesty	N	S		S*	S*	S*	S**	S**	S**	S*	S**	S*	S*
'arental criminality	UN	S2	S		S	S2	S2	S	S	UN	S2	S	UN
'amily income	N	UN	UN	US		N	S2	S2	N	S2	S2	N	S2
ntelligence	N	S2	UN	S2	S2		S2	S	N	S*	S	UN	S
'amily size	UN	S*	UN	S2	US	US		S	S2	S2	S	US	S
arental behaviour	S2	S	UN	S*	S	S*	S		S	US	S	UN	US
:lumsiness	N	S	N	UN	S2	N	S2	US		UN	S2	UN	S2
'arental supervision	UN	N	UN	UN	UN	N	US	S2	S		S2	S2	US
eparations	N	S2	N	N	UN	S2	US	S2	S2	S2		UN	S2
arental authoritarianism	N	N	N	S2	N	N	N	N	UN	UN	UN		N
Catholic' families	N	N	N	N	N	N	UN	UN	UN	N	N	N	
'opularity	N	US	N	N	N	N	N	N	N	N	N	N	N
ervous-withdrawal	N	N	N	N	N	N	N	S2	N	N	N	UN	N
1aternal neuroticism	N	N	N	N	N	N	N	N	UN	N	N	N	N
leurotic-extraversion	N	N	N	N	N	N	N	N	N	N	N	UN	N
aternal neuroticism	N	N	N	N	N	N	N	N	N	N	N	N	N
hysique	N	N	N	N	N	N	N	N	N	N	N	N	N
bstetric abnormalities	N	N	N	N	N	N	N	N	N	N	N	N	N

ey =
** = Very highly significant (all three results significant at p = ·001).
* = Very significant (all three results significant at p = ·01).
= Significant (all three results significant at p = ·05).
2 = Just significant (two results significant at p = ·05, one not significant).
S = Uncertain, but probably significant (one result significant at p = ·01, two not significant).
N = Uncertain, but probably not significant (one result significant at p = ·05, two not significant).
= Not significant (all three results not significant).

associated with delinquency. After matching for parental behaviour, it emerged that delinquents were significantly less often nervous-withdrawn than non-delinquents. This negative association had been cancelled out by the positive association of poor parental behaviour with both delinquency and nervous-withdrawal. The matching analyses served to reveal that, so long as they were not subjected to worse parental behaviour, delinquents were less likely than non-delinquents to have a nervous-withdrawn temperament.

With the exception of the example just quoted, the results of all the matching analyses were in the direction of the delinquents being 'worse' than the matched non-delinquents. For example, the delinquents were more troublesome, less intelligent and came from larger-sized families than the income-matched non-delinquents.

APPENDIX C

Inter-Relationships of Important Factors

Table Cl shows the extent to which 13 important factors were inter-related, and the sizes of their associations with juvenile delinquency. As in Appendix A, the boys rated on each factor were divided as far as possible into the 'worst' quarter and the remainder. For example, the 92 most troublesome boys were contrasted with the remaining 319. The size of the association between each pair of factors is indicated by the value of χ^2 calculated from the 2 × 2 table relating them. For example, the value of χ^2 resulting from the comparison between troublesomeness and daring is 52·9, which is significant at $p = \cdot 001$. This level of significance is indicated by the dagger. Such a high level does not necessarily mean that troublesomeness and daring are interchangeable labels; only 55 of the 121 most daring boys were in fact among the 92 most troublesome.

The value of χ^2 indicates the extent of a relationship, but not its direction. However, in every case a significant χ^2 was associated with the overlapping of the 'worst' quarters. There was no instance of a significant χ^2 following from the overlapping of the 'worst' quarter on one factor and the remaining three-quarters on another.

Table Cl shows that every one of the 13 factors was significantly linked with juvenile delinquency, and that many of them were significantly interrelated. Troublesomeness was significantly associated with every other factor, in agreement with the idea that it indicates a predisposition towards delinquency. Low family income was very significantly correlated with every factor except 'Catholic' families, and poor parental supervision was significantly related to every factor except authoritarianism.

TABLE C1

Inter-Relationships of Important Factors

	Troublesomeness	*Daring*	*Dishonesty*	*Criminal parents*	*Poor parental behaviour*	*Low family income*	*Large family size*	*Clumsiness*	*Separations*	*Low intelligence*	*Poor parental supervision*	*'Catholic' families*	*Parental authoritarianism*
Troublesomeness (92)													
Daring (121)	52·9†												
Dishonesty (88)	34·8†	10·50*											
Criminal parents (97)	12·7†	3·23	8·69*										
Poor parental behaviour (96)	9·92*	6·41*	5·35*	2·05									
Low family income (93)	25·0†	16·3†	13·4†	12·1†	11·2†								
Large family size (99)	18·0†	7·47*	7·89*	16·9†	1·66	83·3†							
Clumsiness (104)	24·6†	2·45	2·34	2·53	0·46	23·7†	14·7†						
Separations (90)	8·78*	4·90*	2·87	16·0†	4·62*	18·6†	2·64	2·47					
Low intelligence (103)	11·6†	0·15	3·35	9·00*	4·97*	17·8†	11·4†	31·5†	2·68				
Poor parental supervision (74)	25·9†	19·3†	11·7†	12·6†	17·9†	40·9†	22·7†	9·24*	7·73*	15·0†			
'Catholic' families (73)	4·97*	2·13	0·57	16·3†	2·60	1·50	0·85	0·85	2·92	2·54	5·99*		
Parental authoritarianism (73)	7·71*	0·68	3·54	0·04	3·48	17·2†	11·6†	0·85	4·87*	0·72	0·82	1·87	
Juvenile delinquency (84)	40·5†	33·5†	23·5†	17·9†	12·3†	11·3†	10·39*	10·01*	8·94*	8·70*	7·23*	5·27*	4·89*

Note: The figure in each cell is the value of χ^2 resulting from a 2 × 2 table relating the two factors defined in the row and column. The number in brackets after each factor gives the number of boys placed in the 'worst' category.
* = Significant at p = ·05.
† = Significant at p = ·001.

APPENDIX D

The Picture Frustration Test

Picture 1: John Smith misses the school bus. He walks instead but is late. Teacher remarks 'You *never* try to get here on time!'

Comment A I don't run the London Transport system, do I?
Comment B I missed the first bus. I knew I had to wait a long time so I walked.
Comment C Go away and shut up.
Comment D I'm sorry but I missed the bus.
Comment E I am sorry M'am, I missed the bus, so as it started to rain I ran to school.

Picture 2: John Smith's friends are waiting to take him out. Mother stops him—'Your room *is* untidy. You'll clear it up before you go.'

Comment A Aw come on, mum. My room's as tidy as any of my mates.
Comment B I am going out, so shut your face.
Comment C All right, mum.
Comment D Ah mum, will you do it for me? I've got to rush.
Comment E I can find my things when I want them. My room does not need to be altered.

Picture 3: John Smith tries out his new guitar. Father says 'I don't want that row when I get home from work.'

Comment A I've saved up for months for this. Please let me play it; I'll try not to make too much noise.
Comment B I might as well sell it. I can never do what I want.
Comment C I've just saved up all my money for this guitar and there's nowhere else to practise.
Comment D Well you told me to get a hobby and now when I got one you complain.
Comment E Shut up, you silly old man.

Picture 4: The headmaster said he would see John Smith after school. Very late, he found him at his desk. 'Are you pretending you don't know where my office is?'

Comment A Oh get lost.
Comment B No I was just coming when you came in.
Comment C You never said come to your office. I waited here for you.
Comment D Sorry, sir, but I thought you wanted to see me here.
Comment E Well I have waited here for over half-an-hour to see you.

Picture 5: John Smith wanders round an empty building while his friends go inside. A voice behind him says 'Trespassing, are you?'

Comment A What do you mean, trespassing?
Comment B But sir, I wasn't going to steal, sir. I was just going.
Comment C No, sir.
Comment D I would watch what you were saying.
Comment E No I am not, I'm only walking around. It's a free country, ain't it?

Picture 6: John Smith gives his place to a lady but clumsily knocks a parcel out of her hand. The conductor says 'Any trouble and you'll be off this bus.'

Comment A That's what you get for giving your seat to an old lady. I'll never do it again.
Comment B Everybody's moaning at me, even for accidents. I lead a 'dog's life'!
Comment C Oh——, 'ere we go.
Comment D I was only trying to help. It was the driver's fault.
Comment E Sorry, miss.

Picture 7: John Smith runs to give teacher her glasses. He falls and the teacher says 'And now you'll know why running downstairs is forbidden.'

Comment A You can get your own glasses next time.
Comment B You're right, I was silly. I won't do it again, miss.
Comment C Right, that's the last thing I'll do for you.
Comment D I was only trying to help.
Comment E You get on my —— nerves.

Picture 8: John Smith brings a friend home to watch their favourite T.V. programme. Father comes home and changes it, saying 'Right, let's have the news!'

Comment A Aw Dad, it's not fair. I brought my friend home particularly to watch that programme. Can we turn back, please?
Comment B All right but let's turn it over as soon as the news is finished.
Comment C You wouldn't like it if we did that to you, would you?
Comment D Turn it back, you old git.
Comment E The news is on this side after the film.

Picture 9: John Smith collects his shopping and holds it ready in the queue. The shop-keeper says 'Can't you wait your turn?'

Comment A If you want to be like that I'll take my custom elsewhere.
Comment B Shut up.
Comment C What a cheek, I didn't push in.

Comment D Well I was trying to help you, sir.
Comment E I am, aren't I?

Picture 10: John Smith is busy reading a magazine. When his younger brother asks for help with homework. Mother adds 'It's time you were doing something useful.'
Comment A Do I have to, Mum? I am reading my book.
Comment B Go and wash the pots. You should be doing something useful too.
Comment C My blasted brother!
Comment D Oh well, I would like to read this but I suppose I might as well.
Comment E What am I, your slave? You won't learn if I do it for you.

APPENDIX E

Attitudes to the Police

Item	Attitude statement	Age 14–15 Per cent 'True' Delinquents (N = 83)	Age 14–15 Per cent 'True' Non-Delinquents (N = 322)	Age 16–17 Per cent 'True' Delinquents (N = 81)	Age 16–17 Per cent 'True' Non-Delinquents (N = 316)
1	The police threaten you to try to make you admit you did whatever they have run you in for. (X)	71·1	47·8†	76·5	44·9†
2	If you need a policeman urgently you can't find one: but they interfere when they are not wanted. (X)	71·1	58·7	80·3	57·9†
3	The police usually try to persuade boys to plead 'guilty' in court, even if it's against the boy's interests. (X)	74·7	37·0†	61·7	37·3*
4	Police methods of obtaining information from boys are usually quite fair.	60·2	77·3*	45·7	74·7†
5	The evidence police give in court about boys is usually quite fair.	69·9	82·3*	75·3	79·8
6	The police pick on boys. (X)	59·0	34·0†	65·4	41·5*
7	The charges policemen bring against boys are usually quite fair.	63·9	74·5	61·7	76·6*
8	A lot of policemen take money or gifts for letting people off small offences, like parking or exceeding the speed limit. (X)	53·0	32·0*	60·5	37·0*
9	Policemen act as if there's one law for the rich and another for the poor, at least as far as boys are concerned. (X)	48·2	41·6	46·9	28·2*
10	The young policemen are specially down on boys. (X)	50·6	43·8	63·0	41·8*
11	The police are always roughing people up. (X)	42·2	19·3*	48·2	19·0†
12	The police spend so much time over petty little things that the people who do big crimes often get away with them. (X)	71·1	56·8*	71·6	51·9*
13	Policemen very rarely use more force than is necessary.	68·7	70·2	61·7	64·9
14	I'd go to the police if I was in trouble—threatened or beaten up.	39·8	54·0*	29·6	44·6

Item	Attitude statement	*Age 14–15 Per cent 'True'* Delinquents (*N* = 83)	*Age 14–15 Per cent 'True'* Non-Delinquents (*N* = 322)	*Age 16–17 Per cent 'True'* Delinquents (*N* = 81)	*Age 16–17 Per cent 'True'* Non-Delinquents (*N* = 316)
15	If I were in a punch-up and the police were called, I'd be more likely to join in fighting the police than to keep on fighting the other side. (X)	45·8	31·7	37·0	23·1
16	If I saw someone breaking into a shop, I'd probably tell the police.	50·6	71·4†	27·2	52·5†
17	If I saw someone stealing an old woman's purse, I'd tell the police.	74·7	85·7*	66·7	80·1*
18	If I saw a couple of toughs roughing someone up, I'd tell the police.	47·0	60·6*	34·6	48·7
19	If I saw someone trying the door handles of parked cars, I'd tell the police.	36·1	51·2*	18·5	35·4*
20	The police never take bribes.	38·6	37·3	21·0	20·9
21	I hate the police. (X)	44·6	14·3†	35·8	8·2†
22	Hardly any policemen would take bribes or presents to help people get away with serious crimes.	59·0	64·9	55·6	58·5
23	Policemen have far too many jobs.	49·4	65·2*	56·8	71·8*
24	I respect the police.	43·4	69·6†	48·2	73·7†
25	The British police are the best in the world.	45·8	64·0*	46·9	73·4†
26	Policemen never use their truncheons unless absolutely necessary.	69·9	82·0*	70·4	80·1
27	So far as taking bribes is concerned, the British police are much less corrupt than most police forces in other countries.	66·3	70·2	65·4	69·9
28	If a friend of mine joined the police, he wouldn't be a friend much longer. (X)	31·3	14·0*	29·6	10·8*
29	The police are a lousy lot. (X)	42·2	14·9†	33·3	13·0*
30	The police are well organized and efficient.	86·8	82·6	75·3	78·2
31	The police have a difficult job to do.	75·9	92·2†	84·0	94·9*
32	The police ought to get more support from the public.	68·7	87·6†	67·9	85·8†

(X) = Unfavourable items to be scored if rated 'probably true'.
* = Significant difference between per cent of delinquents and per cent of non-delinquents (2 × 2 χ^2 test) at p = ·05.
† = Significant difference at p = ·001.

APPENDIX F

Secondary School Teachers' Ratings

Question	*Age 12–13* N (% *delinquents*)	*Age 14–15* N (% *delinquents*)
Has this boy been punctual in attending school during the last year?		
Never late unless with good reason	283 (14·8)*	177 (9·6)*
Sometimes late	99 (25·3)	155 (23·2)
Persistently late	22 (63·6)	48 (50·0)*
Has this boy played truant during the last year?		
Never	349 (15·8)*	254 (12·6)*
Yes, occasionally	35 (40·0)	79 (27·9)
Yes, frequently	18 (61·1)	42 (50·0)*
Do you think that he tries to be a credit to his parents?		
Is very concerned	64 (9·4)*	62 (6·5)*
About average	297 (19·5)	258 (17·8)
Just doesn't care	38 (36·8)*	55 (43·6)*
When he comes to school in the morning is he clean and tidy?		
Noticeably clean and tidy	159 (14·5)*	158 (11·4)*
About average	207 (22·2)	194 (24·2)
Noticeably below average	38 (31·6)	31 45·2)*
Do you regard this boy as:		
Extremely energetic, never tired?	44 (27·3)	26 (30·8)
Normally energetic?	333 (20·4)	311 (17·0)
Always tired and 'washed out'?	27 (3·7)*	38 (39·5)*
Which statement best describes this boy?		
A very hard worker	74 (9·5)*	48 (6·3)*
Average—works moderately well	242 (19·0)	223 (16·1)
A poor worker or lazy	85 (31·8)*	109 (36·7)*
Which statement best describes this boy?		
One with high power of concentration	25 (20·0)	21 (19·1)
Average—concentrates moderately well	271 (16·2)	252 (11·9)
Little or no power of sustained concentration	107 (29·9)*	106 (42·5)*
Which statement best describes this boy?		
Extremely neat and tidy in class work	55 (10·9)	46 (10·9)
Average—moderately neat and tidy	263 (20·2)	274 (18·6)
Very untidy in class work	80 (25·0)	49 (36·7)*
Which statement best describes this boy?		
Seldom or never disobedient	216 (12·0)*	211 (11·9)*
Sometimes disobedient	160 (25·6)	135 (23·0)
Frequently disobedient	26 (50·0)*	32 (62·5)*

Question	Age 12–13 N (% delinquents)	Age 14–15 N (% delinquents)
Which statement best describes this boy?		
Seldom or never difficult to discipline	319 (17·2)*	276 (13·0)*
Sometimes difficult to discipline	71 (25·4)	73 (31·5)
Frequently difficult to discipline	14 (57·1)	28 (60·7)*
Which statement best describes this boy?		
Seldom or never restless in class	164 (11·0)*	156 (12·8)*
Sometimes restless in class	193 (23·8)	167 (16·2)
Frequently restless in class	46 (37·0)*	51 (54·9)*
Which statement best describes this boy?		
Seldom or never daydreams in class	157 (19·1)	155 (16·8)
Sometimes daydreams in class	201 (20·9)	176 (19·9)
Frequently daydreams in class	46 (19·6)	42 (35·7)*
Which statement best describes this boy?		
Seldom or never cribs	304 (18·1)	243 (14·0)*
Sometimes cribs	86 (23·3)	102 (28·4)
Frequently cribs	8 (37·5)	13 (69·2)
Which statement best describes this boy?		
Seldom or never evades the truth to keep out of trouble	293 (14·3)*	220 (10·0)*
Sometimes evades the truth to keep out of trouble	90 (32·2)	120 (25·0)
Frequently evades the truth to keep out of trouble	21 (47·6)	35 (65·7)*
Which statement best describes this boy?		
Very popular with other children	49 (20·4)	47 (19·2)
Of average popularity	322 (19·6)	286 (17·8)
Tends to be ignored by other children	33 (24·2)	44 (36·4)*
Which statement best describes this boy?		
Liable to get unduly rough during playtime	20 (35·0)	17 (58·8)
Takes a normal part in rough games	333 (19·2)	295 (18·3)
Rather frightened of rough games	51 (19·6)	62 (17·7)
Which statement best describes this boy?		
Avoids attention, hates being in the limelight	36 (8·3)	51 (9·8)
Does not unduly avoid or seek attention	318 (17·9)	279 (16·9)
Shows off, seeks attention	50 (42·0)*	46 (50·0)*
Which statement best describes this boy?		
A dare-devil	33 (42·4)*	26 (53·9)*
As cautious as the average child	357 (17·9)	337 (17·2)
Extremely fearful	14 (21·4)	12 (25·0)
Which statement best describes this boy?		
Over-competitive with other children	4 (0·0)	4 (50·0)
Normally competitive	334 (19·8)	275 (15·6)
Diffident about competing with other children	66 (22·7)	97 (30·9)*
Which statement best describes this boy?		
Usually happy and contented child	24 (29·2)	16 (18·8)
Generally cheerful and in good humour	354 (18·6)	315 (19·1)
Usually gloomy and sad	26 (30·8)	44 (27·3)

Question	*Age 12–13* N (% *delinquents*)	*Age 14–15* N (% *delinquents*)
Which statement best describes this boy?		
A quarrelsome and aggressive child	20 (60·0)	24 (62·5)*
Average—not particularly quarrelsome	345 (18·6)	321 (16·8)
A timid child	39 (12·8)	28 (17·9)
Which statement best describes this boy?		
Makes friends extremely easily	75 (24·0)	54 (33·3)*
Takes usual amount of time to make friends	304 (18·8)	291 (15·5)
Does not seem able to make friends	25 (14·0)	31 (38·7)
Would you describe this boy as an anxious child—i.e. apprehensive, worrying and fearful?		
Not at all anxious	218 (20·6)	199 (18·6)
Somewhat anxious	164 (17·1)	150 (18·7)
Very anxious	22 (36·4)	19 (42·1)
How does this boy react to criticism or punishment?		
Tends to become unduly resentful	36 (41·7)*	58 (53·5)*
Normal attitude to criticism and punishment	329 (17·6)	296 (13·5)
Tends to become unduly miserable or worried	39 (20·5)	23 (21·7)

* = Percentage of delinquents in this category significantly different from percentage in other two.

APPENDIX G

The Discipline Schedule

A draft schedule of questions was revised in the light of discussions with the psychologists in the research team, and then applied in interviews with a pilot group of 24 mothers. These were women not connected with the Study, but living nearby and having boys of similar age to our own. Two social workers each conducted 12 interviews, asking the questions verbally.

Each interview was tape-recorded in its entirety. Both social workers listened to each tape and rated the mother's responses independently. The interviews and ratings were then discussed and compared, in an attempt to evolve a uniform interview and a consistent standard of rating responses. The procedure was repeated when one of the social workers left and was replaced by another.

Following the first 24 pilot interviews, the discipline schedule was slightly revised, and then administered during interviews to Study mothers who could be persuaded to cooperate. The social workers gave a preliminary explanation, saying that they were interested to know about the kinds of rules parents made and the difficulties that arose. They put the questions verbally, as far as possible always in the same words, but not necessarily in the same order as on the questionnaire. Further clarifying questions were asked when necessary. The enquiry related to the present, but behaviour over the preceding six months was counted as relevant. The interviews were not taped, but a record form for rating the parents' responses, or occasionally recording their actual comments, was completed by the social worker shortly after each interview.

The parents of 69 boys did not complete the discipline schedule, usually because they refused or were considered unapproachable, but in a few cases because they were living aboard, in a mental hospital, or otherwise not available. Four-fifths of the 342 completed interviews about discipline were with the boy's mother only, and the majority of the remainder were with both parents rather than with the father alone. In two cases the schedule was completed from information given by the boy himself, because language difficulties prevented direct communication with his Cypriot parents.

At regular intervals during the discipline enquiry, preliminary analyses were carried out on the questionnaires currently completed, and apparent differences between social workers in their rating standards, which were sometimes considerable, were pointed out and discussed. Where necessary and feasible, some assessments were revised as a result of these discussions. Discrepant trends in the administration of the questionnaire were also corrected.

The first measures were based on one set of 13 questions:

1. Has he any sorts of friends you object to his bringing into the house?
2. Are there any sorts of friends you object to his going out and about with?
3. What sort of time in the evening do you think he should be home by in general?
4. What sort of time do you think he should be in bed by?
5.(a) Do you have to make him look after his appearance as far as being clean?
5.(b) Do you have to make him look after his appearance as far as being properly dressed?
6. Does he want to wear clothes that you object to?
7. Do you have to make him mind his manners? Is he ever rude to you? Does he answer back?
8. Do you have to make him keep things tidy at home?
9. Does he have a regular job?; e.g. jobs around the home or errands?
10. Does he ever try to get off going to school?
11. When he goes off on his own do you expect him to tell you where he is going?
12. What would you feel about his smoking?

The responses to each of the 13 questions were classified into five mutually exclusive categories, namely boy conforms, always obeys, mostly obeys, often defiant or parents lax. Questions rated 'parents lax' were excluded from consideration when calculating the percentage of responses rated 'often defiant'. This was because a boy whose parents were lax about a particular rule would have no opportunity to show his defiance to it.

An index of parental laxity was derived from the 13 questions simply by counting the number of times the 'parents lax' category was used. There was some evidence of a relationship between laxity and delinquency, but it did not quite reach statistical significance (24·3 per cent of 103 boys whose parents were rated lax in two or more cases becoming delinquents, in comparison with 15·5 per cent of the remaining 239 boys rated: $\chi^2 = 3{\cdot}18$, $p < {\cdot}10$). These results are roughly comparable with those obtained with the rating of lax parental rules when the boys were aged 8–9 (28·8 per cent of 66 boys with lax parents becoming delinquents; see p. 55). It seems that parental laxity was only slightly associated with delinquency in the present sample.

Evidence of conflict between the boy and his parents was obtained from the above 13 questions and from question 14 (Does he do anything that makes you or your husband really angry?). If there did appear to be conflict, the parents were asked about the sanctions they applied and about the boy's reaction. From the replies given, the mother's usual sanction and the boy's usual reaction were coded. Three-quarters (263) of the mothers concerned usually told the boy off or applied no sanction, but a minority (79) threatened or punished him, either physically or by depriving him in some way. It was found that boys in this latter group were slightly more delinquent-prone than average (25·3 per cent of 79, as opposed to 16·0 per cent of 263: $\chi^2 = 2{\cdot}97$, $p < {\cdot}10$). In most cases, the boy's reaction to sanctions was to obey, usually with verbal protest. However, a small minority (31) were said to continue defying, protest violently, or ignore the mother. Once again, the boys falling into this group were only slightly more often delinquents than average (25·8 per cent).

Question 15 asked about methods of punishment, and sought to elicit the severest sanction used by the parents. About one in five of the boys were said to be physically punished sometimes, but there was no evidence that they were an especially delinquent-prone group (19·4 per cent delinquents out of 67, in comparison with 17·8 per cent of 275: $\chi^2 = {\cdot}02$, not significant). It will be recalled that a definite association between cruel parental discipline and delinquency was discovered at age 8–9 (see pp. 50–2). However, there was no great overlap between the parents previously rated cruel in attitude, or harsh in discipline, and those who later admitted using physical punishment.

The last three questions on the discipline questionnaire were as follows:

21. If your son wants to do something and you have refused, does he run to your husband and try to get round him? *OR* if your husband has refused, does he run to you and try to get round you?
22. Do you and your husband have disagreements over the boy?
23. What about disagreements generally? Would you say that you and your husband have more disagreements than the average couple? (i) more than average, (ii) about average, (iii) less than average.

These questions were all concerned with conflicts between the parents. It was found that boys whose parents had general disagreements were particularly likely to be delinquents (28·6 per cent of 42, as opposed to 14·6 of 246: $\chi^2 = 4{\cdot}06$, $p < {\cdot}05$). Much the same findings were obtained in relation to parents whose disagreements were about the boy himself. These results follow the pattern found earlier (p. 53) in connection with the marital disharmony rating when the boys were 8–9 years of age. Question 21 on the discipline schedule enquired about inconsistency between the parents in their handling of the boy, and could be compared with the earlier rating of parental inconsistency (p. 54). The 102 boys who could successfully play off one parent against another at 13–14, like the corresponding boys at age 8–9, included a somewhat higher percentage who were delinquents than the remainder rated (22·6 per cent as opposed to 15·1 per cent: $\chi^2 = 2{\cdot}05$, not significant).

In general, the results obtained with the discipline questionnaire were not impressive, despite the immense amount of time and effort invested in its construction. Very few of the relationships with delinquency reached an acceptable level of statistical significance. Indeed, the significance levels were never greater than, and often less than, those obtained with the rather unsystematic and subjective assessments made at age 8–9. This was surprising, in view of the fact that some of the social workers' ratings at age 13–14 were made on boys known to have become delinquents. The influence of retrospective bias would have been expected to increase the apparent associations between social workers' judgments and delinquency. One reason for the comparatively poor outcome of the discipline enquiry may have been the fact that as many as 69 boys could not be rated on account of parental uncooperativeness or non-availability. These boys included a rather high proportion (31·9 per cent) who were delinquents. However, this could not be the whole explanation.

If the discipline schedule was a reliable measure, it would appear that parental discipline is a less important factor in delinquency than is generally believed. On the other hand, it may be that this closely structured interview making use of set questions was a less effective method of extracting significant information about parent–child relationships than the more free-ranging and unstructured approach employed by the psychiatric social workers in their earlier interviews. We are inclined towards this latter conclusion. It is an important point for future research. In view of the criticisms recorded in this report, and in the earlier publication (West, 1969), of PSWs' impressionistic assessments, it is only fair to emphasize that a serious attempt to use more systematic methods yielded no better results.

APPENDIX H

Other Longitudinal Surveys

In the introduction to this book, several longitudinal delinquency surveys were cited, but none of them had followed a normal population by personal contact over an extended period. It seems that this is a peculiarly difficult task. Although there are none so comparable to the present Study as those cited in the Introduction, it is worth listing some other longitudinal surveys in order to show the range of work along these lines that has been reported.

Among British investigations worthy of note, the Scottish Mental Survey had some similarities with the National Survey (p. xiv). A representative sample (1,200) of all children born in Scotland in 1936 was followed up from age 11 to age 27 (MacPherson, 1958; Maxwell, 1969). The children and their families were continuously studied, although not usually by members of the research team, and detailed case histories were not taken. The focus of interest was on the relationship between intelligence test results at age 11 and later educational and occupational progress. There was some slight mention of delinquency, although official records were not searched.

Spence and his collaborators (Spence *et al.*, 1954; Miller *et al.*, 1960) followed up 1,100 children, comprising all those born in Newcastle-upon-Tyne in two months of 1947, for 15 years after their births. They were particularly interested in the development of illnesses, and provided no information about delinquency. The researchers maintained continuous personal contact with the boys and with their families.

A more intensive smaller-scale study has been carried out by the Centre for the Study of Human Development in London (Moore, 1959, 1966). About 200 children were first investigated at the time of their births in 1951–3, and they and their families have been followed up ever since. Case histories have been compiled from regular interviews with mothers. The sample was not randomly chosen, but is reasonably representative socio-economically of the population of central London. The focus of interest has been the development of personality, and no information about delinquency has yet been provided.

The Nottingham child development study (Newson and Newson, 1963, 1968) has also generated a great deal of case history material. The 700 children under investigation represent a stratified random sample of all those born in Nottingham in 1959–60, excluding illegitimates, immigrants and those with gross mental and physical handicaps by their first birthdays. The mothers have been seen at intervals by members of the research team, and no information about delinquency has yet emerged.

Turning from Britain to America, a particularly impressive long-term survey is that of the gifted child (Terman and Oden, 1959; Oden, 1968). Over 1,500 Californian schoolchildren were selected in 1921 when they were aged 7–14, on the basis of their unusually high IQs. The researchers have maintained personal contact with them ever since. Delinquency was almost non-existent among this group.

Two other surveys have intensively studied a comparatively small number of children. At the Fels Research Institute in Ohio, 89 children and their mothers were continuously observed from birth to the age of 20 (Kagan and Moss, 1962). In California, a representative sample of 126 children were studied between the ages of 21 months and 14 years by repeated interviews with their mothers (Macfarlane *et al.*, 1954). However, no information about delinquency has emerged in either of these investigations.

Other American surveys are less comparable to our own. In the Cambridge–Somerville Youth Study in Massachusetts (Powers and Witmer, 1951), two matched groups of 300 boys aged 8–12 were followed up for an average of five years. The main purpose originally was to see whether continuous counselling treatment given to one group would reduce the number of delinquents in it. Each group consisted of some boys judged to be pre-delinquents and some 'average' boys. The criminal records of both treatment and control groups were examined many years later (McCord *et al.*, 1959).

The Maximum Benefits Project in Washington (Hodges and Tait, 1963; Tait and Hodges, 1962, 1971) was also primarily concerned with delinquency prevention. Nearly 200 children aged 5–14, said to show behaviour problems, were followed up for more than 10 years, and the majority were given treatment.

A survey concerned with the relationship between personality and delinquency was carried out in Minnesota by Hathaway and Monachesi (1957). An unselected group of 2,000 boys aged about 15 was given the Minnesota Multiphasic Personality Inventory, and then followed up for four years. Information was obtained from the boys themselves, from their parents and from a variety of official agencies. A sub-group of 300 boys was then followed up for a further four years, until they were 23 (Wirt and Briggs, 1959).

Two other longitudinal surveys which were not specifically concerned with delinquency are worth mentioning. The first, carried out by Peck and his associates (Peck, 1958; Peck and Havighurst, 1960) in a mid-Western city, is notable because it represents an intensive survey of a small group of 34 children between the ages of 10 and 18, almost exactly the age range of the present Study. The second is a longitudinal survey of child development in New York (Rutter *et al.*, 1964; Thomas *et al.*, 1968), and is worth mentioning because it has focussed on behaviour disorders in the early years of life. Over 100 children and their parents are being intensively studied, and, when they reach adolescence, some useful information about delinquency may emerge. A recent research report (Thomas *et al.*, 1970) traced the children's progress up to age 10.

There are a number of other follow-up surveys in which continuous contact was not maintained with those investigated. For example, Robins (1966) tried to trace and interview over 500 persons who had been treated at a St Louis child guidance clinic more than 30 years before, the majority for anti-social behaviour. Another long-term follow-up survey was carried out by Morris and his collaborators (1956), who tried to trace 90 persons who had been treated 20 years before at a Pennsylvania hospital for aggressive behaviour disorders. Finally, the follow-up survey described by Himmelweit and Swift (1969) can be mentioned. More than 600 London boys were interviewed at age 13–14 in 1952, and then an attempt was made to retrace and re-interview them 11 years later. Among the data collected were court appearances during the interim period (Bebbington, 1970).

APPENDIX J

Some Reflections on the Longitudinal Method of Research

A survey such as this, which traces the development of individuals over long periods of time, has obvious advantages over cross-sectional methods of social investigation. It is possible to show to what extent, at any given stage, contemporary characteristics govern the future course of life. For instance, we have been able to show that being well behaved or badly behaved at primary school is associated with very different likelihoods of delinquency in later years. Since the observations of school behaviour were recorded contemporaneously, the result cannot be accounted for by the distortions liable to occur when people are asked to remember the past conduct of known delinquents. The effects of particular events, such as the loss of a parent, upon the course of development may also be investigated, by comparing the affected individuals with their peers before and after the events and noting consequential changes.

In the present Study, the delinquent minority developed naturally out of the total sample, which was in itself an unselected group of neighbourhood boys. This meant that all gradations of delinquency were present, in the proportions in which they occur in real life. The place of the delinquents among their social peers was therefore more easily evaluated here than in researches dependent upon contrasting extreme delinquents with artificially selected non-delinquent 'controls'.

It is usual in the early stages of a longitudinal survey to cast the net widely and measure as many factors as possible which might conceivably prove to be important. We adopted this approach (West, 1969, pp. 1–3), and collected information simultaneously about a wide variety of factors, both psychological and social. This enabled us to assess the relative importance of different factors in the genesis of delinquency, as well as to investigate how factors interacted to produce their effects.

However advantageous in theory, longitudinal surveys present many difficulties in practice. The benefits of a properly conducted and successfully completed longitudinal research project have to be weighed against the risk that uncontrollable events may intervene to ruin the design and waste the very considerable investment of money and effort that such surveys represent. In the present instance, we have been singularly lucky in that nothing has prevented the completion of the Study, but if all the problems had been fully appreciated at the outset it is doubtful whether the project would ever have been undertaken.

Data collected in the early stages of a longitudinal survey are intended to throw light upon events in the distant future. If there is an intervening gap of some years, as in this Study, ideas and theories are apt to change in the meantime. When the results are finally available, an investigator may feel that the factors which were thought most relevant when the project was planned are not the ones he would choose in the light of the most recent research. This is one reason why, in devising a long-term survey, as many factors as possible need to be considered, in order not to leave out those which future researchers may want to know about. Even so, no one can foresee everything that will become of interest, and we have been repeatedly frustrated by having to tell subsequent enquirers that the particular points in which they were interested were not part of the research. Moreover, as the work progresses, and it becomes evident that certain factors are of unexpected importance, there is inevitably regret that these were not investigated in greater detail. In a longitudinal survey, decisions taken at the start are unalterable, and for better or worse affect the research for years to come.

As well as choice of factors, methods of measurement must also be decided firmly at the beginning. Since many features change as the subjects grow older, the opportunity to measure them is lost if the initial assessments are unsatisfactory. This means that pilot studies to check upon the feasibility and reliability of interview techniques and tests assume an even greater importance in longitudinal surveys than they do in other kinds of research. A large amount of the early interview data might have proved more valuable if it had been possible to carry out more extensive preparatory work. Unfortunately, realization of the length of time needed for a longitudinal survey places research workers under some pressure to get started quickly.

The organization of a long project is far from simple. A stable research team is essential for continuity of assessments and for maintaining the cooperation of the subjects under investigation. This is not so easy to achieve when staff are on annually renewable research grants and when the leaders of a research team must move on or lose their place on some academic career ladder.

Social research demands the cooperation of both the subjects and the administrative authorities who have access to information. A great deal of labour can be saved, and more data obtained, if it is possible to collaborate fully and continuously with all the services and departments concerned—education, health, mental welfare, employment, housing, taxation, penal, police, probation, community services and voluntary organizations. Our experience suggests that some departments jealously tend to guard their own channels of information against each other as well as against probing outside investigators. No doubt this policy is sometimes necessary and desirable. Confidential information, especially that detrimental to individuals, has to be kept from authorities who might take punitive action, or from critical relatives or unsympathetic employers who have the power to make life difficult. From the point of view of research, however, the obstacles in the way of information gathering appear arbitrary and excessive. The degree of collaboration that can be secured too often seems to depend on the personal contacts and individual professional affiliations of the researchers.

These considerations assume a special importance in a longitudinal survey. The collaboration of various authorities is desirable in order to preserve contact with subjects who would otherwise drift away and be lost without trace. Assistance in tracking down families who have changed their addresses is liable to vary. In one area an official may be willing to divulge an address, whereas in another the corresponding official will not. Some departments will forward letters but do no more, so that, if no reply is received, the investigators are left wondering whether the subjects declined to respond or whether they were never successfully reached. In tracing our boys and their families, we have relied more upon repeated personal enquiries, from relatives, neighbours or individual officials, than upon formal arrangements with social agencies or government departments. This policy has been successful, but the time and cost involved were considerable.

The release of confidential information by official agencies, and the use of information acquired in confidential interviews, does raise ethical considerations. At one stage, even the members of the research team differed among themselves as to the correct attitude, certain social workers taking the view that enquiries about families made without their knowledge or consent were unjustified. Unfortunately, in delinquency research the information needed is not always of a kind likely to be given voluntarily, certainly not by the more evasive and uncooperative families. We have justified the enquiries we made on the grounds that stringent precautions have been taken to preserve the anonymity of the families and the privacy of case records, so that no individual can be harmed by leakage of personal information.

A long-term survey needs long-term support, in regard to both finance and facilities for investigation. The present Study depended in large part upon the access to schoolboys provided by the Local Education Authority. We were therefore compelled to limit the enquiry to matters which that Authority saw fit to allow. Since some of the topics we were interested in, such as educational standards and the prevalence of delinquency, were 'sensitive' areas politically, we were obliged to tread warily and to try to avoid publicity. There were many anxious moments, especially when journalists discovered the office telephone number and kept demanding information. The worst crisis of this sort arose when a journalist, by devious means, managed to secure some of our data about the schools and printed them in garbled form, thereby providing material for a highly publicised but quite unfounded political squabble.

Research is most easily carried out on captive populations, in schools or institutions, where the subjects are all in one place in a situation that exposes them to observation. In most longitudinal surveys, even if the subjects are captives to begin with, they do not remain so, and contact can only be maintained with a disappointingly small proportion of the original sample. A satisfactory follow-up of individuals in the community depends not only upon tracing their whereabouts, but also upon persuading them to consent to be interviewed. In this Study, when the boys were 16 and 18, we were able to pay them a reasonably generous fee for their cooperation. While this has been most helpful, it would have been of little use in itself without the persistence, tact and powers of persuasion exercised by the interviewers. The high proportion of subjects interviewed at later ages was achieved by a very special effort. Some of the more reluctant or elusive subjects were seen finally only after many preliminary enquiries and failed attempts to secure cooperation. This necessity considerably increased the labour and the cost of the enquiry.

It is not usual for research reports to dwell upon the difficulties and embarrassments encountered by the investigators. In this case, it seemed necessary to do so in order to warn others who may be too easily tempted by the methodological attractiveness of longitudinal research.

List of References

AKERS, R. L. (1964), 'Socioeconomic status and delinquent behavior: a retest', *Journal of Research in Crime and Delinquency*, **1,** 38–46.

ALBEE, G. W., and GOLDMAN, Rosaline (1950), 'The picture frustration study as a predictor of overt aggression', *Journal of Projective Techniques*, **14,** 303–8.

ANDERSON, J. W. (1958), 'Recidivism, intelligence and social class', *British Journal of Delinquency*, **8,** 294–7.

ANDRY, R. G. (1960), *Delinquency and Parental Pathology*. London: Methuen.

ANTHONY, H. Sylvia (1960), 'Anxiety as a function of psychomotor and social behaviour', *British Journal of Educational Psychology*, **51,** 141–52.

ANTHONY, H. Sylvia (1972), *An Experiment in Personality Assessment of Young Men Remanded in Custody*. London: H.M.S.O.

ASUNI, T. (1963), 'Maladjustment and delinquency: a comparison of two samples', *Journal of Child Psychology and Psychiatry*, **4,** 219–28.

BALDWIN, A. L. (1967), *Theories of Child Development*. New York: Wiley.

BALL, J. C., ROSS, A., and SIMPSON, A. (1964), 'Incidence and estimated prevalence of recorded delinquency in a metropolitan area', *American Sociological Review*, **29,** 90–3.

BANDURA, A., and WALTERS, R. H. (1959), *Adolescent Aggression*. New York: Ronald Press.

BANKS, Charlotte (1965), 'Boys in detention centres', in Banks, Charlotte and Broadhurst, P. L. (eds.), *Studies in Psychology*. London University Press.

BARRATT, E. S. (1956), 'The relationship of the progressive matrices (1938) and the Columbia Mental Maturity Scale to the WISC', *Journal of Consulting Psychology*, **20,** 294–6.

BARTHOLOMEW, A. A. (1959), 'Extraversion-introversion and neuroticism in first offenders and recidivists', *British Journal of Delinquency*, **10** 120–9.

BEBBINGTON, A. C., (1970), 'The effect of non-response in the sample survey with an example', *Human Relations*, **23,** 169–80.

BECKER, W. C. (1964), 'Consequences of different kinds of parental discipline', in Hoffman, M. L., and Hoffman, Lois W. (eds.), *Review of Child Development Research*, vol. 1. New York, Russell Sage: pp 169–208.

BELSON, W. A. (1968), 'The extent of stealing by London boys and some of its origins', *Advancement of Science* (British Association), **25,** 171–84

BERNARD, J. (1949), 'The Rosenzweig picture-frustration study', *Journal of Psychology*, **28,** 325–43.

BESWICK, D. G., and COX, F. N. (1958), 'Reputed aggression and dependence in children', *Australian Journal of Psychology*, **10,** 144–50.

BHAGAT, M., and FRASER, W. I. (1970), 'Young offenders' images of self and surroundings: a semantic enquiry', *British Journal of Psychiatry*, **117,** 381–7.

BHAGAT, M., and FRASER, W. I. (1971), 'The effect of low intelligence on the emotional and environmental concepts of retarded offenders', *British Journal of Psychiatry*, **119,** 639–46.

BILES, D. (1971), 'Birth order and delinquency', *Australian Psychologist* **6,** 189–93.

BIZE, P. R. *et al.*, (1964, 1965), 'Etude comparative de la psychomotricité', *Annales de Vaucresson*, **2,** 3–56; **3,** 81–96.

BLACK, W. A. M. (1972), 'Extraversion, neuroticism and criminality', *Australian and New Zealand Journal of Criminology*, **5,** 99–106.

BLACKLER, Charmian (1968), 'Primary recidivism in adult men: differences between men on first and second prison sentence', *British Journal of Criminology*, **8,** 130–67.

BLOCH, H. A. (1958), 'Juvenile delinquency: myth or threat?', *Journal of Criminal Law, Criminology and Police Science*, **49,** 303–9.

BRODY, Grace F. (1965), 'Relationship between maternal attitudes and behavior', *Journal of Personality and Social Psychology*, **2,** 317–23.

BRONFENBRENNER, U. (1958), 'Socialization and social class through time and space', in Maccoby, E. E., Newcomb, T. M., and Hartley, E. L. (eds.), *Readings in Social Psychology*, 3rd ed. New York, Holt, Rinehart and Winston: pp. 400–25.

BRUCE, N. (1970), 'Delinquent and non-delinquent reactions to parental deprivation', *British Journal of Criminology*, **10,** 270–6.

BURGESS, P. K. (1972), 'Eysenck's theory of criminality: a new approach', *British Journal of Criminology*, **12,** 74–82.

BUSS, A. H. (1961), *The Psychology of Aggression*, New York: Wiley.

BUTCHER, J. N. (1965), 'Manifest aggression: MMPI correlates in normal boys', *Journal of Consulting Psychology*, **29**, 446–54.

BYNNER, J. M. (1969), *The Young Smoker*. London: H.M.S.O.

CAPLAN, N. S., and SIEBERT, L. A. (1964), 'Distribution of juvenile delinquent intelligence test scores over a thirty-four year period (N = 51,808)', *Journal of Clinical Psychology*, **20,** 242–7.

CAPLAN, N. S. (1965), 'Intellectual functioning', in Quay, H. C. (ed.), *Juvenile Delinquency: Research and Theory*. Princeton: Van Nostrand.

CHILTON, R. J., and MARKLE, G. E. (1972), 'Family disruption, delinquent conduct and the effect of subclassification', *American Sociological Review*, **37,** 93–9.

CHOROST, S. B. (1962), 'Parental child-rearing attitudes and their correlates in adolescent hostility', *Genetic Psychology Monographs*, **66,** 49–90.

CHRISTENSEN, R. (1967), 'Projected percentage of U.S. population with criminal arrest and conviction records', *President's Commission on Law Enforcement and Administration of Justice: Task Force Report*, *Science and Technology*. Washington: Government Printing Office. pp. 216–28.

CHRISTIE, N., ANDENAES, J., and SKIRBEKK, S. (1965), 'A study of self-reported crime', in Christiansen, K. O. (ed.), *Scandinavian Studies in Criminology*, vol. 1. London: Tavistock.

CLARK, J. P., and TIFFT, L. L. (1966), 'Polygraph and interview validation of self-reported deviant behavior', *American Sociological Review*, **31,** 516–23.

CLARK, J. P., and WENNINGER, E. P. (1964), 'The attitude of juveniles toward the legal institution', *Journal of Criminal Law, Criminology and Police Science*, **55,** 482–9.

CLOWARD, R. A., and OHLIN, L. E. (1960), *Delinquency and Opportunity: A Theory of Delinquent Gangs*. Glencoe: Free Press.

COHEN, A. K. (1955), *Delinquent Boys: The Culture of the Gang*. Glencoe: Free Press.

COHEN, J. (1972), *Psychological Probability*. London: Allen & Unwin.

CONGER, J. J., and MILLER, W. C. (1966), *Personality, Social Class and Delinquency*. New York: Wiley.

COWIE, J., COWIE, Valerie, and SLATER, E. (1968), *Delinquent Girls*. London: Heinemann.

CRAIG, Maude M., and BUDD, Laila A. (1967), 'The juvenile offender: recidivism and companions', *Crime and Delinquency*, **13,** 344–51.

CRAIG, Maude M., and GLICK, Selma J. (1963), 'Ten years' experience with the Glueck Social Prediction Table', *Crime and Delinquency*, **9,** 249–61.

CRAIG, Maude M., and GLICK, Selma J. (1964), 'A manual of procedures for application of the Glueck prediction table'. New York City Youth Board.

CRITCHLEY, E. M. R. (1968), 'Reading retardation, dyslexia and delinquency', *British Journal of Psychiatry*, **114,** 1537–47.

CROFT, I. J. and GRYGIER, T. G. (1956), 'Social relationships of truants and juvenile delinquents', *Human Relations*, **9,** 439–66.

CULPAN, R. H., DAVIES, B. M., and OPPENHEIM, A. N. (1960), 'Incidence of psychiatric illness among hospital outpatients: an application of the Cornell Medical Index', *British Medical Journal*, **1,** 855–7.

DAVIE, R., BUTLER, N. R., and GOLDSTEIN, H. (1972), *From Birth to Seven. The Second Report of the National Child Development Study*. London: Longman.

DENTLER, R. A. and MONROE, L. J. (1961), 'Social correlates of early adolescent theft', *American Sociological Review*, **26,** 733–43.

DILLER, Juliet C. (1955), 'A comparison of the test performance of male and female delinquents', *Journal of Genetic Psychology*, **86,** 217–36.

DOCTER, R. F. and WINDER, C. L. (1954), 'Delinquent versus non-delinquent performance of the Porteus Qualitative Maze Test', *Journal of Consulting Psychology*, **18,** 71–3.

DOUGLAS, J. W. B. (1964), *The Home and the School*. London: MacGibbon and Kee.

DOUGLAS, J. W. B. (1966), 'The school progress of nervous and troublesome children', *British Journal of Psychiatry*, **112,** 1115–16.

DOUGLAS, J. W. B. (1970), 'Discussion', in Hare, E. H. and Wing, J. K. (eds.), *Psychiatric Epidemiology*. London: Oxford University Press.

DOUGLAS, J. W. B., ROSS, Jean M., HAMMOND, W. A., and MULLIGAN, D. G. (1966), 'Delinquency and social class', *British Journal of Criminology*, **6,** 294–302.

DOUGLAS, J. W. B., ROSS, Jean M., and SIMPSON, H. R. (1968), *All our Future*. London: Peter Davies.

EIDNER, V. (1966), 'Effect of parents in the home on juvenile delinquency', *Public Health Reports* (Washington), **81**, 905–10.

EILENBERG, M. D. (1961), 'Remand home boys 1930–1955', *British Journal of Criminology*, **2,** 111–31.

ELLIOTT, D. S. (1962), 'Delinquency and perceived opportunity', *Sociological Enquiry*, **32,** 216–27.

EMPEY, L. T. and LUBECK, S. G. (1971), *Explaining Delinquency*. Lexington, Mass.: D. C. Heath.

ERICKSON, M. L. (1972), 'The changing relationship between official and self-reported measures of juvenile delinquency: an exploratory-predictive study', *Journal of Criminal Law, Criminology and Police Science*, **63,** 388–95.

ERICKSON, M. L., and EMPEY, L. T. (1963), 'Court records, undetected delinquency and decision-making', *Journal of Criminal Law, Criminology and Police Science*, **54,** 456–69.

ERICKSON, M. L., and EMPEY, L. T. (1965), 'Class position, peers and delinquency', *Sociology and Social Research*, **49,** 268–82.

EYNON, T. G., and RECKLESS, W. C. (1961), 'Companionship at delinquency onset', *British Journal of Criminology*, **2,** 162–70.

EYSENCK, H. J. (1970), *Crime and Personality*. London: Paladin (rev. ed.).

EYSENCK, H. J., and EYSENCK, Sybil B. G. (1964), *Manual of the Eysenck Personality Inventory*. University of London Press.

EYSENCK, Sybil, B. G., and EYSENCK, H. J. (1970), 'Crime and personality: an empirical study of the three-factor theory', *British Journal of Criminology*, **10,** 225–39.

FARRINGTON, D. P. (1972), 'Delinquency begins at home', *New Society*, **21,** 495–7.

FARRINGTON, D. P. (1973), 'Self-reports of deviant behavior: predictive and stable?', *Journal of Criminal Law and Criminology*, **64**, 99–110.

FARRINGTON, D. P., and WEST, D. J. (1971), 'A comparison between early delinquents and young aggressives', *British Journal of Criminology*, **11,** 341–58.

FERGUSON, T. (1952), *The Young Delinquent in his Social Setting*. London: Oxford University Press.

FERRACUTI, F. (1966), *Intelligence and Criminality: a Bibliography*. Milan: Giuffré.

FITCH, J. H. (1962), 'Two personality variables and their distribution in a criminal population: an empirical study', *British Journal of Social and Clinical Psychology*, **1,** 161–7.

FOOKS, G., and THOMAS, R. R. (1957), 'Differential qualitative performance of delinquents on the Porteus Maze', *Journal of Consulting Psychology*, **21**, 351–3.

FOSTER, A. L. (1959), 'A note concerning the intelligence of delinquents', *Journal of Clinical Psychology*, **15**, 78–9.

FOULDS, G. A. (1968), 'Neurosis and character disorder in hospital and in prison', *British Journal of Criminology*, **8**, 46–9.

FREDERICKS, M. A., and MOLNAR, M. (1969), 'Relative occupational anticipations and aspirations of delinquents and non-delinquents', *Journal of Research in Crime and Delinquency*, **6**, 1–7.

FROST, B. P., and FROST, Ruth (1962), 'The pattern of WISC scores in a group of juvenile sociopaths', *Journal of Clinical Psychology*, **18**, 354–5.

FRY, F. D. (1952), 'A normative study of the reactions manifested by college students and by state prison inmates in response to the MMPI, the Rosenzweig Picture-Frustration study and the TAT, *Journal of Psychology*, **34**, 27–30.

FURNEAUX, W. D., and GIBSON, H. B. (1961), 'A children's personality inventory designed to measure neuroticism and extraversion', *British Journal of Educational Psychology*, **31**, 204–7.

FURNEAUX, W. D., and GIBSON, H. B. (1966), *The New Junior Maudsley Inventory*. University of London Press.

GATH, D., TENNENT, G., and PIDDUCK, R. (1970), 'Educational characteristics of bright delinquents', *British Journal of Educational Psychology*, **40**, 216–19.

GATLING, F. P. (1950), 'Frustration reactions of delinquents using Rosenzweig's classification system', *Journal of Abnormal and Social Psychology*, **45**, 749–52.

GERHART, Ursula C., and GEISMAR, L. L. (1969), 'The PARI as a predictor of parental behavior', *Child Welfare*, **48**, 602–5.

GIBBENS, T. C. N. (1958), 'The Porteus Maze test and delinquency', *British Journal of Educational Psychology*, **28**, 209–16.

GIBBENS, T. C. N. (1963), *Psychiatric Studies of Borstal Lads*. London: Oxford University Press.

GIBSON, H. B. (1964a), 'A lie scale for the Junior Maudsley Personality Inventory', *British Journal of Educational Psychology*, **34**, 120–4.

GIBSON, H. B. (1964b), 'The validity of the lie scale of a children's personality inventory', *Acta Psychologica*, **22**, 241–9.

GIBSON, H. B. (1964c), 'The Spiral Maze: a psychomotor test with implications for the study of delinquency', *British Journal of Psychology*, **55**, 219–25.

GIBSON, H. B. (1965a), *Manual of the Gibson Spiral Maze*. University of London Press.

GIBSON, H. B. (1965b), 'A new personality test for boys', *British Journal of Educational Psychology*, **35**, 244–8.

GIBSON, H. B. (1967a), 'Self-reported delinquency among schoolboys, and their attitudes to the police', *British Journal of Social and Clinical Psychology*, **6**, 168–73.

GIBSON, H. B. (1967b), 'Teachers' ratings of schoolboys' behaviour related to patterns of scores on the New Junior Maudsley Inventory', *British Journal of Educational Psychology*, **37**, 347–54.

GIBSON, H. B. (1968), 'The measurement of parental attitudes and their relation to boys' behaviour,' *British Journal of Educational Psychology*, **38**, 233–9.

GIBSON, H. B. (1969a), 'The Tapping Test: a novel form with implications for personality research', *Journal of Clinical Psychology*, **25**, 403–5.

GIBSON, H. B. (1969b), 'The Gibson Spiral Maze Test: retest data in relation to behavioural disturbance, personality and physical measures', *British Journal of Psychology*, **60**, 523–8.

GIBSON, H. B. (1969c), 'Early delinquency in relation to broken homes', *Journal of Child Psychology and Psychiatry*, **10**, 195–204.

GIBSON, H. B. (1969d), 'The significance of "lie responses" in the prediction of early delinquency', *British Journal of Educational Psychology*, **39**, 284–90.

GIBSON, H. B., and HANSON, Ruth (1969), 'Peer ratings as predictors of school behaviour and delinquency', *British Journal of Social and Clinical Psychology*, **8**, 313–22.

GIBSON, H. B., HANSON, Ruth, and WEST, D. J. (1967), 'A questionnaire measure of neuroticism using a shortened scale derived from the Cornell Medical Index', *British Journal of Social and Clinical Psychology*, **6**, 129–36.

GIBSON, H. B., MORRISON, Sylvia, and WEST, D. J. (1970), 'The confession of known offences in response to a self-reported delinquency schedule', *British Journal of Criminology*, **10**, 277–80.

GIBSON, H. B., and WEST, D. J. (1970), 'Social and intellectual handicaps as precursors of early delinquency', *British Journal of Criminology*, **10**, 21–32.

GILDEA, Margaret C-L., GLIDEWELL, J. C., and KANTOR, Mildred B. (1961), 'Maternal attitudes and general adjustment in school children', in Glidewell, J. C. (ed.), *Parental Attitudes and Child Behavior*. Springfield, Illinois, C. C. Thomas: pp. 42–89.

GITTINS, J. (1952), *Approved School Boys*. London: H.M.S.O.

GLIDEWELL, J. C., GILDEA, Margaret C-L., DOMKE, H. R., and KANTOR, Mildred B. (1959), 'Behavior symptoms in children and adjustment in public school', *Human Organization*, **18**, 123–30.

GLUCK, M. R. (1955), 'The relationship between hostility in the TAT and behavioral hostility', *Journal of Projective Techniques*, **19**, 21–6.

GLUECK, S., and GLUECK, Eleanor T. (1930), *500 Criminal Careers*. New York: Knopf.

GLUECK, S., and GLUECK, Eleanor T. (1937), *Later Criminal Careers*. New York: Commonwealth Fund.

GLUECK, S., and GLUECK, Eleanor T. (1943), *Criminal Careers in Retrospect*. New York: Commonwealth Fund.

GLUECK, S., and GLUECK, Eleanor T. (1950), *Unraveling Juvenile Delinquency*. Cambridge, Mass: Harvard University Press.

GLUECK, S., and GLUECK, Eleanor T. (1956), *Physique and Delinquency*. New York: Harper.

GLUECK, S., and GLUECK, Eleanor T. (1962), *Family Environment and Delinquency*. London: Routledge & Kegan Paul.

GLUECK, S., and GLUECK, Eleanor T. (1968), *Delinquents and Non-delinquents in Perspective*. Cambridge, Mass.: Harvard University Press.

GOLD, M. (1963), *Status Forces in Delinquent Boys*. Ann Arbor, Michigan: University of Michigan Institute for Social Research.

GOLD, M. (1967), 'On social status and delinquency', *Social Problems*, **15,** 114–16.

GOODACRE, Elizabeth (1967), 'Going to secondary school—how do parents choose?', *Where* (Advisory Centre for Education, Cambridge), **32,** 4–6.

GORDON, J. E. (1957), 'The validity of Shoben's parent attitude survey', *Journal of Clinical Psychology*, **13,** 154–6.

GORDON, R. A., SHORT, J. F., CARTWRIGHT, D. S., and STRODTBECK, F. L. (1963), 'Values and gang delinquency: a study of street-corner groups', *American Journal of Sociology*, **69,** 109–28.

GRAHAM, E. E., and KAMANO, D. (1958), 'Reading failure as a factor in the WAIS sub-test patterns of youthful offenders', *Journal of Clinical Psychology*, **14,** 302–5.

GRYGIER, T. (1955), 'Leisure pursuits of juvenile delinquents: a study in methodology', *British Journal of Delinquency*, **5,** 210–28.

GRYGIER, T., CHESLEY, Joan, and TUTERS, Elizabeth W. (1969), 'Parental deprivation: a study of delinquent children', *British Journal of Criminology*, **9,** 209–53.

HARDT, R. H., and PETERSON, Sandra J. (1968), 'Arrests of self and friends as indicators of delinquency involvement', *Journal of Research in Crime and Delinquency*, **5,** 44–51.

HARGREAVES, D. H. (1967), *Social Relations in a Secondary School*. London: Routledge & Kegan Paul.

HATHAWAY, S. R., and MONACHESI, E. D. (1957), 'The personalities of pre-delinquent boys', *Journal of Criminal Law, Criminology and Police Science*, **48,** 149–63.

HATHAWAY, S. R., MONACHESI, E. D., and YOUNG, L. A. (1960), 'Delinquency rates and personality', *Journal of Criminal Law, Criminology and Police Science*, **50,** 433–40.

HATHAWAY, S. R., and MONACHESI, E. D. (1963), *Adolescent Personality and Behavior*. Minneapolis: University of Minnesota Press.

HENNING, J. J., and LEVY, R. H. (1967), 'Verbal-performance IQ differences of white and negro delinquents on the WISC and WAIS', *Journal of Clinical Psychology*, **23,** 164–8.

HIMMELWEIT, Hilde T., and SWIFT, Betty, (1969), 'A model for the understanding of the school as a socializing agent', in Mussen, P. H., Langer, J., and Covington, M. (eds.), *Trends and Issues in Developmental Psychology*. New York, Holt, Rinehart and Winston: pp. 154–81.

HODGES, E. F., and TAIT, C. D. (1963), 'A follow-up study of potential delinquents', *American Journal of Psychiatry*, **120,** 449–52.

HOGHUGHI, M. S., and FORREST, A. R. (1967), 'Aspects of psycholo-

gical and educational functioning in juvenile offenders', *Approved Schools Gazette*, **61,** 13–20.
HOGHUGHI, M. S., and FORREST, A. R. (1970), 'Eysenck's theory of criminality: an examination with Approved School boys', *British Journal of Criminology*, **10,** 240–54.
HOLZBERG, J. D., and HAHN, F. (1952), 'The picture-frustration technique as a measure of hostility and guilt reactions in adolescent psychopaths', *American Journal of Orthopsychiatry*, **22,** 776–95.
HOOD, R., and SPARKS, R. (1970), *Key Issues in Criminology*. London: Weidenfeld and Nicolson.
HORROCKS, J. E., and GOTTFRIED, N. W. (1966), 'Psychological needs and verbally expressed aggression of adolescent delinquent boys', *Journal of Psychology*, **62,** 179–94.
HURLEY, J. R. (1955), 'The Iowa Picture Interpretation Test: a multiple-choice version of the TAT', *Journal of Consulting Psychology*, **19,** 372–6.
JAAKKOLA, R. (1966), 'Social background and criminality', in Anttila, I., and Jaakkola, R., *Unrecorded Criminality in Finland*. Helsinki: Institute of Criminology.
JONSSON, G. (1967), *Delinquent Boys, their Parents and Grandparents*. Copenhagen: Munksgaard.
KAGAN, J. and MOSS, H. A. (1962), *From Birth to Maturity*. New York: Wiley.
KASWAN, J., WASMAN, M., and FREEDMAN, L. Z. (1960), 'Aggression and the picture-frustration study', *Journal of Consulting Psychology*, **24,** 446–52.
KHLEIF, B. B. (1964), 'Teachers as predictors of juvenile delinquency and psychiatric disturbance', *Social Problems*, **11,** 270–82.
KRAFT, A. (1966), 'Personality correlates of rebellion-behaviour in school', *Adolescence*, **1,** 251–60.
KULIK, J. A., STEIN, K. B., and SARBIN, T. R. (1968), 'Dimensions and patterns of adolescent antisocial behavior', *Journal of Consulting and Clinical Psychology*, **32,** 375–82.
KVARACEUS, W. C. (1960), 'Forecasting delinquency: a three-year experiment', *Exceptional Children*, **27,** 429–35.
KVARACEUS, W. C. (1966), *Anxious Youth: Dynamics of Delinquency*. Columbus, Ohio: C. E. Merrill.
LEES, J. P., and NEWSON, L. J. (1954), 'Family or sibship position and some aspects of juvenile delinquency', *British Journal of Delinquency*, **5,** 46–65.
LITTLE, A. (1963), 'Professor Eysenck's theory of crime: an empirical test on adolescent offenders', *British Journal of Criminology*, **4,** 152–63.
LITTLE, A. (1965), 'The "prevalence" of recorded delinquency and recidivism in England and Wales', *American Sociological Review*, **30,** 260–3.
LUNDEN, W. A. (1967), *Crimes and Criminals*. Ames: Iowa State University Press.
LUNZER, E. A. (1960), 'Aggressive and withdrawing children in the

normal school. I. Patterns of Behaviour', *British Journal of Educational Psychology*, **30**, 1–10.

McClintock, F. H. (1963), *Crimes of Violence*. London: Macmillan.

McClintock, F. H., and Avison, N. H. (1968), *Crime in England and Wales*. London: Heinemann.

McCord, W., and McCord, Joan (1958), 'The effects of a parental role model on criminality', *Journal of Social Issues*, **14**, 66–75.

McCord, W., McCord, Joan, and Zola, I. K. (1959), *Origins of Crime*. New York: Columbia University Press.

McCullough, Mary (1967), 'Criminal families', *New Society*, **10**, 256–7.

McDonald, Lynn (1969), *Social Class and Delinquency*. London: Faber.

Macfarlane, Jean W., Allen, Lucile, and Honzik, Marjorie P. (1954), *A Developmental Study of the Behavior Problems of Normal Children between 21 months and 14 years*. Berkeley: University of California Press.

Mack, J. A. (1972), 'The able criminal', *British Journal of Criminology*, **12**, 44–54.

McKennell, A. C., and Bynner, J. M. (1969), 'Self images and smoking behaviour among school boys', *British Journal of Educational Psychology*, **39**, 27–39.

McKissack, I. J. (1967), 'The peak age for property crimes', *British Journal of Criminology*, **7**, 184–94.

McNeil, E. B. (1962), 'Aggression in fantasy and behavior', *Journal of Consulting Psychology*, **26**, 232–40.

MacPherson, J. S. (1958), *Eleven-year-olds Grow Up*. University of London Press.

Madoff, J. M. (1959), 'The attitudes of mothers of juvenile delinquents toward child rearing', *Journal of Consulting Psychology*, **23**, 518–20.

Mannheim, H. (1965), *Comparative Criminology* (2 vol.) London: Routledge & Kegan Paul.

Marcus, B. (1955), 'Intelligence, criminality and the expectation of recidivism', *British Journal of Delinquency*, **6**, 147–51.

Marsh, R. W. (1969), 'The validity of the Bristol social adjustment guides in delinquency prediction', *British Journal of Educational Psychology*, **39**, 278–83.

Masters, F. G., and Tong, J. E. (1968), 'The semantic differential test with Borstal subjects', *British Journal of Criminology*, **8**, 20–31.

Matza, D., and Sykes, G. M. (1961), 'Juvenile delinquency and subterranean values', *American Sociological Review*, **26**, 712–19.

Maxwell, J. (1969), *Sixteen Years On*. University of London Press.

Megargee, E. I., and Cook, P. E. (1967), 'The relation of TAT and Inkblot aggressive content scales with each other and with criteria of overt aggressiveness in juvenile delinquents', *Journal of Projective Techniques and Personality Assessment*, **31**, 48–60.

Miller, F. J. W., Court, S. D. M., Walton, W. S., and Knox, E. G. (1960), *Growing up in Newcastle upon Tyne*. London: Oxford University Press.

MILLER, W. B. (1958), 'Lower class culture as a generating milieu of gang delinquency', *Journal of Social Issues*, **14,** 5–19.

MONAHAN, T. P. (1960), 'On the incidence of delinquency', *Social Forces*, **39,** 66–72.

MOORE, T. (1966), 'Difficulties of the ordinary child in adjusting to primary school', *Journal of Child Psychology and Psychiatry*, **7,** 17–38.

MOORE, T. (1959), 'Studying the growth of personality', *Vita Humana*, **2,** 65–87.

MORRIS, H. H., ESCOLL, P. J., and WEXLER, R. (1956), 'Aggressive behavior disorders of childhood: a follow-up study', *American Journal of Psychiatry*, **112,** 991–7.

MOSHER, D. L., and MOSHER, Joan B. (1965), 'Relationships between authoritarian attitudes in delinquent girls and the authoritarian attitudes and authoritarian rearing practices of their mothers', *Psychological Reports*, **16,** 23–30.

MULLIGAN, G., DOUGLAS, J. W. B., HAMMOND, W. A., and TIZARD, J. (1963), 'Delinquency and symptoms of maladjustment', *Proceedings of the Royal Society of Medicine*, **56,** 1083–6.

MURPHY, F. J., SHIRLEY, Mary M., and WITMER, Helen L. (1946), 'The incidence of hidden delinquency', *American Journal of Orthopsychiatry*, **16,** 686–96.

MURSTEIN, B. I., and WIENS, A. N. (1965), 'Diagnostic and actuarial correlates of thematic and questionnaire measures of hostility', *Journal of Projective Techniques and Personality Assessment*, **29,** 341–7.

MUSSEN, P. H., and NAYLOR, H. K. (1954), 'The relationships between overt and fantasy aggression', *Journal of Abnormal and Social Psychology*, **49,** 235–40.

MYLONAS, A. D., and RECKLESS, W. C. (1968), 'Attitudes toward law enforcement in Greece and the United States', *Journal of Research in Crime and Delinquency*, **5,** 81–8.

NAAR, R. (1965), 'A note on the intelligence of delinquents', *British Journal of Criminology*, **5,** 82–5.

NAESS, S. (1962), 'Mother separation and delinquency', *British Journal of Criminology*, **2,** 361–74.

National Foundation for Educational Research (1964), *Local Authority Practices in the Allocation of Pupils to Secondary Schools*. London: N.F.E.R.

NEWSON, J., and NEWSON, Elizabeth (1963), *Infant Care in an Urban Community*. London: Allen & Unwin.

NEWSON, J., and NEWSON, Elizabeth (1968), *Four Years Old in an Urban Community*. London: Allen & Unwin.

NYE, F. I. (1958), *Family Relationships and Delinquent Behavior*. New York: Wiley.

NYE, F. I., SHORT, J. F., and OLSEN, V. (1958), 'Socioeconomic status and delinquent behavior', *American Journal of Sociology*, **63,** 381–9.

ODEN, Melissa H. (1968), 'The fulfilment of promise: 40-year follow-up of the Terman gifted group', *Genetic Psychology Monographs*, **77** (1) 3–93.

OSGOOD, C. E., SUCI, G. J., and TANNENBAUM, P. H. (1957), *The Measurement of Meaning*. Urbana: University of Illinois Press.

PALMAI, G., STOREY, P. B., and BRISCOE, O. (1967), 'Social class and the young offender', *British Journal of Psychiatry*, **113**, 1073–82.

PARKE, R. D. (1970), 'The role of punishment in the socialization process', in Hoppe, R. A., Milton, G. A., and Simmel, E. C. (eds.), *Early Experiences and the Processes of Socialization*. New York, Academic Press, pp. 81–108.

PASAMANICK, B., ROGERS, Martha E., and LILIENFELD, A. M. (1956), 'Pregnancy experience and the development of behavior disorder in children', *American Journal of Psychiatry*, **112**, 613–18.

PASSINGHAM, R. E. (1968), 'A study of delinquents with children's home background', *British Journal of Criminology*, **8**, 32–45.

PECK, R. F. (1958), 'Family patterns correlated with adolescent personality structure', *Journal of Abnormal and Social Psychology*, **57**, 347–350.

PECK, R. F., and HAVIGHURST, R. J. (1960), *The Psychology of Character Development*. New York: Wiley.

PETERSON, D. R., and BECKER, W. C. (1965), 'Family interaction and delinquency', in Quay, H. C. (ed.), *Juvenile Delinquency: Research and Theory*. Princeton, New Jersey, Van Nostrand: pp. 63–99.

PILIAVIN, I., and BRIAR, S. (1964), 'Police encounters with juveniles', *American Journal of Sociology*, **70**, 206–14.

PORTEUS, S. D. (1942), *Qualitative Performance in the Maze Test*. Vineland, N.J.: Smith Printing House.

PORTEUS, S. D. (1965), *Porteus Maze Test: Fifty Years' Application*. Palo Alto, California: Pacific Books.

POWER, M. J. (1965), 'An attempt to identify at first appearance before the courts those at risk of becoming persistent juvenile offenders', *Proceedings of the Royal Society of Medicine*, **58**, 704–5.

POWER, M. J., BENN, R. T., and MORRIS, J. N. (1972), 'Neighbourhood, school and juveniles before the courts', *British Journal of Criminology*, **12**, 111–32.

POWERS, E., and WITMER, Helen (1951), *An Experiment in the Prevention of Delinquency*. New York: Columbia University Press.

PRENTICE, N. M., and KELLY, F. J. (1963), 'Intelligence and delinquency: a reconsideration', *Journal of Social Psychology*, **60**, 327–37.

PRINGLE, Mia L. K., BUTLER, N. R., and DAVIE, R. (1966), *11,000 Seven-year-olds*. London: Longman.

PURCELL, K. (1956), 'The TAT and antisocial behavior', *Journal of Consulting Psychology*, **20**, 449–56.

RAVEN, J. C. (1960), *Guide to the Standard Progressive Matrices*. London: H. K. Lewis.

RAWNSLEY, K. (1966), 'Congruence of independent measures of psychiatric morbidity', *Journal of Psychosomatic Research*, **10**, 84–93.

RECKLESS, W. C., and DINITZ, S. (1967), 'Pioneering with self-concept as a vulnerability factor in delinquency', *Journal of Criminal Law, Criminology and Police Science*, **58**, 515–23.

RHODES, A. L., and REISS, A. J. (1969), 'Apathy, truancy and delinquency as adaptations to school failure', *Social Forces*, **48**, 12–22.

RICHARDSON, Helen M., and SURKO, Elise F. (1956), 'WISC scores and status in reading and arithmetic of delinquent children', *Journal of Genetic Psychology*, **89**, 251–62.

RICHARDSON, K., SPEARS, D., and RICHARDS, M. (1972, eds.), *Race, Culture and Intelligence*. Harmondsworth: Penguin.

ROBERTS, A. H., and ERIKSON, R. V. (1968), 'Delay of gratification, Porteus maze test performance and behavioral adjustment in a delinquent group', *Journal of Abnormal Psychology*, **73**, 449–53.

ROBINS, Lee N. (1963), 'The reluctant respondent', *Public Opinion Quarterly*, **27**, 276–86.

ROBINS, Lee N. (1966), *Deviant Children Grown Up*. Baltimore: Williams and Wilkins.

ROBINS, Lee N., and HILL, Shirley Y. (1966), 'Assessing the contributions of family structure, class and peer groups to juvenile delinquency', *Journal of Criminal Law, Criminology and Police Science*, **57**, 325–334.

RODMAN, H., and GRAMS, P. (1967), 'Juvenile delinquency and the family: a review and discussion', *President's Commission on Law Enforcement and Administration of Justice. Task Force Report: Juvenile Delinquency and Youth Crime*. Washington, Government Printing Office: pp. 188–221.

ROSE, G. N. G. (1968), 'The artificial delinquent generation', *Journal of Criminal Law, Criminology and Police Science*, **59**, 370–85.

ROSENTHAL, R., and JACOBSEN, L. (1968), *Pygmalion in the Classroom*. New York: Holt, Rinehart and Winston.

ROSENZWEIG, S. (1945), 'The picture-association method and its application in a study of reactions to frustration', *Journal of Personality*, **14**, 3–23.

ROSENZWEIG, S., FLEMING, Edith E., and CLARKE, Helen J. (1947), 'Revised scoring manual for the Rosenzweig picture-frustration study', *Journal of Psychology*, **24**, 165–208.

ROSENZWEIG, S., FLEMING, Edith E., and ROSENZWEIG, Louise (1948), 'The children's form of the Rosenzweig picture-frustration study', *Journal of Psychology*, **26**, 141–91.

RUTTER, M., BIRCH, H. G., THOMAS, A., and CHESS, Stella (1964), 'Temperamental characteristics in infancy and the later development of behaviour disorders', *British Journal of Psychiatry*, **110**, 651–61.

RUTTER, M., TIZARD, J., and WHITMORE, K. (1970), *Education, Health and Behaviour*. London: Longman.

RYLE, A. (1967), *Neurosis in the Ordinary Family*. London: Tavistock.

SARBIN, T. R., WENK, E. A., and SHERWOOD, D. W. (1968), 'An effort to identify assault-prone offenders', *Journal of Research in Crime and Delinquency*, **5**, 66–71.

SAVITZ, L. (1970), 'Delinquency and migration', in Wolfgang, M. E., Savitz, L., and Johnson, N. (eds.), *The Sociology of Crime and Delinquency* (2nd ed.), New York: Wiley.

SCHAEFER, E. S., and BELL, R. Q. (1958), 'Development of a parental attitude research instrument', *Child Development*, **29**, 339–61.

SCHMIDEBERG, Melitta (1970), 'The socio-psychological impact of IQ tests', *International Journal of Offender Therapy*, **14**, 91–7.

SCHNELL, R. R., and DWARSHUIS, L. (1967), 'Progressive matrices—scores and time', *Educational and Psychological Measurement*, **27**, 485–487.

SCOTT, P. D. (1956), 'Gangs and delinquent groups in London', *British Journal of Delinquency*, **7**, 4–26.

SCOTT, P. D. (1966), 'Medical aspects of delinquency', *Hospital Medicine*, **1**, 219–23, 259.

SEARS, R. R., MACCOBY, E. E., and LEVIN, H. (1957), *Patterns of Child Rearing*. Evanston, Illinois: Row, Peterson.

SELLIN, T. (1958), 'Recidivism and maturation', *N.P.P.A. Journal*, **4**, 241–50.

SELLIN, T., and WOLFGANG, M. E. (1964), *The Measurement of Delinquency*. New York: Wiley.

SHAW, Margaret (1971), Delinquency in London: the court histories of juveniles born in March 1946 (personal communication).

SHIPMAN, W. G. (1965), 'The validity of MMPI hostility scales', *Journal of Clinical Psychology*, **21**, 186–90.

SHIPMAN, W. G., and MARQUETTE, C. H. (1963), 'The manifest hostility scale: a validation study', *Journal of Clinical Psychology* **19**, 104–6.

SHOBEN, E. J. (1949), 'The assessment of parental attitudes in relation to child adjustment', *Genetic Psychology Monographs*, **39**, 101–48.

SHORE, M. F., MASSIMO, J. L., and MORAN, Janet K. (1967), 'Some cognitive dimensions of interpersonal behavior in adolescent delinquent boys', *Journal of Research in Crime and Delinquency*, **4**, 243–7.

SHORT, J. F. (1957), 'Differential association and delinquency', *Social Problems*, **4**, 233–9.

SHORT, J. F. (1958), 'Differential association with delinquent friends and delinquent behavior', *Pacific Sociological Review*, **1**, 20–5.

SHORT, J. F., and NYE, F. I. (1958), 'The extent of unrecorded juvenile delinquency: tentative conclusions', *Journal of Criminal Law, Criminology and Police Science*, **49**, 296–302.

SHORT, J. F., and STRODTBECK, F. L. (1965), *Group Process and Gang Delinquency*. University of Chicago Press.

SIEGEL, S. M. (1956), 'The relationship of hostility to authoritarianism', *Journal of Abnormal and Social Psychology*, **52**, 368–72.

SILBER, D. E., and COURTLESS, T. F. (1968), 'Measures of fantasy aggression among mentally retarded offenders', *American Journal of Mental Deficiency*, **72**, 918–23.

SKABERNE, B., BLEJEC, M., SKALAR, V., and VODOPIVEC, Katja (1965), 'Criminal prevention and elementary schoolchildren', *Revija za Kriminalistiko in Kriminologijo*, **16**, 8–14.

SLOCUM, W. L., and STONE, Carol L. (1963), 'Family culture patterns and delinquent-type behavior', *Marriage and Family Living*, **25**, 202–8.

SPENCE, J., WALTON, W. S., MILLER, F. J. W., and COURT, S. D. M.

(1954), *A Thousand Families in Newcastle upon Tyne*. London: Oxford University Press.

STEER, D. J. (1970), *Police Cautions*. Oxford: Blackwell.

STOTT, D. H. (1960), 'Delinquency, maladjustment and unfavourable ecology', *British Journal of Psychology*, **51**, 157–70.

STOTT, D. H. (1962), 'Evidence for a congenital factor in delinquency and maladjustment', *American Journal of Psychology*, **118**, 781–94.

STOTT, D. H. (1963), *The Social Adjustment of Children: Manual to the Bristol Social Adjustment Guides*. University of London Press (2nd edn.).

STOTT, D. H. (1964), 'Prediction of success or failure on probation: A follow-up study', *International Journal of Social Psychiatry*, **10**, 27–9.

STOTT, D. H., and WILSON, D. M. (1968), 'The prediction of early adult criminality from school-age behaviour', *International Journal of Social Psychiatry*, **14**, 5–8.

SUGARMAN, B. (1968), 'Social norms in teenage boys' peer groups: a study of their implications for achievement and conduct in four London schools', *Human Relations*, **21**, 41–58.

SUTCLIFFE, J. P. (1955), 'An appraisal of the Rosenzweig picture-frustration study', *Australian Journal of Psychology*, **7**, 97–107.

SUTHERLAND, E. H., and CRESSEY, D. R. (1970), *Criminology*. New York: Lippincott (8th edn).

SVERI, K. (1965), 'Group activity', in Christiansen, K. O. (ed.), *Scandinavian Studies in Criminology*, vol. I. London: Tavistock.

TAIT, C. D., and HODGES, E. F. (1962), *Delinquents, their Families and the Community*. Springfield: Thomas.

TAIT, C. D., and HODGES, E. F. (1971), 'Follow-up study of predicted delinquents', *Crime and Delinquency*, **17**, 202–13.

TAYLOR, A. J. W. (1968), 'A brief criminal attitude scale', *Journal of Criminal Law, Criminology and Police Science*, **51**, 37–40.

TAYLOR, R. S. (1960), 'The habitual criminal', *British Journal of Criminology*, **1**, 21–36.

TEELE, J. E., SCHLEIFER, M. J., CORMAN, Louise, and LARSON, Karin (1966), 'Teacher ratings, sociometric status and choice reciprocity of antisocial and normal boys', *Group Psychotherapy*, **9**, 183–97.

TERMAN, L. M., and ODEN, Melissa H. (1959), *The Gifted Group at Mid-life*. London: Oxford University Press.

THOMAS, A., CHESS, Stella, and BIRCH, H. G. (1968), *Temperament and Behavior Disorders in Children*. University of London Press.

THOMAS, A., CHESS, Stella and BIRCH, H. G. (1970), 'The origin of personality', *Scientific American*, **223** (2), 102–9.

TIZARD, J. (1951), 'The Porteus Maze test and intelligence: a critical survey', *British Journal of Educational Psychology*, **21**, 172–85.

TOBY, J. (1961), 'Early identification and intensive treatment of pre-delinquents: a negative view', *Social Work*, **6**, 3–13.

TOWNSEND, Jeannette K. (1967), 'The relation between Rorschach signs of aggression and behavioral aggression in emotionally disturbed boys, *Journal of Projective Techniques and Personality Assessment*, **31** (6), 13–21.

TRASLER, G. B. (1962), *The Explanation of Criminality*. London: Routledge & Kegan Paul.
TRASLER, G. B. (1970), 'Delinquency', in Butcher, H. J., and Pont, H. B. (eds.), *Educational Research in Britain*, 2. University of London Press.
TUCKMAN, J., and REGAN, R. A. (1967), 'Size of family and behavioral problems in children', *Journal of Genetic Psychology*, **111**, 151–60.
VANE, Julia R. (1954), 'Implications of the performance of delinquent girls on the Rosenzweig Picture-Frustration study', *Journal of Consulting Psychology*, **18**, 414.
VERNON, P. E. (1969), *Intelligence and Cultural Environment*. London: Methuen.
VEVERKA, M. (1971), 'The Gluecks' social prediction table in a Czechoslovak research', *British Journal of Criminology*, **11**, 187–9.
VOSS, H. L. (1964), 'Differential association and reported delinquent behavior: a replication', *Social Problems*, **12**, 78–85.
WADSWORTH, M. E. J. (1972), Personal communication.
WAGNER, E. E. (1969), *The Hand Test Manual*. Los Angeles: Western Psychological Services.
WAGNER, E. E., and HAWKINS, R. (1964), 'Differentiation of assaultive delinquents with the hand test', *Journal of Projective Techniques and Personality Assessment*, **28**, 363–5.
WALDER, L. O., ABELSON, R. P., ERON, L. D., BANTA, T. J., and LAULICHT, J. H. (1961), 'Development of a peer-rating measure of aggression', *Psychological Reports*, **9**, 497–556.
WALDO, G. P., and HALL, N. E. (1970), 'Delinquency potential and attitudes toward the criminal justice system', *Social Forces*, **49**, 291–8.
WALKER, N., HAMMOND, W., and STEER, D. (1967), 'Repeated violence', *Criminal Law Review*, 465–72.
WALKEY, F. H., and BOSHIER, R. (1969), 'Semantic differential response bias in psychopathic, delinquent and normal boys', *Psychological Reports*, **24**, 91–4.
WALLIS, C. P., and MALIPHANT, R. (1967), 'Delinquent areas in the county of London: ecological factors', *British Journal of Criminology*, **7**, 250–84.
WALTERS, R. H., and ZAKS, M. S. (1959), 'Validation studies of an aggression scale', *Journal of Psychology*, **47**, 209–18.
WALTON, D. (1955), 'The validity and interchangeability of Terman–Merrill and Matrices test data', *British Journal of Educational Psychology*, **25**, 190–4.
WARDER, J. (1969), 'Two studies of violent offenders', *British Journal of Criminology*, **9**, 389–93.
WARDER, J., PRESLY, A. S., and KIRK, Joan (1970), 'Intelligence and literacy in prison and hospital populations', *British Journal of Criminology*, **10**, 286–7.
WEST, D. J. (1963), *The Habitual Prisoner*. London: Macmillan.
WEST, D. J. (1969), *Present Conduct and Future Delinquency*. London: Heinemann Educational Books.
WIGGINS, J. S., and WINDER, C. L. (1961), 'The peer nomination

inventory: an empirically derived sociometric measure of adjustment in preadolescent boys', *Psychological Reports*, **9**, 643–77.

WINDER, C. L., and RAU, Lucy (1962), 'Parental attitudes associated with social deviance in preadolescent boys', *Journal of Abnormal and Social Psychology*, **64**, 418–24.

WIRT, R. D., and BRIGGS, P. F. (1959), 'Personality and environmental factors in the development of delinquency', *Psychological Monographs*, **73** (15), whole no. 485.

WOLFGANG, M. E., FIGLIO, R. M., and SELLIN, T. (1972), *Delinquency in a Birth Cohort*. University of Chicago Press.

WOODMANSEY, A. C. (1971), 'Understanding delinquency', *British Journal of Criminology*, **11**, 155–66.

WOODWARD, M. (1963), *Low Intelligence and Delinquency*. London: I.S.T.D.

WOOTTON, Barbara (1959), *Social Science and Social Pathology*. London: Allen & Unwin.

ZAKS, M. S., and WALTERS, R. H. (1959), 'First steps in the construction of a scale for the measurement of aggression', *Journal of Psychology*, **47**, 199–208.

ZUCKERMAN, M., BARRETT, Beatrice H., and BRAGIEL, R. M. (1960), 'The parental attitudes of parents of child guidance cases. I. Comparisons with normals, investigations of socioeconomic and family constellation factors, and relations to parents' reactions to the clinics', *Child Development*, **31**, 401–17.

Index of Names

Index of Subjects